DIGITAL SAMARITANS

DIGITAL RHETORIC COLLABORATIVE

The Sweetland Digital Rhetoric Collaborative Book Series publishes texts that investigate the multiliteracies of digitally mediated spaces both within academia as well as other contexts. We encourage submissions that address, among others, topics such as:

- new convergences and economies;
- shifting ideologies and politics;
- global contexts and multilingual discourses;
- reconstructions of race, class, gender, sexuality, and (dis)ability;
- emerging theories and technologies; and
- reconfigured divisions and connections within these spaces.

We welcome born-digital as well as digitally enhanced submissions—in the form of collections, monographs, or teaching materials of varying lengths and genres—that engage with digital rhetoric's histories and futures; its border-fields and transdisciplines; its ethics and aesthetics; its materialities, networks, praxes and pedagogies.

Series Editors:
Anne Ruggles Gere, University of Michigan
Naomi Silver, University of Michigan

Digital Samaritans

RHETORICAL DELIVERY AND ENGAGEMENT
IN THE DIGITAL HUMANITIES

Jim Ridolfo

University of Michigan Press
ANN ARBOR

Published in the United States of America by the
University of Michigan Press
Printed and bound by CPI Group (UK) Ltd, Croydon, CR0 4YY

2018   2017   2016   2015   4   3   2   1

A CIP catalog record for this book is available from the British Library.

DOI: http://dx.doi.org/10.3998/drc.13406713.0001.001

Ridolfo, Jim, 1979– author.
    Digital Samaritans : rhetorical delivery and engagement in the digital humanities / Jim Ridolfo.
        pages   cm. — (Digital rhetoric collaborative)
        Includes bibliographical references and index.
        ISBN 978-0-472-05280-6 (pbk. : alk. paper) — ISBN 978-0-472-07280-4 (hardcover : alk. paper) — ISBN 978-0-472-12133-5 (ebook)
        1. Samaritans—Historiography.   2. Learning and scholarship—Technological innovations.   3. Library materials—Digitization.   4. Tsedaka, Benyamim.   I. Title.
    BM910.R53   2015
    296.8'17072—dc23
                                                                        2015018378

Acknowledgments

This book would not be possible without the support of the National Endowment for the Humanities Office of Digital Humanities, Michigan State University MATRIX, Michigan State University WIDE Research Center, the William T. Taft Foundation at the University of Cincinnati, the Council for International Exchange of Scholars Fulbright Middle East and North Africa Regional Research program, and University of Kentucky. I am grateful for the support of the program officers at the Middle East and North Africa desk in Washington, DC, and Jaclyn Assryian, Aminah Shah, and Gary Garrison. Their guidance and support made my Fulbright experience a truly productive one. The US Consulate in Jerusalem was especially helpful, and I am thankful to Maureen Marroum, Cultural Affairs Specialist for Exchanges in the Public Affairs Office for her support while I was in the West Bank Fulbright program. In the US-Israel Educational Foundation Fulbright program, I would like to thank Deputy Director Judy Stavsky and Executive Director Neal Sherman for their assistance.

To conduct the research for much of this book, I received a 2012 Middle East and North Africa (MENA) Regional Research Fulbright split between the West Bank and Israel. I would especially like to thank Basem Ra'ad, professor emeritus of Al Quds University; Walid Shomaly and the Palestinian Center for Research and Cultural Dialogue; Ruth "Stella" Amossy and the Analyse du Discours, Argumentation, Rhétorique (ADARR) group at Tel Aviv University; and Benyamim Tsedaka, director of the A.B. Samaritan Institute in Holon.

Projects such as this book do not develop in a vacuum. I'm fortunate to have worked with many talented and supportive faculty at Michigan State University. I am especially thankful for the support of rhetoric and writing faculty, especially my doctoral chair Julie Lindquist. From Julie, I gained a greater appreciation for the study of languages and the nuance of language in everyday rhetorical situations. I would also like to thank Malea Powell, Danielle DeVoss, Dean Rehberger, Ellen Cushman, Jeff Grabill, and especially WIDE chief software developer Michael McLeod. At Michigan State University, the confluence of scholar-researchers interested in digital technology and cultural rhetoric are no doubt the reason for this project's existence today, but I am especially thankful to WIDE codirector Bill Hart-Davidson, who has been my co-PI on the Michigan State University digitization project since its earliest stages.

Bill Hart-Davidson deserves special acknowledgment and thanks for being supportive of the initial Samaritan grant project from the beginning. Many senior faculty would have balked at the idea of a graduate student proposing such a project. He didn't. Bill took a chance working with me, and this book would not be possible without his collaboration and early vote of confidence. I'm also grateful for the support of my friends Collin Craig, Donnie Sackey, Kendall Leon, Robyn Tasaka, Angela Haas, Qwo-Li Driskill, and Stacey Pigg. I especially thank Stacey Pigg for reading many drafts of this manuscript. A supportive graduate cohort is a rare gift. Their support and feedback has made my work stronger. I would also like to acknowledge Jessica Enoch and David Gold, who responded to multiple drafts as editors of my 2013 piece in *College English*. Their insights helped me to shape this book project. Additionally, I also want to thank the editors and staff at University of Michigan Press, especially series editors Anne Ruggles Gere, Naomi Silver, the Digital Rhetoric Collaborative, University of Michigan Press editor Aaron McCullough, and the anonymous manuscript reviewers. Without their critical feedback, vision, support, and editorial expertise, this book would not be possible.

I also want to acknowledge the support of the many language instructors that made this work possible. For Hebrew, I thank Ellen Rothschild, Marc Bernstein, and the Ulpan faculty at Hebrew University and the University of Haifa. For Arabic, I am grateful for Mohamed Elayyadi at the University of Cincinnati, Nada El Majzoub, Maher Alkhateeb, and Ghadeer Shaheen Zannoun at the University of Kentucky, and Wael Kubtan from Jaffa for his tutorship in colloquial Palestinian Arabic. I would also like to thank Shlomi Daskal for his Hebrew and Arabic assistance and expertise.

This project would not be possible without Michigan State University Emeritus Professor Robert Anderson's support and translation assistance of Samaritan Hebrew. His work over the last four decades with the MSU Chamberlain Warren Collection and his extensive body of scholarship are important foundations for my work. I would also like to thank Peter Berg, director of special collections at Michigan State University, and David Gilner, director of libraries at Hebrew Union College–Jewish Institute of Religion, for their collaboration. I am also thankful for the friendship and collaboration of Sharon Sullivan Eretz for her assistance on the National Endowment for the Humanities Office of Digital Humanities Start-Up Grant. In addition, a special thanks to my fall 2013 undergraduate research assistant Charles James Carter for helping me prepare bibliography and spreadsheet data.

I thank Benyamim Tsedaka for his friendship, humor, and vast knowledge and the many elders in the Samaritan community for their support of my work. In Holon and Mount Gerizim, I have been welcomed on countless occasions; I consider it a true honor to have had the opportunity the past six years to learn and collaborate with Tsedaka. I have had the privilege to meet and visit with two of the most recent High Priests before their passing, Elazar ben Tsedaka ben Yitzhaq and Aharon ben Ab-Chisda ben Yacob. While they are gone now from this earth, I hope that what I have written in this book honors each of their memories. I wish the current High Priest Aabed-El ben Asher ben Matzliach many long years of leadership and prosperity.

Lastly, I especially want to thank my wife and life partner Janice Fernheimer for her support during all stages of this project. Without her love, support, humor, and feedback on numerous drafts, this book would not be possible. In the process of completing this book, our son Lior was born. This book is dedicated to him.

Contents

Preface: Rhetorical Serendipity

My involvement with the Samaritans and their collections did not begin with an extensive rhetorical understanding of their history or present situation. Rather, it began as a digital humanities project I initiated as a graduate student. In late December 2007, I was halfway through my PhD in Rhetoric and Writing at Michigan State University, and I was in my fourth year of employment as a graduate research assistant at the Writing in Digital Environments (WIDE) Research Center. With some free time between semesters, I found myself one evening browsing the online catalogue for Michigan State University Special Collections. Having recently taught two undergraduate courses with assignments based around research projects on the Radicalism Collection at Special Collections, I was searching for collections that could be useful for new undergraduate research assignments. At the time, I also was deep into my dissertation research and writing about the Hebrew work of fifteenth-century rabbi and rhetorician Judah Messer Leon.[1] Consequently, I had several semesters of university Hebrew under my belt and was very interested in Semitic manuscripts. Not surprisingly, the MSS 287 finding aid for the Chamberlain Warren Samaritan Collection of Samaritan Hebrew materials immediately piqued my curiosity; I found myself wondering about the collection's history.

The finding aid described the collection as "the most extensive set of Samaritan materials in the United States," consisting of over two dozen Samaritan cultural artifacts, including scrolls, codices, a third–sixth-century marble inscription, and a sixteenth-century brass scroll case. To me, the finding aid also gestured toward the beginning of a story. How, when, and under what circumstance did this large "variety of religious and liturgical materials used by the Samaritans" end up in Michigan? Though it suggested such a story existed, it provided only the barest bones of a narrative:[2]

The Chamberlain Warren Samaritan Collection . . . [was] acquired by E.K. Warren, a wealthy businessman of Three Oaks, Michigan in the early 20th century. Warren . . . first met the Samaritans during a visit to Palestine in

1901. He took great interest in helping the Samaritans preserve their religious artifacts. (Abood)

In my attempt to flesh out those bare bones, I learned that during the thirty-five years that followed the rediscovery of the Chamberlain Warren Collection, only a handful of scholars had taken an interest in it. For the most part, the Samaritan materials did not have many visitors, though there are two significant exceptions. The first was Robert Anderson's discovery of the Samaritan manuscripts in 1968, which piqued his own interest in Samaritan studies. In the years that followed, he researched and composed numerous books, articles, and chapters on the Chamberlain Warren Collection, including his 1978 *Studies in Samaritan Manuscripts and Artifacts: The Chamberlain Warren Collection.*[3] The second was the interest of Benyamim Tsedeka, a Samaritan and community scholar, who began traveling from his home in the Samaritan neighborhood of Holon, Israel, to visit archives with Samaritan collections in North America in 1982. These trips included visits to Columbia University, the Annenberg Institute at the University of Pennsylvania, the Library of Congress, and Michigan State University. During his 1982 visit to North America, he met Michigan State University religious studies professor Robert Anderson in East Lansing and saw the Chamberlain Warren Collection for the first time. According to Robert Anderson, the Chamberlain Warren Collection includes "a fine selection of relatively scarce artifacts and manuscripts," including three fifteenth-century Samaritan Pentateuchs on parchment from Egypt and Damascus, many modern liturgical works on paper, a brass scroll case, and a third to sixth-century marble inscription of Exodus 15:13 (Anderson, "Museum Trail" 41–43). In total, twenty complete and partial Pentateuchs in scroll and codex form, the marble inscription and brass scroll case, one book of law, and six additional liturgical texts made up the collection; the languages of the manuscripts include Samaritan Hebrew, Aramaic, and Arabic ("MSS 287"), a collection representative of the kind of Samaritan texts in diaspora.

Impressed with the Chamberlain Warren Collection, Tsedaka returned in 1984 and 2003 to do additional research on the history of his people.[4] On his third trip to East Lansing in 2003, he visited more than the Special Collections. Learning that there was a MSU Board of Trustees meeting scheduled for that day, Tsedaka attended the "Public Participation on Issues Not Germane to the Agenda" segment of the trustee meeting and stood to address MSU's trustees about the MSU Chamberlain Warren Collection of Samaritan manuscripts and artifacts. The meeting notes record that he introduced and explained some basic facts about himself and his people, specifically, that he was a descendant of the ancient Northern Israelite Kingdom. According to the meeting notes, he then explained to the trustees that "MSU received one of the largest collections in the world of Samaritan manuscripts; they are located in the Library." On behalf of his people, Tsedaka made a request, encouraging "the University to utilize this collection to promote Samaritan Studies" ("Michigan State University Board of Trustees").[5] After Tsedaka spoke at the Board of Trustees meeting, there was some activity on the part of Peter Berg at MSU Special Collections to display key pieces of the Chamberlin Warren Collection, but the university did not move forward with any larger initiatives.

Four years later in December 2007, I discovered the finding aid to the Michigan State Chamberlain Warren Collection. Curious about the collection, a quick Google search led me first to Professor Robert Anderson's article "The Chamberlain Warren Samaritan Collection at MSU: The Museum Trail," which details the history of the MSU collection and, a few hours later, to Tsedaka's November 2003 Michigan State University Board of Trustees address. After reading the meeting notes and Tsedaka's request to do something with the collection, I searched to see if MSU had responded to Tsedaka; I did not find any evidence that they had. I did, however, find Tsedaka's e-mail address, and a few days later I wrote to him:

I am interested in potentially digitizing some or all of the three Pentateuch texts in the collection, and making them available online off msu.edu . . . for educators, researchers, and your own Samaritan community. I wanted to know if first and foremost such an endeavor is respectful of your culture's values regarding these texts. I am aware that these are sacred texts, and I would not proceed with such an endeavor unless it honors the values of your people. Any feedback you could give would be greatly appreciated. (Ridolfo)

Tsedaka responded back almost immediately with his support for a digitization project:

In regards to the question you have asked. We will be much honored with your blessed work. Go ahead with this and you have my pure blessings. The texts in your hands are very important and need a professional use. Displaying them before the public will be a great contribution to the world's culture. (Tsedaka)[6]

What developed over the next few years became the first in several stages that ultimately led to this current project about rhetorical delivery, cultural sovereignty, and the digital humanities. The exigence for this book emerged as I began to notice the difference between digital humanities work at the intersection of rhetorical studies and the interests of more traditional scholars in textual studies. For example, in the summer of 2013, Samaritan Benyamim Tsedaka translated and published the first English edition of the Samaritan Torah,[7] *The Israelite Samaritan Version of the Torah*. For the first time ever, English-speaking scholars and lay people would be able to access and compare the Jewish Masoretic Torah (MT) and the SP (Samaritan Pentateuch) side-by-side. In Tsedaka's introduction to the translation, he writes that

> For the first time in history we present the English translation of the Israelite Samaritan text of the Pentateuch (SP), parallel to the English translation of the Masoretic Text (MT) based on *The Holy Scriptures*, the 1917 Jewish Publication Society edition, in two columns emphasizing the differences between the two versions and explained by commentary in marginal notes by the author, emphasizing the most important differences from a Samaritan point of view (because the Jewish commentary is already widely known in the field of Biblical Studies). (Tsedaka, *The Israelite Samaritan Version of the Torah: First English Translation Compared with the Masoretic Version*, xxxiii)

This publication coincided with scholars Terry Giles, Stefan Schorch, Emmanuel Tov, and Ingrid Lilly's panel proposal to the 2013 Society for Biblical Literature (SBL) on "Current Issues in the Study of the Samaritan Pentateuch." Since Professor Giles, a renowned scholar in his own right and a student of Robert Anderson, was familiar with my work on the digitization of Samaritan manuscripts at Michigan State University and Hebrew Union College–Jewish Institute of Religion in Cincinnati, he invited me to share his time on the panel. On November 23, 2013, I traveled to Baltimore for the SBL to talk about the digitization of Samaritan manuscripts, not only for scholars to access, but also for the Samaritan community in the West Bank and Israel to view, share, and use.

During the panel session, accomplished Samaritan scholar Professor Stefan Schorch responded to Tsedaka's translation of the Samaritan Pentateuch into English. Although he found much to praise about the book, he also critiqued Tsedaka's project. For Schorch, Tsedaka's choice of English as the translation language for the Samaritan Pentateuch demonstrated that the book "isn't intended for the Samaritan community."[8] And if the translation is not for the community, then, Schorch reasoned, the translation must be intended for biblical scholars. Following this line of reasoning, Schorch assumed that text was aimed at biblical scholars and consequently, the project fell short of its intended audience. He also noted a number of translation problems, which he attributed to language influences present in Tsedaka's translation. At the panel and then later in a public Facebook post, Tsedaka responded to the concerns Schorch raised about the intended audience of the translation and value of the book to the Samaritan community:

> The main purpose of the book is to open the Samaritan version of the Torah for the first time to readers of the most spoken language in the world today—English. More than four billion people in the world speak this language and there is room to expose them to the [Samaritan] version that was previously only available to 10 million speakers of Hebrew.

According to Tsedaka, the book was not only aimed at scholars but also at opening up global access to Samaritan culture and religious beliefs, as well as the need for Samaritan cultural sovereignty. In contrast to the more particular audience of Biblical scholars Schorch assumed for the book, Tsedaka's introduction to *The Israelite Samaritan Version of the Torah* makes clear that a key concern for his English translation is to communicate the "Samaritan point of view" to outside audiences. In his foreword to the translation, Professor Steven Fine also notes that the goal of Tsedaka's translation is to more widely circulate Samaritan culture, history, and traditions outside the 770-person Samaritan community:[9]

> Benyamim Tsedaka has reached beyond the bounds of the Holy Land, the "Sacred Tongue," and the "Holy Nation" to present Samaritanism to the broader world of scholars and interested lay people. His work has coincided with a period of new prominence for Samaritan studies in Israel and abroad . . . [He] has presented a Samaritan perspective on Samaritan life, culture and politics as well as a forum for scholarly research on Samaritan history, religion, and culture. (xiv)

Schorch called attention to issues he saw with the use of the book for Samaritan scholarship, such as Tsedaka's Modern Hebrew influencing how he translated particular passages from the Biblical Hebrew (Tsedaka, "Panel on the Samaritan Version of the Torah"). Yet, Schorch's questions about the value of Tsedaka's English translation for the Samaritan community do not account for the possibility that the book does more than simply communicate to scholars.

The issues that sparked disagreement at this panel—the proposed audience for Tsedaka's translation and definitions of what constitutes a Samaritan translation—highlight the central issues *Digital Samaritans* explores. What might texts *do*, especially texts in diaspora, for cultural stakeholders such as the Samaritans to help them communicate their unique identity and need for cultural sovereignty to a global audience in the digital age? What is the role of rhetoric at the crossroads of the digital humanities in that mission, and what might engaged research look like at the intersection of rhetorical studies and the digital humanities? At the core of this book is the idea that beyond digitizing manuscripts, there remains an unanswered question about the role of rhetorical delivery in digital humanities. Digital humanists have been regularly digitizing and sending out texts for more than three decades: but what do those texts *do* once they enter digital circulation and for *whom*?

The panel at the SBL brought to light a key difference in how scholars consider Samaritan texts. In the eyes of some textual scholars, texts are first and foremost objects of study. In the eyes of many Samaritans, however, texts form part of their cultural heritage and provide one of the primary ways they may communicate their identity and need for cultural sovereignty to faraway audiences. In other words, texts enable Samaritans to engage in a process that I term leveraging *textual diaspora*, which is the process by which cultural communities strategically theorize the future delivery and circulation of their texts in diaspora, a concept I discuss more in chapters 1 and 3 of this book. For Tsedaka, his translation of the Samaritan Pentateuch is first and foremost a means to convey in a more "accessible" global tongue the uniqueness of Samaritan cultural heritage. For Schorch, the text is first and foremost an object of textual study, most important to the community itself (the Samaritans) and the elite group of Biblical/textual scholars trained to appreciate the text as an object of scholarly study. These two views may complement one another most of the time; however, in the case of Schorch and Tsedaka's argument about the intended audience for Tsedaka's translation of the Samaritan Pentateuch, they differ. The difference between what each values is one of the central tenants of the book. While Tsedaka privileges access and the ability to communicate with as broad an audience as possible, his imagined purpose for his translation bumps up against the more limited and particular conception of the translation's audience that Schorch assumes. What this minor clash of values demonstrates is the central focus of this book: the difference between what textual scholars, largely the dominant voice in the digital humanities to date, might want from texts, and what cultural communities such as the Samaritans might want from their texts, a key area of interest for scholars in rhetorical studies. The clash of values that Tsedeka and Schorch found themselves in at the SBL is similar to the competing values inherent in more traditional approaches to the digital humanities that do not imagine diverse audiences and purposes for texts in future circulation. Rhetorical training provides the tools to better understand where Tsedeka and Schorch miss each other even though they're talking about the same issues—audience—and the same text.

While the digital humanities typically is interested in developing tools for scholars, and understanding how digitization may benefit the work of scholars, *Digital Samaritans* is interested in the historical and contemporary reasons for Tsedaka's *rhetorical* goals and objectives. More broadly, *Digital Samaritans* investigates the history of the Samaritans' textual diaspora and asks Samaritans what they think about and want from their diaspora of manuscripts, and why. In rhetorical terms, these questions about what Samaritans want from their textual diaspora translate into questions about the kind of future digital delivery and distribution they want from their texts, why they want them circulated in the first place, and for what rhetorical circumstances? As part of the ongoing digitization project to make Samaritan manuscripts available on the Internet, the book also explores how members of the community are theorizing their textual diaspora as digital objects in order to help them communicate their cultural sovereignty to the world.

Based on archival research and interviews with the Samaritan community, *Digital Samaritans* explores what some Samaritans *want* from this diaspora of manuscripts, and how these goals and objectives relate to the contemporary existential and rhetorical situation of the Samaritans as a living, breathing people existing "between the raindrops" and "between the two fires" of the Israeli-Palestinian conflict, phrases Samaritans use to describe their delicate geopolitical position in the region. The exigence for this book is rooted in a practical digital humanities project: a digitization project involving the Samaritan community. What do some Samaritans want to *communicate* to outside audiences with their manuscripts? Why do Samaritans want to engage the outside world with their culture, history, and religious texts? How does the circulation of Samaritan manuscripts, especially in digital environments, relate to their rhetorical circumstances and future goals and objectives as one of the smallest religious/ethnic minorities in the region "walking between the raindrops" or "two fires" in one of the most tumultuous regions in the world?[10] What does it mean for scholars and community members to research and engage the digitization of Samaritan manuscripts from a rhetorical perspective? Where do engaged digitization projects intersect with current conversations in rhetorical studies and the digital humanities? For rhetoric scholars, there have been a number of calls (Grabill; Cushman) to consider the relationship of the humanities in community-university partnerships, the role of public intellectuals (Weisser), and public engagement (Cushman). *Digital Samaritans* provides an additional case example of university-community engagement for scholars in rhetoric, and especially the digital humanities, to consider.

Digital Samaritans argues that digital humanists could benefit from engaging conversations around theoretically informed practice or *praxis*, with projects developed in conjunction with communities outside the academy, or what is referred to as *stakeholders* in this book.[11] There are benefits for humanists engaging with digital humanities projects through the disciplinary lens of rhetoric, especially rhetorical delivery. Just as rhetoricians typically seek to understand what texts *do*, as much as scholars in literature seek to understand what texts *mean* (Bazerman), rhetoricians working at the intersection of the digital humanities and rhetorical studies seek to understand *digital projects themselves* as rhetorical activities of value to specific audiences. For each digital humanities project, there's a rhetorical history informing the contemporary rhetorical situation and potential consequences or outcomes for each individual and community with a stake in the project. When we upload and hit send on digital projects, there's the potential for something to happen as a result of those acts of rhetorical delivery. Perhaps that act of delivery will lead to a ripple effect, triggering other discrete acts of delivery and broader circulation as the project is shared across networks, referenced on Facebook, responded to in e-mail, or criticized on Twitter. In exploring the intersection of digitization and the communication of cultural identity, the digital humanities and rhetorical studies intersect in meaningful and productive ways. This is a book about those ways.

Chapter 1 begins with a brief introduction to the Samaritans, their current situation on Mount Gerizim, a digital humanities project, and their rhetorical sovereignty. In chapter 2, "Between the Raindrops and Two Fires: A Brief History of the Samaritans and Their Diaspora of Manuscripts," I investigate the history of the Samaritans' diaspora of manuscripts in relationship to their recent history and contemporary rhetorical situation in Israel and Palestine. In chapter 3, "From Parchment to Bytes: Digital Delivery as a Rhetorical Strategy," I examine the complexity of nine Samaritan reactions to the diaspora of Samaritan manuscripts in order to argue that the way Samaritans strategize the future circulation of their manuscripts in diaspora is rhetorically complex and has conceptual connections to rhetorical sovereignty and delivery. Chapter 4, "Leveraging Textual Diaspora: Rhetoric and the Digital Humanities as Engaged Scholarship," examines two instances of engaged research in rhetoric and the digital humanities. In the concluding chapter, I outline not only the rhetorical implications of Samaritan calls for digitization and engagement but also the implications for the relationship of rhetorical studies to the digital humanities.

While *Digital Samaritans* is a static print project representing over six years of research with the Samaritan community, the book also references digital resources produced for the Samaritan community and this book. These resources includes a dozen digitized manuscripts from Michigan State University and Hebrew Union College–Jewish Institute of Religion's Klau Library, geocoded maps of the Samaritan diaspora of manuscripts with (when available) links to library finding aids, a geocoded map of known digitized Samaritan manuscripts, and a geocoded map of current Samaritan centers of population in relationship to many of their former locations. In addition, I also include links to a UNICODE Samaritan keyboard I am developing for OS X and Windows and a recent open source Samaritan font with vowel markers developed by Yoram Gnat of the OpenSiddur project. All resources are hosted on http://samaritanrepository.org, a server I host in London, United Kingdom, in order to be as equidistant as possible in terms of Internet traffic patterns between Israel and the West Bank, North America, and Europe: the former are centers of the Samaritan population, and the latter are home to large concentrations of Samaritan scholars. As Henry Jenkins, Sam Ford, and Joshua Green emphasize, digital participation is a complicated matter:

> even if we get our messages through, there is often a question of whether anyone is listening. None of this allows us to be complacent about the current conditions of networked communications, even if the expanded opportunities for participation give us reasons for hope and optimism. (194)

The digital content referenced in this book takes advantage of the electronic medium to reach as many stakeholder audiences as possible. The digital content referenced is not static; rather, the digitized manuscripts and interactive maps are part of a growing project and will continue to improve over time. As David Bodenhamer, John Corrigan, and Trevor Harris note in *The Spatial Humanities: Gis and the Future of Humanities Scholarship*, "seeking to fuse GIS with the humanities is challenging in the extreme, but already we have glimpses of what this technology can produce when applied to the problems in our disciplines" (24). For rhetorical studies and the digital humanities, mapping technologies hold the promise to geocode and consider the spatial dimension of the relationship of people to their texts. In turn, this visualization has implications for thinking about rhetorical delivery and the circulation of texts. Initially, what interactive maps of manuscripts and other texts have to show rhetorical studies is not necessarily why texts are where they are or where they have been, but where texts are said to be in a particular moment in time. As more is discovered about the history of texts, interactive maps may be complicated, improved, and built upon, or put into conversation with other maps.

In the years to come and with the help of Samaritan Benyamim Tsedaka, I plan to update the map of the Samaritan diaspora of manuscripts to include more detailed information about when each manuscript was acquired by each institution. For now, the map of Samaritan textual diaspora includes additional information on library holdings from Jean-Pierre Rothschild's bibliography, information from Tsedaka, and updated links to library catalogue websites. When I started writing *Digital Samaritans*, there was to my knowledge no other digitized Samaritan manuscripts available and thus no activity to map. Over the last two years, the situation has changed for the better, and I now make available a geocoded map of digitized Samaritan manuscripts. With time, my hope is that this map too will grow exponentially, as the late High Priest Elazar ben Tsedaka ben Yitzhaq had wished in 2009 when he told the Michigan State University project team on Mount Gerizim that he wanted all Samaritan manuscripts abroad digitized.

ONE

Introduction to *Digital Samaritans*

Always there is a person inside any community that is telling stories about his or her people. There's nothing special about that. My father was a very good storyteller. He had the habit to visit the old people of the community and pull from them a lot of stories about their family, his family. Some of them left something in writing, some of them didn't.
—Benyamim Tsedaka

This is a story.
—Malea Powell

Rhetoric and the Digital Humanities

The Samaritans are one of the smallest religious and ethnic communities in the Middle East with a population of only 770. While the Samaritans once numbered in the hundreds of thousands in the Roman period and are legendary for the Parable of the Good Samaritan in the Gospel of Luke 10:29–37, today they have just two centers of population: Kiryat Luza on Mount Gerizim next to the ancient West Bank city of Nablus (also known in Hebrew as Shechem) and the small Samaritan neighborhood of Holon, Israel. Kiryat Luza is defined as area "B" under the 1993 Oslo Accords or Declaration of Principles on Interim Self-Government Arrangements as territory governed by Palestinian Authority civil administration and joint Israeli-Palestinian security administration (Newman 61). While the Samaritan people live only in these two population centers, their diaspora of manuscripts is spread out in major museums, libraries, and universities across the globe.[1] This geographic reality situates the Samaritans squarely in the midst of the contemporary Israel-Palestinian conflict, and also, because of their textual diaspora of manuscripts, in the midst of the digital humanities at the intersection of rhetorical studies.

   Given their unique situation of textual diaspora, the Samaritans stand to benefit from increased access to their manuscripts through digitization. Of course, in order to understand the broader possibilities that such digitization opens up for them and us (as rhetorical and digital humanities [DH] scholars), a rhetorical understanding of digitization and the leveraging and circulation of digital materials is necessary. Manuscript digitization along with the creation of other digital cultural heritage resources such as Samaritan language fonts and keyboard layouts help the Samaritan people to reference those materials abroad and, on their own terms, articulate their place in a region fraught with conflict and sectarian division. In order to understand the broader impact of manuscript digitization and the far-reaching political, educational, and cultural effects of digitization, a rhetorical understanding of delivery, audience, and circulation is essential for the digital humanities because the digital humanities and the making of cultural heritage resources are not neutral activities but are *rhetorical* (see Cushman 2013; Graban).

Unlike other research in the digital humanities, *Digital Samaritans* is framed with an emphasis on the implications of the Samaritan digitization project for multiple audiences and the canon of rhetorical delivery. A broader humanities understanding of rhetoric's value for the digital humanities has been less visible in many seminal digital humanities collections to date, and in the studies that do feature some discussion of it, they have misrepresented the role rhetoric may play in the digital humanities. For example, in Schreibman, Siemens, and Unsworth's 2004 *A Companion to Digital Humanities*, Rockwell and Mactavish define a multimedia "rhetorical artifact" as "a computer-based rhetorical artifact in which multiple media are integrated into an interactive whole" (109). Rockwell and Mactavish's description of a rhetorical artifact is neither helpful nor accurate for scholars working at the intersection of rhetorical studies and the digital humanities because it provides a very limited definition of rhetoric and fails to articulate benefits for the digital humanities such as rhetorical delivery and studying the circulation of texts. Implicit in their definition of a multimedia work is a limited sense of the scope of rhetoric. They elaborate their definition of multimedia rhetorical artifact as follows:

> A multimedia work is one designed to convince, delight, or instruct in the classical sense of rhetoric. *It is not a work designed for administrative purposes or any collection of data in different media.* Nor is it solely a technological artifact. This is to distinguish a multimedia work, which is a work of human expression, from those works that may combine media and reside on the computer, but are not designed by humans to communicate to humans. (109, emphasis mine)

Missing from Rockwell and Mactavish's definition of a rhetorical artifact are basic tenants of rhetorical theory such as the notion of purpose, audience, and rhetorical situation that would allow scholars in the digital humanities to think about how DH projects are situated in relationship to multiple audiences. Their limited definition of rhetoric also discounts digital objects designed for "administrative purposes or any collection of data" (109) and thus de facto excludes a large body of work in technical communication, human computer interaction (HCI), and professional writing, as well as any research involving data collection. In *Digital Samaritans*, the role rhetoric plays in the Samaritan case example—especially in aspects of rhetorical situation and delivery—includes many of the areas discounted by Rockwell and Mactavish and thus expands the reach of the digital humanities to include these heretofore unexamined areas and the rhetorical questions they open up about rhetorical situation, multiple audiences, and especially digital delivery and circulation's value to digital humanists.

More promising, Matthew Gold's 2012 *Debates in the Digital Humanities* includes work by scholars working at the intersection of computers and writing and the digital humanities. In the first chapter of the collection, Matthew Kirschenbaum's piece acknowledges the historical connection between computers and writing and the digital humanities by citing Cindy Selfe's 1988 "Computers in English Departments: The Rhetoric of Technopower" (3). Additionally, Alexander Reid's and Elizabeth Losh's important contributions to *Debates in the Digital Humanities* articulate the role of the digital humanities in graduate education (Reid) and the broader relationship of computers and writing to digital humanities (Losh). Reid's and Losh's pieces provide a bridge from rhetorical studies to the more mainstream digital humanities conversations, but more work remains to articulate projects in rhetorical terms to broader DH audiences. For example, a quick survey of the NEH Office of Digital Humanities library of funded projects shows that rhetorical studies is not a major area of funding. The rhetorical studies contributions of Gold, Losh, and Reid in *Debates in the Digital Humanities* helped William Hart-Davidson and me envision the 2015 collection *Rhetoric and the Digital Humanities*. As we state in our Introduction to that collection, while "scholars working in either rhetoric studies or computers and writing (C&W) have received a number of National Endowment for the Humanities (NEH) Office of Digital Humanities (ODH) Digital Humanities Start-Up grants (e.g., Potts and Gossett 2012; Carter 2011; Ball, Eyman, and Gossett 2010; and Hart-Davidson and Ridolfo 2008) and a NEH Digging into Data grant (Rehberger 2010)," there is still much work to do to facilitate cross-talk between rhetorical studies and the digital humanities, and *Digital Samaritans* is one additional step toward broader field connections between rhetorical studies and the digital humanities (1). The payoff for the digital humanities is a more enhanced sense of the multiple audiences projects might have, and a method for thinking about each of those audiences as a specific research project. With a rhetorical understanding, the digital humanities is able to more clearly address multiple publics in more intentional and effective ways.

Working with my coeditor of *Rhetoric and the Digital Humanities*, William Hart-Davidson, as an editorial team we developed the collection with the specific disciplinary objective that "rhetoric and writing studies' recent attention to DH not only demonstrates the need for this collection to put scholars in conversation with one another but also suggests that there is much work to be done" (3). As a first step, we contend that the "collection aims to provide a first step toward building interdisciplinary discussions between rhetoric studies and DH by defining shared research trajectories, methods, and projects between DH and the federation of rhetoric studies, composition, C&W, and areas of TPW" (9). *Digital Samaritans* is a complement to *Rhetoric and the Digital Humanities*, because it extends a single case example at the intersection of rhetoric and the digital humanities to consider more broadly the role of rhetorical delivery in the digital humanities. While the collection aims to survey a broad range of work happening between both fields through short pieces, *Digital Samaritans* offers a deeper meditation on the rhetorical connections to a single digital humanities project, the digitization of Samaritan manuscripts. In *Digital Samaritans*, I situate the digitization of Samaritan manuscripts in textual diaspora and creation of digital tools and resources for the community as a theoretical and rhetorical object of research. By connecting this practical engaged work with a specific community to broader questions of audience, delivery, and circulation in the field of rhetoric, I show how rhetorical research and theory is necessary to understand not only the historical and contemporary context of the project but also the digital delivery of the texts in relationship to the goals and rhetorical objectives of members of the living cultural community: the two Samaritan communities in Israel and the Palestinian Authority.

In *Digital Samaritans*, I use the term *textual diaspora* to describe how some Samaritans are strategically talking about the future rhetorical potential of their diaspora of manuscripts and its digitization as a matter of rhetorical sovereignty. This concept evolves out of my earlier work on rhetorical velocity and strategizing the future potential of texts (see Ridolfo and DeVoss) and my fieldwork with the Samaritans themselves.[2] However, thinking about the future rhetorical potential of digital objects may not only be limited to the digitization of manuscripts. *Textual diaspora* situates the past, present, and future of texts. Situating texts in diaspora and their digital potential involves thinking about the changing rhetorical goals and the particular objectives of cultural stakeholders.[3] Such stakeholders might want or need to theorize the strategic importance of the present location of manuscripts, and resources around those manuscripts, in relationship to the cultural stakeholders' cultural/rhetorical sovereignty, future repatriation and/or digitization and additional amplification of collections.

The Samaritans want to draw cultural strength from their diaspora; however, unlike Jewish and other peoples, their diaspora is comprised of manuscripts and artifacts, not people. The circumstance of textual diaspora can be understood within the broader context of rhetorical delivery and circulation (Helsley; Kathleen Welch; Trimbur; DeVoss and Porter; Prior et al.; and others), because manuscripts deposited in libraries and archives across the world may once again be accessed by the Samaritans and redistributed or shared via their own use of social and print media. In other words, the Samaritans see their textual diaspora as a rhetorical source of strength. Echoing Cameron and Kenderine's sentiments about power residing in institutions and "the specific roles that museums and cultural heritage institutions play in interpretation and representation using new and emerging digital media," the Samaritans understand the global locations of the manuscripts as critical to generating additional scholarly attention to their community and its practices, and they recognize that this increased awareness of their spiritual/religious texts leads to increased knowledge about their cultural heritage and political situation in the region (Cameron and Kenderdine 2). Rather than desiring the repatriation of these valuable manuscripts, some Samaritans prefer that these texts remain in diaspora. *Digital Samaritans* argues that a range of Samaritan positions on their diaspora of manuscripts demonstrates a complex understanding of delivery by showing how the texts' current geographic and institutional location can be used to further advance the Samaritans' interests.

Digital Samaritans connects field conversations in rhetorical studies on rhetorical delivery and circulation (Helsley; Kathleen Welch; Trimbur; DeVoss and Porter; Prior et al.; and others) to the digital humanities by describing how cultural stakeholders may theorize and strategically *leverage* their material in diaspora with the advent of the digital. To theorize such a rhetorical situation, I develop the concept of *textual diaspora* to explain the situation of Samaritan manuscripts and a range of Samaritan desires for those manuscripts. Textual diaspora is a term used to describe the situation whereby the Samaritans' complex historical circumstances led to the dispersal of their manuscripts around the globe. The distance of the texts from the community that would study them, use them in ritual practice, and interact with them has created additional rhetorical needs and desires for the Samaritans to exercise cultural sovereignty, or rhetorically leverage their texts in digital environments. In the chapters to come, I describe how the majority of their manuscripts exist today in libraries, archives, and museums abroad and show how these manuscripts in diaspora relate to rhetorical strategies of future delivery, what I term the *leveraging of textual diaspora.* While the case example derives from the specific situation of the Samaritans, the questions the example raises and the theoretical insights it helps to develop are applicable to the broader intersection of digital humanities and rhetorical studies. We send texts out to *do something* in the world. Digitization both enacts and enables specific kinds of *doing*; it enables the delivery of digitized manuscripts that may then be referenced on Samaritan websites and shared in Samaritan Facebook groups.

After tracking the movement of Samaritan manuscripts from the Samaritan community out into a worldwide diaspora, it is easier to understand how textual diaspora becomes a key component in understanding the Samaritans' ever-evolving attitudes toward the composition and distribution of their texts. Although the Samaritans are divided between Israeli and Palestinian civil societies, Samaritans must be able to reference their historic relationship to the land, their culture, languages, and identity as an ancient Israelite people to both audiences.[4] More than that, they must also be able to explain their unique cultural heritage to outsiders within and beyond Israeli and Palestinian society, and they can do that best by referring to "their own writing . . . their own language . . . and historical tradition" through cultural artifacts (Tsedaka and Tsedaka 1). Theorizing the digital delivery of textual diaspora creates a double-linkage between how texts came to be where they are and how they will be used in the future. Making this connection explicit offers productive ways to understand rhetorical historiography and delivery as interrelated aspects of a text's movement in time and across culture.

The Samaritans' textual diaspora challenges scholars of rhetoric to consider the relationship of rhetorical delivery to rhetorical sovereignty, what Scott Lyons defines as "the inherent right and ability of *peoples* [sic] to determine their own communicative needs and desires in this pursuit, to decide for themselves the goals, modes, styles, and languages of public discourse" (449–50), a term that describes Samaritan calls for cultural sovereignty in the "Seven Principles" document discussed in chapters 2 and 3 and relates to rhetorical sovereignty over how they are able to communicate their cultural identity. In turn, rhetorical sovereignty is directly related to the future of their textual diaspora. In the sixteenth and seventeenth centuries, European scholars resorted to deceiving Samaritans out of their manuscripts by, in some cases, pretending to be their long lost brethren from Europe. I discuss the origins of the Samaritans' textual diaspora further in the next chapter. Based on interviews with Samaritans, archival documents, travel narratives, and secondary literature in Samaritan studies, I show that some Samaritans prefer the current state of these manuscripts in diaspora because their sovereignty as a people is contingent on the Samaritans' ability to make reference to and interpret their cultural heritage. For example, Samaritans are increasingly referencing their cultural heritage through Facebook and other online resources, and doing so allows them to share examples of their cultural heritage and to explain more clearly to other people where the Samaritans came from, how long they have been in the region, and how they understand their position in the region as a bridge for peace. While one might assume that Samaritans would prefer to have large numbers of the manuscripts abroad returned and repatriated, this is not universally the case. For Benyamim Tsedaka, the manuscripts do more work for the Samaritans *in diaspora*; however, Yacop Cohen wants some of the manuscripts returned to Mount Gerizim in order to fill their library with Samaritan books. *Digital Samaritans* explores these rhetorical positions on a case-by-case basis and argues that these responses to the diaspora of Samaritan manuscripts constitute complex and strategic reactions to the Samaritans' recent history, current geopolitical situation, and future as a growing, thriving people and culture.

Implicit in *Digital Samaritans* is the idea that digital humanists need to understand the rhetorical situation of digital projects, as well as the rhetorical context for making digital projects public and thinking about how they will be rhetorically leveraged by different groups. When North American and European funding agencies place grant resources, dollar bills, and Western institutional ethos behind digital projects, they are making implicit arguments about what cultures and histories Western institutions value. As Cameron and Kenderdine argue in their introduction to the 2007 collection *Theorizing Digital Cultural Heritage: A Critical Discourse*, Western museums and heritage organizations

hold a significant part of the "intellectual capital" of our information society. The use of emerging digital technologies to activate, engage, and transform this "capital" is paralleled by shifts in the organizational and practice culture of the institutions entrusted with its case. In a symbiotic relationship, cultural heritage "ecologies" also appropriate, adopt, incorporate, and transform the digital technologies they adopt. Why and how this transformation occurs in our cultural organizations requires serious investigation and is the subject of this compilation. (1)

For example, from the moment NEH Office of Digital Humanities' funded grant lists are published, digital projects are delivered and, rhetorically, become more than their digital parts and dollars. They take on the ethos and endorsement of a government agency, educational or cultural heritage institution, and scholarly backing. Scholars know, for example, that Western institutions value Shakespeare enough to recast Shakespeare in digital environments dozens of times in dozens of projects. The same is also true to a degree for Jeremy Bentham, Walt Whitman, and many other Western authors. In many cases, when universities recast cultural heritage material in digital environments they are adding their ethos to the project and are communicating the cultural value of the material to larger audiences.

As Digital Samaritans demonstrates, digitization is not a culturally or politically neutral act. In the case of the Samaritans, digitization helps the living community reference their cultural heritage in digital environments. Practically speaking, http://www.the-samaritans.com, a website run by Osher Sassoni, a member of the Samaritan community in Holon, links to digital manuscripts to provide examples of their cultural heritage and uniqueness to the region. In doing so, the Samaritans behind http://www.the-samaritans.com are leveraging their digital cultural heritage made available by institutions abroad. Other Samaritan-run websites such as the Arabic-English Samaritan Legend Association (http://www.sl-a.org) and the Hebrew-English homepage of the A.B. Institute of Samaritan Studies (http://www.israelite-samaritans.com) advance knowledge about the Samaritans to the world through digital technology. The tagline of the A.B. Institute of Samaritan Studies reads "Ancient Tradition Thriving in the 21st Century," signifying on the one hand the Samaritan ethos of tradition, and on the other their present-day use of digital technology to communicate Samaritan identity.

In the Samaritan example, the relationship of digitization, digital tools, and digital delivery to the past and present rhetorical situation of the Samaritans is integral to understanding why Samaritans want their manuscripts abroad digitized and made available to the world, especially from Western institutions that have seized, purchased, and collected their texts. Such digitization helps them to advance arguments about their cultural, political, and economic sovereignty in one of the most contentious regions in the world (Powell).

As the Samaritan example shows, project teams need to consider that they are not funded and digitally delivered in a rhetorical vacuum and the rhetorical context of funding is of utmost importance to digital humanists more broadly. As multicultural information studies scholar Kimberly Christen reminds us: "[S]hifting the focus away from information as bits and bytes . . . indigenous cultural protocols and structures for information circulation remind us that information neither wants to be free nor wants to be open; human beings must decide how we want to imagine the world of knowledge-sharing and information management in ways that are at once ethical and cognizant of the deep histories of engagement and exclusion that animate this terrain" (2889). In calling attention to the idea that information does not "inherently want" to be free, Christen makes room for a rhetorical understanding of digital objects and the "contentious issues of access to knowledge and information freedom as they play out through assertions of control over digital materials, clarion calls for a more robust public domain, and expansive definitions of open access" (2874). Christen's ideas about information availability relate to Samaritan desires to express their rhetorical sovereignty through their textual diaspora of manuscripts. As cultural heritage is spread out across the globe while Samaritan centers of population remain in two geographic locations, an important component of Tsedaka's efforts has been to encourage institutions to make Samaritan cultural heritage available and accessible. In doing so, Tsedaka is exemplifying Christen's idea of engaging in matters of "access to knowledge and information freedom." His work is not only related to the digital. Tsedaka's advocacy to libraries and museums abroad includes calls to put Samaritan material on display. Furthermore, to digitize and make Samaritan material available often requires the expenditure of resources on the part of the institution. This conservation and digitization work does not always happen without external prompting and resources. In this regard, what's made available on the Internet by institutions is often a reflection of their own values and needs, and not necessarily that of the communities far away whose cultural heritage material they possess.

Thinking about digital cultural objects in rhetorical terms also addresses Walter Benjamin's idea that "even the most perfect reproduction of a work of art is lacking in one element: its presence in time and space, its unique existence at the place where it happens to be" (220). For the digitized manuscript, there's enhanced potential "for replicas to transcend originals" (Schwartz 297) and even begin, as Hillel Schwartz theorizes, to anticipate when "the copy will transcend the original" and become something else entirely (iii). What Christen, Benjamin, and Schwartz have in common then is the idea that copies of cultural heritage are something different than the original. For Christen, this means that protocols should be developed to understand what cultural stakeholders want from their digital materials. Building upon Christen's insistence on attention to stakeholders' needs and values, *Digital Samaritans* argues that even though "digital copies" differ from original textual materials, part of their added advantage, at least from the Samaritans' understanding of the value of their textual diaspora, is that they provide much-needed and valued material for circulation and recomposition. Consequently, this book explores why such a textual diaspora is rhetorically beneficial for the Samaritans and why digital humanists and rhetoricians more broadly speaking have much to learn from the sophisticated ways Samaritans think about, engage, and use their textual diaspora to help them attain greater cultural sovereignty and recognition as a cultural heritage community. For projects with living stakeholder communities such as the Samaritans, acknowledging the rhetorical dimension means scholars must adopt an *ethos* of engaged research and reciprocity with stakeholder communities. Digital cultural projects that are aware of their rhetorical and cultural contexts must, whenever possible, be fully engaged with stakeholder communities and attuned to their past, present, and future desires.

Digital Samaritans contends that a key feature of Samaritan dissemination efforts is their ability to reference and explain their cultural heritage to Palestinians and Israelis in the region and beyond. Dissemination of their own historical narrative, culture, and history is of high importance to them because of the constant need to explain who they are and that they still exist as a living, breathing people to their neighbors and the world. In addition to Samaritan direct advocacy such as the work of Yacop Cohen and the Samaritan Legend Association discussed more in chapter 3, another factor in the rhetorical situation are thousands of Samaritan manuscripts, the majority of which were purchased or stolen from the Samaritans and now reside in more than seventy libraries and archives abroad. This textual diaspora sets the stage for Digital Samaritans.

Based on archival materials and interviews with nine Samaritans, I show that the digitization of the Samaritans' textual diaspora allows them to leverage their cultural heritage in digital environments. Once provided access to these digitized materials, the Samaritans have a greater rhetorical ability to make arguments about their regional identity to their neighbors and the world. As I show in chapter 3, several of the Samaritans I interviewed preferred that the manuscripts remain abroad instead of being returned to Mount Gerizim, because they want scholars to have access to manuscripts all across the world rather than remaining available only to their small, relatively isolated community. Reasons given include that scholarly attention helps to foster greater awareness of the Samaritan people and their unique place in the region, and this is important because it helps to create a record of scholarship on the Samaritans as a people and on their Israelite heritage, distinct although still historically connected to Judaism as an Israelite faith. In chapters 2 and 3, the reasons for Samaritan cultural and religious distinction are discussed in more depth.

This rhetorical understanding demonstrates that some Samaritans are theorizing the rhetorical potential of their textual diaspora to communicate their identity to the world. In addition, Tsedaka's and the late Samaritan Elazar ben Tsedaka ben Yitzhaq's calls for digitizing all Samaritan manuscripts abroad point to the important role digitization plays in helping to increase the reach of this textual diaspora. So long as the texts remain in brick and mortar archives all across the world, the Samaritans' potential to reference them is limited; however, digitization provides greater potential for the Samaritans to leverage their cultural heritage not only by offering remote access to community members but also by providing increased access to scholars and the general public. In the Samaritan context, the digitization of their cultural heritage texts provides a link between rhetoric and the digital humanities and helps to illustrate how the digital humanities can help the Samaritans in their efforts to explain their unique cultural heritage to their neighbors. As Jess Enoch and David Gold argue in their introduction to the November 2013 special issue of *College English* on rhetorical historiography and the digital humanities, scholars in rhetorical studies "are indeed in a methodological moment" in which the digital is not employed "for its own sake" but seeks "to use digital tools to answer extant and evolving historical and historiographic questions" (112). For the Samaritans, these questions are especially prescient, given their unique geopolitical location between the Israelis and Palestinians.

However, the leveraging of cultural heritage in digital environments is not only about making arguments, it's also about viewing unique acrostics in manuscripts abroad. For example, as part of the Samaritan manuscript digitization project, in 2011 I digitized an 1145 CE Samaritan scroll of Deuteronomy at Hebrew Union College in Cincinnati. What makes the average Samaritan manuscript particularly unique is the presence of *tashkil*, or acrostic writing. In a typical *tashkil* for example, from right-to-left will be the text of the Torah and top-down would be a story about the scribe, family, and community. While the story of Exodus or Deuteronomy may be universal to all Samaritans, the letters align to produce a local story unique to the scribe's time and place. In the case of this 1145 CE[5] manuscript of Deuteronomy featured here (for digitally enhanced version see http://samaritanrepository.org), the acrostic tells the story of the previously unknown Samaritan community of Ashkelon (in present-day Israel). Several interviewees worry that if this manuscript and many more like it were centralized in an archive on Mount Gerizim, scholars would not as readily have access to conduct research about it and create new scholarship on the manuscripts. In addition to the manuscripts themselves, each Samaritan manuscript generally contains a unique acrostic or *tashkil* in which Samaritan scribes have written a story about themselves through the vertical alignment of letters. For Samaritans in Holon and Mount Gerizim, a *tashkil* is a direct connection to their people's past and often is the voice of relatives in their family lineage. At this juncture in history, this type of broader access, awareness, and circulation of knowledge, it turns out, is more valuable to the Samaritans than the material, physical text itself. The strategic thinking, then, is that many manuscripts in many hands have a greater rhetorical payoff for the Samaritans than many manuscripts in the hands of very few. The process of scholarly study and digitization provides access not just to non-Samaritans, but also Samaritans within the community who can't leave Israel and the Palestinian Authority to visit archives across the world.

The scholarly work that's done with texts abroad provides additional *ethos* to the manuscripts that the Samaritans working on their own can't fully provide. This increased legitimacy is especially important for outside audiences who have a real impact on the Samaritans' physical existence. Having texts in digital form and widely available for study and circulation enables the Samaritan community to make more respected/authentic/legitimate arguments to their Israeli and Palestinian neighbors and the world beyond. Digital humanities work in the form of digitization and tailoring archives to multiple publics and audiences functions as a rhetorical means to increase access to these collections and further stakeholders' goals of maintaining cultural sovereignty.

Drawing on Aristotle's notion of actualities and potentialities in the *Metaphysics* Z, I argue that the rhetorical power of these diasporic manuscripts has changed and increased with the advent of digital technology and digitization (S. Marc Cohen).[6] While these manuscripts were previously limited to a brick and mortar existence in archives, they have a new rhetorical *potential* as digitized resources that may be cited, referenced, shared, and composed into other Samaritan-authored texts. In museums, libraries, and special collections across the world, there is a large and vast resource of cultural heritage waiting to be digitized—and then *actualized* by the Samaritans. Later in this book, I connect actuality and potentiality to the term textual diaspora to argue that leveraging textual diaspora is not only about the digitization of manuscripts but also, as Hillel Schwartz contends, about how the copy can go beyond the original to become other kinds of texts, to be referenced, drawn upon, and rhetorically leveraged in new and strategic ways (Schwartz).

Thinking about the rhetorical potentiality of texts provides a useful framework to understand the relationship of rhetoric to the digital humanities, because it prompts rhetoricians and digital humanists to ask what kind of sharing and composing a digital archive or repository might enable. In the case of the Samaritans, the more than seventy libraries, archives, and museums that currently possess Samaritan manuscripts also lend *ethos* to those texts for particular Western audiences.[7] Additionally, these institutions have the potential to digitize these manuscripts over the next ten to twenty years. If such digitization work continues to receive funding to move forward at a wider range of institutions, the Samaritans will have greater potential to *actualize* and leverage their cultural heritage in digital environments such as Facebook, the Web, and their own media and ongoing cultural heritage production. In the era of digitization, the Samaritans' textual diaspora has increased potential to aid the Samaritans as a resource in their work to communicate the Samaritans' place in the region. In the case of the Samaritan textual diaspora, manuscripts spread out across the world reside in the libraries of the same governments that continue to be active in regional policy matters. The Samaritans I interviewed look toward the objective of broader public knowledge about the Samaritans rather than the return of the manuscripts. The former, in several of the perspectives, is more likely if the manuscripts remain where colonialism has deposited them, provided that they are studied and, one day, digitized. While many of these concerns have been less visible in the digital humanities, in this book I explore a rhetorical orientation for engaged work in the digital humanities, focusing specifically on rhetorical delivery and investigating the past and future circulation of texts.

Rhetoric and Mount Gerizim

This centrality of why it's important for Samaritans to argue their cultural identity was highlighted recently by a series of events that unfolded during the first week of July 2012. For political commentators, this week could be read as just another set of stories in the ongoing Israel-Palestine conflict. For the Samaritan community in Israel and the West Bank, the week marked a new round of Palestinian and Israeli claims about the Samaritans' heritage, cultural identity, and sovereignty over their holy site on Mount Gerizim in the West Bank. As National Public Radio reporter Daniel Estrin observed: "In the Israeli-Palestinian tug-of-war over heritage sites, it's often the custodians who've looked after these places for centuries who feel the uncomfortable pull." *Digital Samaritans* begins with this latest "pull," because it helps to frame the contemporary rhetorical situation the Samaritans presently confront with two nationalist entities making competing claims about the Samaritans' place in the region. The digitization project helps the Samaritans' larger project of articulating their historical place in the region amidst the contemporary geopolitical conflict, and the need for scholars and institutions to deal ethically with cultural heritage materials in diaspora because of the very salient and real questions of political and cultural sovereignty at stake.

On July 5, 2012, the Israeli government, in a ceremony on top of the Samaritan ruins of Tel er-Ras on Mount Gerizim in the West Bank, transferred control of the ancient archaeological fortress, site of a twenty-four-year-long archaeological excavation by the Israel Antiquities Authority, to the Israel Nature and Parks Authority. The site, which had been open to tourists for one month in August of 2000, closed in September 2000 at the start of the Second Intifada and remained closed for the next twelve years. In June 2010 in *Haaretz*, Samaritan Ovadia Cohen advocated that the Israeli government reopen the site to tourists. Since the end of the Second Intifada in 2004, the threat of violence and shooting around Mount Gerizim had diminished considerably.[8] Cohen told *Haaretz* that the Samaritans "are ready to manage the place" and that they not only "have the capacity to manage it," but they are also "losing a lot of money every year [in admission fees]" because of the closure (Levinson). Cohen claims that the archaeological site was turned over to the Samaritans on Mount Gerizim by the Hashemite King "during the period of Jordanian rule over the West Bank," from 1948–1967, but for the last twelve years the Samaritans had to "obtain permission from the [Israeli] authorities" every time they wanted to officially access the site (Levinson).[9] While the Israelis were making bureaucratic and security arguments that the site needed to be closed, Cohen made historical and financial arguments relating to the well-being of his people, the Samaritan people, and their ability to manage their religious site on Mount Gerizim. This is important not only from the perspective of how the larger Palestinian-Israeli conflict impacts daily life in the West Bank but also from the perspective of how the Samaritans' wishes for cultural sovereignty on their own mountain top are superseded by larger current events.

The July 5, 2012, opening by the Israelis, however, marked a new chapter in the battle for the cultural and political identity of Mount Gerizim and the Samaritans' place in the ongoing Israel-Palestine conflict. While the opening and this brief story may seem far removed from the digital humanities and rhetorical studies, they are connected in that the digital humanities is one way Samaritan cultural knowledge may be delivered to the world. The competing values evident in both Cohen's and the Israeli government's claims illustrate how rhetorical methodology not only helps to unpack the stakes of the argument but also better enables the Samaritans to attain cultural sovereignty, asserting and having their own identity claims recognized not just by the local adversaries in the region but also by the world.

Just two days after Israel transferred authority to the Israel Nature and Parks Authority, allowing the site to resume tourist activity under Israeli government supervision and administration, the Palestinian National Authority (P.A.) was successful in its petition to the United Nations Educational, Scientific, and Cultural Organization (UNESCO) to add the Church of the Nativity to the list of World Heritage sites. More importantly for the Samaritans, the P.A. also announced its intention to petition to add Mount Gerizim, along with other sites in the West Bank, to the UNESCO list of World Heritage sites. At the Israeli opening ceremony for Mount Gerizim, which coincided with the UNESCO Bethlehem decision, Israeli Minister of Environmental Protection Gilad Erdan made a reference to the ongoing UNESCO fight over cultural heritage sites in the West Bank: "As the Palestinians lead a false international campaign to end our connection to the Land of Israel, opening sites like Mount Gerizim will help us show the world that the Palestinian smear campaign is false and that it is impossible to sever the historical connection of the Jewish people to its land" (Benardi and Kempinski).[10] Upon learning of the

Israeli intention to turn Mount Gerizim into a park, the Palestinian Ministry of Tourism and Antiquities issued a press release condemning the Israeli announcement as a violation of the Fourth Geneva Convention of 1949 and the Hague Convention of 1954. Similar to the Israeli claim advancing a historical link to Mount Gerizim, an article in *Ma'an* claimed that the Samaritan village on Mount Gerizim represents the "continuity of Palestinian cultural heritage" from prehistoric times to the present day ("The Ministry of Tourism"). Absent from the Israeli and Palestinian claims, however, are Samaritans' own ideas about their culture and relationship to the land the Israelis and Palestinians were competing to claim.

On July 7, 2012, in Bethlehem, the Palestinian National Authority formally celebrated the decision by UNESCO to make Bethlehem's Church of the Nativity a World Heritage site.[11] For the P.A., the event was hailed as a victory and "recognition of the rights of our people and their independent Palestinian state on the 1967 borders with East Jerusalem as its capital," according to Palestinian Authority presidential spokesman Nabil Abu Rudeineh. P.A. Prime Minister Salam Fayyad also linked the UNESCO decision on Bethlehem to Palestinian nationalist struggles: "This decision reflects the importance to the world of this holy Palestinian city and its holy places and heritage," and the decision "gives hope and confidence to our people of the imminent victory of their just cause" (R.T. and M.S.). Israeli Prime Minister Benjamin Netanyahu responded, "This is proof that UNESCO is motivated by political and not cultural considerations" (Dobkina), interpreting Fayyad's statements to mean that the P.A.'s UNESCO petitions are largely tactical and political. In the midst of this landmark decision for the P.A., three churches that share administration of the Church of the Nativity expressed reservations about the UNESCO decision (Kershner). According to National Public Radio reporter Daniel Estrin, the clergy "were afraid of letting politicians meddle on their turf." This would not be the first or the only instance where religious stakeholders to a historical site would object to the use of UNESCO for Palestinian and Israeli nationalisms.

In response to the Israeli and Palestinian actions regarding Mount Gerizim, on Monday July 9, the Facebook public page for the Samaritan-administered Museum on Mount Gerizim posted that the latest "conflict between the Israelis and the Palestinians to take control of the top of Mount Gerizim aims to exploit the mountain as an archaeological and tourist landmark" and asked "where is the free world to defend" the Samaritans amidst this conflict (Samaritan Museum)? For example, in the first week of July 2012 Israel's *Arutz Sheva* (Channel 7) posted a video of the Israeli ceremony declaring Mount Gerizim a national park. *Arutz Sheva* interviewed a future Israeli tour guide for the park and asked her who the Samaritans are and where they originate:

Fig. 1. Ancient ruins on top of Mount Gerizim / Israeli park, July 2012. (Photograph by Jim Ridolfo.)

Fig. 2. Ancient ruins on top of Mount Gerizim / Israeli park, July 2012. (Photograph by Jim Ridolfo.)

Fig. 3. Israeli military jeep parked at entrance to Mount Gerizim park, July 2012. (Photograph by Jim Ridolfo.)

On the one hand there's . . . one side which will say that they are the original Israelites and they are the ones which have kept the Bible as it is meant to be . . . and on the other hand you have people that will say they were brought here by the Assyrians years later, about 700 B.C.E. (Elad and Kempinski)

The tour guide does not label the sides; however, the first position that the Samaritans are "original Israelites" is the Samaritans' own religious belief. The second position, that the Samaritans were transplants brought to the biblical land of Israel by the Assyrians after their conquest in 722 BCE is the common Jewish interpretation of Samaritan identity found in the Talmud.[12] This is not the first time this schism in religious narrative has been politicized in Israeli

Fig. 4. Mount Gerizim's park rules, July 2012. (Photograph by Jim Ridolfo.)

Fig. 5. Israeli settlement of *Har Bracha* adjacent to the Samaritans. New construction, May 2012. (Photograph by Jim Ridolfo.)

Fig. 6. Still from *Arutz Sheva* report on July 6, 2012, "Mount Gerizim Archaeological Site Reopens." (*Video available at* https://www.youtube.com/watch?v=P4fzcuLNBuY. *A full video transcript is available in Appendix A.*)

civic society. In the beginning of the twentieth century, the Samaritans were embraced by Israeli leaders such as Yitzhak Ben-Zvi because they represent a living, breathing link to the Hebrew Bible and land. Consequently, in the early 1950s Ben Zvi helped found a Samaritan neighborhood in Holon, Israel; however, the Samaritans' own narrative of events differs considerably from Judaism's and key parts of the Jewish religious narrative of the West Bank and Jerusalem.

July 2012's week of dramatic events is part of a much longer rhetorical story about the relationship of the Samaritans to their Palestinian and Israeli neighbors, and how these relationships inform access, use, and interaction with sacred objects, artifacts, and texts. The Israeli narrative of Mount Gerizim tries to qualify the Samaritans' own version of historical events because the Samaritans' religious beliefs and presence in the region challenge the spiritual and political significance of Israeli biblical claims to the West Bank and to the holiness of Jerusalem. The Palestine Liberation Organization has also tried to selectively reference the Samaritan historical narrative in arguments for its own nationalist agenda. For example, Yasser Arafat was quoted as denying Jewish claims for Jerusalem, advancing instead that "if it [the Temple] existed, it must have existed elsewhere," and on several occasions he indicated that this "elsewhere" was, in fact, near Nablus. Arafat also went so far in 1996 as to create a designated Samaritan seat in the eighty-eight member Palestinian National Council, and Palestinian media often reference the coexistence of Muslims, Christians, and Samaritans in Nablus, the city next to Mount Gerizim as evidence of the prospects for religious coexistence. As the next several chapters will elaborate in greater detail, these overlapping nationalist claims put significant cultural pressure on the Samaritan community and are the cause of much speculation on the part of Israelis and Palestinians as to the Samaritans' identity and nationalist loyalties. In turn, the Samaritans' own efforts to explain their place between these two fires is ongoing, and their diaspora of manuscripts, what I term *textual diaspora*, is one resource they can leverage to make clear to their neighbors and the world their history in their land, and their unique culture and heritage.

The Samaritans' own story begins in their Samaritan Torah (five books of Moses), which has its own unique script,[13] pronunciation scheme, and grammatical differences from the Masoretic Hebrew. While their Torah is largely similar in content to that of the Jewish people, it has many textual and theological differences. For example, the Samaritan version of the Torah maintains that Mount Gerizim rather than Jerusalem is the site of the holy temple; consequently, Samaritan religious law and practices differ considerably from Jewish traditions.

At one time, the Samaritans were one of the largest populations in the region. During the Roman-Byzantine period the total Samaritan population was anywhere from 150,000 to 200,000 according to Ottoman tax registers, but by 1538–1539 there were only 220 Samaritans remaining in Ottoman Palestine (Pummer 1; Crown, Pummer, Tal, "Demographics" 71). According to Reinhard Pummer, "Revolts against repressive governments and forced conversions reduced their numbers more and more, until there came a time, in the 19th cent. [sic], when they were at the point of near extinction" (Pummer 1). In fact, in January 1920, *National Geographic* magazine published a feature story on the Samaritans of Nablus. At that time, their population numbered less than 140. *National Geographic* writer John Whiting described the Samaritans as an "almost extinct community" and concluded the article by proclaiming the Samaritans are a "dying people" due to hundreds of years of war, conversion, famine, poverty, and earthquakes (1 and 46). From these low numbers, the Samaritan population began to increase in the 1940s, and it continues to rise due to a combination of better health, economic, and social circumstances. The community has more than quadrupled in size since those grim predictions, and now approximately 405 Samaritans reside in Israel and 365 in the Palestinian Authority. Although the two communities maintain close connections, the geographic split means that younger members of the community in Holon speak Modern Hebrew as a first language and the residents of Kiryat Luza on Mount Gerizim speak Arabic as a first language. Beyond language, this separation places the Samaritans directly between the "two fires," as Samaritan Faruk Rijan Samira refers to the conflict between Palestinians and

Israelis. Within this context, the Samaritans strive to maintain a delicate balance between the Israeli government and Palestinian Authority. Being few in number and vulnerable to larger political trends, they have positioned themselves in the region as seeking peaceful relationships with both government entities.

As the Israeli government attempts to define the tourist narrative of the Samaritans and the P.A. applies for UNESCO status to recognize Mount Gerizim's place in Palestinian civil and historical society, Samaritans are working to determine and to disseminate their own story through the use of Facebook and other social media. Through the case example of digitizing Samaritan manuscripts for future circulation, *Digital Samaritans* provides a rhetorical framework for envisioning relationships between theory and practice in the digital humanities. In addition to providing scholars in the digital humanities with a case example for thinking about the rhetorical history, delivery, circulation, and audiences of projects as a theoretical heuristic to complicate and complement projects, an equally important goal for this book is to provide scholars in digital rhetoric with a model for thinking about the intersection of rhetoric and the digital humanities.

TWO

Between the Raindrops and Two Fires: A Brief History of the Samaritans and Their Diaspora of Manuscripts

We are a small community, and so we try to go between the raindrops.
—Faruk Rijan Samira, Nablus, 1990

We have a big problem—we're between two fires.
—Joseph Cohen, Nablus, 2011

In order to understand the Samaritan textual diaspora, we need to understand the context that gave birth to it and show how the rhetorical concept develops out of Samaritan responses both to material circumstances and to the Samaritans' desire to be their own authors and to have sovereignty over their cultural and religious identity. Over the last five hundred years there have been three stages of Samaritan manuscript removal: deceit and theft, coercion and consent, and writing for tourists. These stages combined with the Samaritans' historical and contemporary rhetorical context directly contribute to the development of some Samaritans' ideas on the present and future of their diaspora of manuscripts. This chapter traces the emergence of the diaspora of Samaritan manuscripts as a historical consequence of Western interest in their Pentateuch (version of the Hebrew Bible) and connects this diaspora to the historical rise/fall/revision of attitudes to writing and their manuscripts.

To this end, I focus on the history of the Samaritan community from the late Ottoman period through the British mandate to their present day position between the Palestinian Authority and Israel. I discuss four significant events: first, *National Geographic*'s 1920 special issue on the Samaritans where the author predicted the Samaritans' extinction by the end of the twentieth century; second, the establishment of the Samaritan neighborhood in Holon by Israel's second president, Yitzhak Ben-Zvi, and his rhetorical move to claim the Samaritans as fellow Israelites; third, the years of isolation, 1949–1967, when there was very little contact between the Samaritan communities in the West Bank and Israel; and fourth, Yasser Arafat's appointment of a Samaritan to the Palestinian Council on December 15, 1995, and his argument to claim the Samaritans as Palestinians. The recent events discussed in the previous chapter, such as the Palestinians' and Israelis' competing claims to the Samaritans' cultural heritage, the isolation of the two Samaritan communities as a result of the war of 1948, and National Geographic's yet-to-be recanted proclamation, are important factors for understanding the situation and context of the Samaritan manuscript digitization project.

I also examine how Westerners acquired Samaritan manuscripts, Samaritan responses to these various stages of Western manuscript acquisition, and Samaritans' contemporary reflections on how their attitudes toward writing have changed. This historical foundation is essential for understanding the context of contemporary digitization and Samaritan calls for their cultural and historical sovereignty. As Mary Louise Pratt says, "If one studies only what the Europeans saw and said, one reproduces the monopoly on knowledge and interpretation that the imperial enterprise sought" (Pratt, 7).[1] In most cases, the sources I rely upon are travel narratives and records of Western contact with the Samaritans. They display, especially in the nineteenth century, all of the traits and characteristics Mary Louise Pratt describes in *Imperial Eyes: Travel Writing and Transculturation*: a Western vision of an "imperial order" in relationship to those whom they're discussing (x).[2] The acquisition of Samaritan manuscripts occurs in tandem with major historical and economic changes in the region that, in turn, directly impact the already small community.[3]

The relationship of Samaritans to their manuscripts has gradually changed over time. By saying that the relationship has changed, I do not mean that their religious or spiritual relationship to their liturgical texts has changed, but rather that economic, political, existential, and colonialist influences have changed, by the necessity of survival, their relationship to their manuscripts in diaspora. Major historical transitions changed their relationship to their scribal practices and manuscripts. First, fragments, and then later full manuscripts, were sold for currency to buy bread and subsist, particularly in the absence of other economic opportunities. Within a short amount of time, the Samaritans adapted to their material surroundings and began to write as a form of survival. Manuscripts were produced for the pilgrim economy of nineteenth- and early twentieth-century Ottoman Palestine, and this professional tourist economy of writing continued well into the Mandate period. Writing was no longer strictly about fulfilling the mitzvah (commandment) to copy the Torah: writing was also a means to feed starving families.

Although the Samaritans began to thrive economically after this difficult period in the early twentieth century, fundamentally their cultural milieu was changed: thousands of their manuscripts and fragments, particularly those from their *Genizah* in Nablus, were overseas, swindled, stolen, or sold off to foreign hands. As these developments progressed, the Ottoman Empire's power over Palestine had waned. It finally collapsed after the end of the First World War. Zionist settlement of British Mandate Palestine increasingly sped up, and the *Yishuv* grew from small settlements in the early twentieth century to the state of Israel in 1948; Arab and Palestinian nationalisms, particularly after the First World War, also began to assert their political visions for future autonomy from British rule. Ever since the 1930s, and especially after the 1936 Arab Revolt in Nablus, the Samaritans found themselves "between the raindrops" as economic hardship subsided and, in its place, mounting political pressure continued to develop. This chapter lays the foundation for understanding the diaspora of Samaritan manuscripts historically in order to better understand their present-day rhetorical context as they enter the digital age[4] and the way some Samaritan attitudes toward their diaspora of manuscripts have evolved.

Samaritans' Early History

Samaritans trace their history to the time of Aaron and understand themselves as the direct descendants of the northern tribes of Israel: Ephraim, Manasseh, and Levi. According to Robert Anderson and Terry Giles, the Samaritans have historically preferred to be called Israelites rather than Samaritans. The Samaritans "claim they originate in the time of the judges (eleventh century B.C.E.), when they say the priest and judge Eli established a cult site at Shiloh to rival that at Shechem," present-day Nablus (Anderson and Giles 10).[5] Citing Feldman, Anderson and Giles quote that "the separation of the Jews and the Samaritans, like that of the Jews and the Christians, was not sudden but took place over a considerable period of time" (13). Over the last two and a half millennia, Samaritan history has touched Jewish, Greek, Roman, and Christian traditions:

> Alexander the Great purportedly financed their Holy Place; the Roman governor, Pontius Pilate, lost his position after a complaint from the Samaritan community; and the emperor Justinian practically decimated the community in the sixth century. Samaritan presence is attested in the Hebrew Bible (Christian Old Testament), the Dead Sea Scrolls, and the New Testament . . . Through Samaritan eyes we can also catch new glimpses of the rise and development of Islam as well as the turbulence in the Middle East during the Crusades and the Mongol invasion. (Anderson and Gilles 6)

As an Abrahamic faith, the Samaritans of today share core similarities with Judaism, and their history has intersected with Judaism as an Israelite faith. Anderson and Giles note that "there are three competing narratives concerning the origin of the Samaritan religious community: that of the Samaritan community itself; that of the ancient Judean community, now encoded in the Hebrew Bible particularly interpreted through the writings of Josephus; and that advanced by modern critical scholars" (7).[6] According to Samaritan Benyamim Tsedaka, "The principles of the Israelite Samaritan faith are four: One Almighty, One Prophet, One Holy Book, and One Chosen Holy Place" (A.B. Samaritan News, "Four Principles of the Israelite Samaritan Faith," Feb. 2012, 58); however, Samaritanism and Judaism diverge first on the location of the "One Chosen Holy Place." While Judaism holds that Jerusalem is holy, Samaritanism holds that "Mount Gerizim or Aargaareezem [emphasis added]" is holy (Tsedaka). Samaritanism holds that Mount Gerizim, also called Har Bracha or the Mountain of Blessings, is "The Chosen Place of the Almighty to dwell His Name there" (58).

The principal differences pertain to the chosen place for the dwelling of the Almighty's Name. It is written in twenty-two verses in the book of Deuteronomy in the Israelite Samaritan Version: "In the place that the Almighty **has chosen**," whereas in the Jewish Masoretic Version it is written in the parallel verses: "In the place that the Almighty **will choose**." The Israelite Samaritans claim that the chosen place has already been chosen at the time of the Pentateuch, and therefore the past tense form "**has chosen**" represents Mount Gerizim, the only mountain in the land of Israel sanctified in the Pentateuch to offer the blessings upon it (Deut. 11:29). It was on Mount Gerizim that Abraham and Jacob built altars. Opposed to the Samaritans, the Jews claim that the chosen place was selected and announced in the period of the Davidic and Solomonic kingdom (1000–930 BCE), and therefore the form written in future tense "**will choose**" refers to the Temple Mount in Jerusalem (Tsedaka, The First English Translation of the Israelite Samaritan Torah xxi).

According to Tsedaka, the Samaritan belief that Mount Gerizim rather than Jerusalem is holy stems from a literacy practice, where Samaritans continue "reading non-stop the end of [sic] chapter 11 and chapter 12" in Deuteronomy, thus leading "to the conclusion . . . that Aargaareeezem is the Place of the Dwelling" (58). In this regard, as Samaritan scholars Robert Anderson and Terry Giles explain, the Samaritans "believe themselves to represent the orthodox faith and Judaism to be deviant" (Anderson and Giles 13).

One of the core historical and theological disputes between Samaritans and Jews is the Assyrian conquest of Samaria and subsequent population transfer in 722 BCE. When Assyrian ruler Shalmaneser V conquered Samaria, or today's northern West Bank, "Shalmanesr's successor, Sargon II, exiled the

Israelites, resettled foreigners (Samaritans) in Samaria and made it an Assyrian provincial administrative center" (Berlin and Grossman 644). The status of the Samaritans for Rabbinic Judaism was in dispute. According to Amit, "Rabbinic Sages did not consider the Samaritans to belong to another religion, but were in their eye a branch of the people of Israel who, for various historic reasons, developed in a direction that was different from the rabbinic tradition until they broke away completely from the community of Israel" (Amit, *Samaritans: Past and Present* 263–64). Anderson and Giles note that in the Judean narrative, "tensions arose between the two groups over the Jerusalemites' insistence that they and they alone were heirs of 'all Israel.' These tensions were expressed in competing claims to a legitimate priesthood and a gradual marginalization of the Shechemites concurrent with the ascendency of Jerusalemite Judaism" (10). Today, the Samaritan population is only 770 while the Jewish population is in the millions.

However, for Jews it is for these historic tensions that the Samaritans, according to Talmudic Judaism, are the "only Jewish group to which a special tractate of the Talmud is dedicated," despite the fact that the Samaritans themselves do not consider themselves Jews (264).[7] The Tractate, called Tractate *Cuthim*, is considered a negative term for Samaritans by the community. However, Jewish attitudes toward Samaritans are not fixed in one text but are spread out across several. As Itzhak Hamitovsky argues, *halakhic* (Jewish religious law) attitudes toward the Samaritans and their status as Jews or outsiders differed considerably between the Babylonian Talmud and the Palestinian Talmud (1–16). According to Magnar Kartveit, the writings of Josephus illuminate the Jewish "narrative about a priest who was forced to leave Jerusalem and move to Samaria because of his exogamous marriage to a Samaritan woman. In this involuntary exodus he was followed by other Jerusalemites who were in a similar situation in regard to their mixed Israelite marriages" (2).[8] In contrast to the Jewish explanation of Samaritan origins, the Samaritans believe that despite the Assyrian conquest and population removal in 722 BCE, "a small group of Israelites [Samaritans] survived the destruction and continued to believe in the sanctity of Mt. Gerizim" (Magen 5–6). According to Tsedaka, "only the elite minority" of Israelite Samaritans were expelled by the Assyrians (A.B. *Samaritan News*, "The Jewish and Samaritan legends about the Lost Tribes," 95). Today, the Samaritans' *Cohen Gadol* (High Priest) is Aharon ben Ab-Chisda ben Yaacob, the 132nd to have the title. The Samaritans claim an uninterrupted succession of priests and worship on Mount Gerizim, preserving the ancient traditions of the "House of Joseph" (Anderson and Giles). According to Anderson and Giles, this understanding of continually "preserving the ancient traditions is reflected in their self-designation: Shomrim ("keepers" of the Torah)" (Anderson and Giles, *The Keepers* 13).

In *Jews and Samaritans: The Origins and History of Their Early Relations*, Gary Knoppers complicates the label "Samaritan" as one that is "largely shunned by the Samaritans, who prefer to call themselves northern Israelite . . . or the community of Samarian Israelites" (15). Anderson and Giles also note that the verse from 2 King 17:29 reveals "that the שמרים of 2 Kgs 17:29 are not the 'Samaritans' at all but rather the 'people of Samaria,' whose relationship to the Samaritan religious group (שמרים) is not clear" (Anderson and Giles 11). To summarize, Samaritans today are Israelite Samaritans, the former label Samaritan is used to distinguish them from Judean Israelites. *Shomrim* means keepers (of the Torah), and Samarian means people of Samaria or what is also known as the northern West Bank of the Jordan River.

Knoppers elaborates on Anderson and Giles and explains that the term Samaritan itself is "basically geographical in origin," referring to Yahwistic Samarians from northern Israel or Samaria, and the label Samaritan is the result of the Septuagint's Greek translation in 2 Kings 17:29 (14–15).[9] While the early history of the Samarians and Judeans foregrounds the "difficult issue of ethnic nomenclature" (14), especially since there was "much that Yahwistic Judeans and Yahwistic Samarians shared in common during earlier periods of Israelite and Judean history in spite of some important differences between them" (217), by the first century CE there are "deteriorating relations" between the two groups" (220).[10]

In the sixteenth and seventeenth centuries, conversations about the Samaritans and their Pentateuch largely happened as a response to the Protestant Reformation and, as we will see in chapter 3, helped to shape Western interests in acquiring Samaritan manuscripts. For example, since the mid-sixteenth century,[11] European and American collectors, clergy, scholars, and tourists have sought Samaritan manuscripts for a wide variety of reasons, ranging from religious motivations to collectors' impulses. Today, the Samaritans' diaspora of manuscripts has become a rhetorically strategic resource that may be leveraged to inform policy makers, laypeople, and neighbors in the Samaritans' region about their unique history and cultural heritage. Now that I've offered a brief introduction to the various narratives surrounding the Samaritans' origins as a people and a religion, in the next section I will demonstrate how scholars' interest in the Samaritans in the sixteenth century led to a period of significant deceit and theft in the seventeenth century.

Deceit and Theft of Samaritan Manuscripts

In the late sixteenth and early seventeeth centuries, the West learned that the Samaritans had a valuable cultural heritage that intrigued Christians in Europe: another version of the Hebrew Pentateuch or Five Books of Moses.[12]

The Samaritans, largely absent from the consciousness of Europe as a living people prior to the era of the Protestant Reformation, caught the eye of Protestant and Catholic intellectuals because their tradition differed from that of the Masoretic Hebrew. In the sixteenth century, European scholarly interest in the acquisition of Samaritan manuscripts was propelled forward by larger religious and political debates between Rome and England: "When the Samaritan version of the Pentateuch was revealed to the Western World . . . it made a very deep impression and inspired a series of debates on its place relative to other versions of the Bible" (Florentin 1).[13] After Europeans learned about the Samaritans' Pentateuch, scholars sought to acquire Samaritan manuscripts for their own Christian religious debates; however, there was a problem. At that time, Samaritans across North Africa and the Middle East were reluctant to sell their sacred manuscripts to non-Samaritans. As is the case with too many other instances of European cultural acquisition during the rise of the colonial era, some European scholars resorted to dishonest means in order to acquire Samaritan holy books. According to Benyamim Tsedaka, European scholars pretended to be members of a long lost Samaritan community, and they cheated Samaritans by making them believe that they had distant brethren in Europe, giving them the hope that they are not alone (Tsedaka, "Personal interview in Holon, Israel, 16 Feb. 2012"). By the time the first wave of European acquisition of Samaritan manuscripts was complete, European scholars succeeded in "purchas[ing] forty Torah manuscripts from Samaritans" (Tsedaka, "Personal interview in Holon, Israel, 16 Feb. 2012").

This process of European scholarly contact and interest in the Samaritans began in 1537 with Postel and 1584 with Joseph Scaliger, and by the early seventeenth century the Italian explorer Pietro della Valle was sent on a political/religious mission to track down a Samaritan manuscript for Rome.[14] In 1616, della Valle was told by the French ambassador to Istanbul that the "Samaritans had a recension of the Pentateuch which differed from that in the possession of Christendom," and he was urged to acquire a copy for the sake of Christendom (Thomson 72). According to Benyamim Tsedaka, "he went to Nablus first and they [the Samaritans] refused to sell to him according to his [own] testimony." Samaritan scholar Nathan Schur argues that della Valle sought to acquire the Pentateuchs for the sake of Christendom in "any way possible: by purchase, or by some trick," and eventually he did find a Samaritan community that was more "amenable to persuasion," and thus he was able to purchase two copies of the Pentateuch (Schur 129). Della Valle travelled to major centers of Samaritan scribal production—Nablus, Damascus, Gaza, and Cairo. In many of the locations, the prevailing Samaritan attitude of several communities was to decline della Valle's request to purchase a copy of the Samaritan Pentateuch. We still do not know exactly what kind of "persuasion" he used or what the circumstances of the exchange were; however, scholars such as Jean-Pierre Rothschild have noted that this process of European acquisition is one "which a few consider to have been a form of colonial appropriation" (771).[15]

Colonial appropriation or not, the process of European manuscript acquisition was not accomplished by outright purchase alone. Because Samaritans were wary of selling their manuscripts at this time to non-Samaritans, there is evidence that European scholars resorted to impersonation and deceit. After della Valle, a group of European scholars insinuated affiliation with a community of long lost Samaritans in Europe. As a result, Europeans were able to acquire Samaritan manuscripts in no small quantity. Perhaps one of the most egregious examples of such deceit was in 1671, when Robert Huntington, then British chaplain at Aleppo, visited the Samaritan community in Nablus.[16] According to Robert Anderson, Huntington, with his working knowledge of Ancient Hebrew script, initially impressed the Samaritans with his ability to read their manuscripts. Huntington's knowledge of Ancient Hebrew prompted the Samaritans of Nablus to ask Huntington if there were "Israelites" in England (Anderson, "Samaritan History During the Renaissance" 105). Huntington then made what appears to be a significant leap in his story and "affirmed that there were" and "they assumed that there were Samaritans in England" (105). However, Huntington went beyond a momentary cultural miscommunication. Sending the Samaritans of Nablus a letter, Huntington "gave the Samaritans an account of their English brethren" (S.C. 537). The correspondence between Huntington and the Nablus Samaritans continued for several years. Huntington, it seems, decided to exploit the Samaritans' confusion about his affiliation rather than correct their false impressions. For Huntington, deceit paid off. For his efforts, he received "at least one copy of the [Samaritan] Pentateuch" (Anderson, "Samaritan History During the Renaissance," 105). The Samaritans, however, received in trade a lie that would, on the one hand, provide them with a hope that their people's circumstances were not so dire, and on the other, make them vulnerable to the ruse of Western scholars and pilgrims that followed Huntington and used his deceit to their own advantages.[17]

According to Benyamim Tsedaka, the Samaritans of Nablus wanted to believe Huntington's story was true, "because it encouraged them to know that they have brothers in some other place in the world, like London, Paris, and Germany" (Tsedaka, "Personal interview in Holon, Israel, 8 June 2012"). The impact of Huntington's story reverberated for the next several hundred years.[18] For example, in 1684, Jacob Levi of Hebron travelled to Europe to collect alms and met German orientalist and linguist Job Ludolph. Levi told Ludolph about the condition of the Samaritans in Nablus and, according to Silvestre de Sacy, Ludolph himself then began correspondence with the Samaritans:

> Ludolf took advantage of his [Levi's] return to enter into a correspondence with the Samaritans of Naplouse, and transmitted to them, by him, a letter written in the Hebrew language, and in Samaritan characters. This letter was safely delivered to those to whom it was addressed, by the Jew who kindly undertook to be the bearer of it; and having received from the Samaritans two replies, written also in Hebrew and in Samaritan characters, addressed, *To Frankfort, to M. Job Ludolf*, he likewise got them safely transmitted to the place of their destination. Ludolf having translated them into Latin, and added some hasty notes, communicated them to Cellarius, by whom they were published in both languages, at Zeitz, iu 1688. To these he subjoined Edward Bernard's Latin translation of the first letter that the Samaritans wrote to their supposed brethren in England. (de Sacy, "On the Samaritans" 128)

Because of the deceit of scholars such as Huntington and Ludolph,[19] well into the mid-nineteenth century the Samaritans of Nablus believed that they had long lost brothers and communities in Europe. As a consequence, European scholars continued to exploit the Samaritans' belief that they were assisting their people in Europe. For example, Robert Anderson notes that in de Sacy's *Correspondence*, there's an early nineteenth-century letter to the Samaritans of Nablus requesting a copy of their religious calendar on behalf of the "Samaritans of Paris" (107). The Samaritans, in turn, responded and expressed a sense of brotherhood to their nonexistent counterparts in Europe:

> I give you notice that your letter reached us, and that there has been from us much joy, and what you said was already in our hearts . . . You say, my brother, that he is among you anyone of us brothers who keep the Law of Moses, our prophet is the one thing that we do not believe, consequently we have sent to you a Torah (to your country). You are to us our brothers. (de Sacy 101)[20]

Beyond de Sacy's *Correspondence*, well into the mid-nineteenth century visitors to Nablus write about how the Samaritans inquired about their brothers in Europe and beyond.[21] In de Sacy's *Correspondence*, the history of deceit and Samaritan manuscript acquisition relates directly to Samaritan decline in numbers over the last two millennia. This history of deception and appropriation has influenced the way the Samaritans' textual diaspora was formed, and yet, despite this difficult history, now more than ever Samaritans wish to preserve this diaspora and hopefully rhetorically capitalize on its ability to communicate Samaritan identity.

Mounting Economic Pressures and Coerced Consent

Well past the end of the eighteenth century, Samaritans did not easily part with their manuscripts to non-Samaritans; however, beginning in the mid-nineteenth century the Samaritans' economic situation in Nablus became more desperate, and in turn Samaritans resorted to selling their manuscripts as an economic means of survival. For the Samaritans, there was demand from Western tourists and collectors interested in purchasing manuscripts as souvenirs, for libraries and museums, or for personal study and private collections.[22] The process of "letting go" of Samaritan manuscripts occurred over a period of several decades in the nineteenth century.[23]

For example, in the early nineteenth century there are cases in which travel writers report that they were unable to purchase Samaritan manuscripts. In a December 1821 travel account of Ottoman Palestine, Joseph Wolff describes how in Jaffa he was introduced to a Samaritan by the name of Israel.[24] According to Wolff, Israel showed him three Samaritan manuscripts. When Wolff asked Israel if he would sell his books, Wolff says that Israel replied: "No Samaritan will ever sell his books!" (238).[25] The Samaritans' prohibition against selling Samaritan manuscripts is also echoed in a similar account two years later by William Jowett. In 1823, Jowett traveled to Nablus where he "saw several Samaritan manuscripts on a shelf, wrapped up in cloth: they were written on skin. On our asking their price, a young man said that they were not to be sold; that to sell them was 'Haram,' 'prohibited'; and that every letter was worth a sequin" (150).[26]

By the 1830s, there is evidence that some Samaritans began to sell manuscript fragments and charge visitors to view the Abisha scroll,[27] the Samaritans' oldest Pentateuch. For example, in Charles Boileau Elliott's 1838 *Travels in the Three Great Empires of Austria, Russia and Turkey*, he writes that he was successful in purchasing a fragment of a Samaritan manuscript, saying the following disturbing remarks about his acquisition and the Samaritans: "The 'cohen' suffered me to purchase a small Samaritan fragment, written in the ancient character; a highly interesting memorial of a people now almost past out of existence" (Elliott 399).[28] Elliott's disregard for the rank of the priest and his choice of words to describe the piece of writing as a "memorial" is echoed in many of these travel accounts.

In James Wilson's 1847 *The Lands of the Bible: Visited and Described*, there's an equally disturbing account of a traveler making outright threats at the refusal of the Samaritans to sell him a manuscript. According to the writer, he "endeavoured, without success, to purchase a copy of the Pentateuch from the Samaritans," and his conversation "went along this strain" (Wilson 74). This "conversation" included a veiled threat against the Samaritans, alluding to the colonial ambitions of England and the potential repercussions for denying these travelers a copy of their Pentateuch:

> **Travelers.** — "Will you allow us to purchase a copy of the Torah?"
> **Priest.** — "No, one is worth its weight in gold."
> **T.** — "Well, we shall give you a good price for it, say 5000 piastres." (£50)
> **P.** — "We shall on no account whatever sell a copy of the books of our prophet."
> **T.** — "Take care what you say; if the English come and take possession of the country, and restore to you Mount Gerizim, won't you give them a copy of the Law in token of your gratitude?"
> **P.** — "The English, we know, will come and take possession of the country, and we shall beg Mount Gerizim from them."

The traveler, apparently aware of the past transfer of Samaritan manuscripts in the seventeenth century under the guise of trickery, argues that because the Samaritans "sold" manuscripts to Europeans in the past, they should also sell to him; however, the Samaritans display an awareness of the European past deceit and refuse to sell their manuscripts to the tourists:

> **T.** — "You do not appear to us to have the spirit of Moses. He said עמו גוים,הרנינו 'Rejoice, O ye nations, with his people.'"
> **P.** — "Well, come and rejoice with us. Become Samaritans; and we shall give you a copy of the Law."
> **T.** — "You say, Become Samaritans. But, according to your principle of withholding the Law from us, how could we ever, except from independent sources, know what the Law is, and what the Samaritans are?"
> **P.** — "It is in vain to ask us to sell a copy of the Law."
> **T.** — "Your fathers sold the copies which are now in the possession of Europeans."
> **P.** — "They did not sell them. They must have been stolen from them." (Wilson 74)[29]

By 1857, William Prime reports in his travel narrative that the Samaritans were selling modern manuscripts but would not sell older manuscripts (335); however, the purchase of modern manuscripts was not enough for Westerners, and the Samaritans continued to receive more direct pressure to part with older and more valued copies of their sacred books.[30] As interest in Samaritan manuscripts became more intense on the part of Westerners, there appear to have been incidents that cross the line from idle threats. In 1864, just three years after this forced consent, Semitic manuscript collector Abraham Firkovich traveled from the Russian Empire to Jerusalem and purchased, in a single trip, 1,341 manuscripts and fragments, almost the entirety of the Samaritans' Genizah, the place where older manuscripts are stored.[31] This massive collection would become the cornerstone for the St. Petersburg University collection, one of the largest single collections of Samaritan manuscripts.[32] According to Benyamim Tsedaka, Firkovich bought in one trip the "most important collection of Samaritan manuscripts [in the world]" (Tsedaka, "Personal interview in Holon, Israel, 16 Feb. 2012").[33]

In the late 1860s and 1870s, travelers such as James Finn begin to write about the large exodus of Samaritan manuscripts from Mount Gerizim thanks to the likes of Firkovich and others, and the destruction of Samaritan cultural treasure:[34]

> I hear that of late years several more books have been purchased from the Samaritans, and so eager have the poor people been to turn them to money account that they have not seldom torn up these rare manuscripts, and sold a few pages at a time to such travellers as have been more ambitious of acquiring bits of things, because they are understood to be rare, than erudite enough to perceive the mischief done by thus dissevering a connected work, and concealing mysteriously those fragments in their private houses of England, Germany, or America. (Finn 229)

Finn's account, similar to many of the other Western travel narratives referenced in this chapter, is quick to judge the Samaritans for their economic state and the situation of their manuscripts. For example, in his 1884 travel narrative *Among the Holy Fields*, Henry Martin describes the Samaritans as a "feeble folk, so few and so poor, that the high priest (a descendant of the tribe of Levi) ekes out a living by showing travellers the synagogue and the sacred scroll, and even offered to sell us his photograph!" (90).[35] While the sale of Samaritan manuscripts and fragments fed Samaritans, the benefits of these manuscript sales were not long lasting, nor did they substantially change the Samaritan community's economic situation in the decades to come.[36]

Decline of Samaritan Populations in the Middle East and North Africa

In order to understand the significance of the diaspora of Samaritan manuscripts from a Samaritan perspective, it's important to understand that the

Samaritans were not always located in only Mount Gerizim, Palestine, and Holon, Israel. Rather, they were once a much larger people with dozens of communities spanning at the very least from Alexandria in the west to Damascus and Aleppo in the east. Their contraction as a people, as illustrated in the map below based on Benyamim Tsedaka's data, reaches its nadir around the time when their manuscripts are becoming more dispersed into foreign hands. These two processes, contraction of population and expansion of manuscript diaspora, are related: the former historical forces relate in direct ways to later economic and colonial vulnerability. In order to understand the relationship of these two processes in greater detail, in this section I provide an overview of Samaritan contraction.

Samaritan population figures are difficult to locate prior to the availability of Ottoman tax records in the sixteenth century (Schur 123). However, it is known from the archaeological records that the Samaritans were once a much larger people in the first century than they were by the medieval period, when 1170 CE Jewish traveler Benjamin of Tudela "found 1000 Samaritans in Nablus, two hundred in Caesarea, and three hundred in Ascalon, 1500 in all," and not including Samaritan populations in other major cities and former centers of Samaritan scribal production such as Damascus and Cairo (Kedar, "The Frankish Period" 84). While this twelfth-century population estimate may seem high when compared to today's figures, Reinhard Pummer notes that "[a]lthough it is difficult to estimate what their numbers were at this early stage of their history, a probable figure is 150,000 to 200,000" (Pummer, *Samaritan Marriage Contracts and Deeds of Divorce* 1). Pummer attributes Samaritan population decline to the reality that the Samaritans "were subject to hostilities virtually from the beginning of their existence as a distinct entity" and that this decline happened during the Byzantine and Muslim rule of Ottoman Palestine (Pummer 1). From the twelfth century to the sixteenth century, the Samaritan population continued to decline even more. According to Nathan Schur in *History of the Samaritans*, Turkish tax records for Palestine 1538 CE indicate a combined total of 220 Samaritans in Nablus and Gaza (Schur 123).[37] Additionally, Robert Anderson and Terry Giles note that these figures combined with the total "populations of Egypt (ca. 200) and Damascus (ca. 100) would yield a population in the mid-sixteenth century" of approximately 520 Samaritans (91). However, 520 Samaritans in the sixteenth century was not the end of Samaritan population decline. By the middle of the nineteenth century, the Samaritan communities of Gaza, Egypt, and Damascus were no more, and the total Samaritan population of approximately two hundred souls resided only in Nablus. By the end of the nineteenth century, only four families remained (Tsedaka, "Samaritan Israelite Families and Households that Disappeared" 222).

In "Samaritan Israelite Families and Households that Disappeared," Benyamim Tsedaka follows "in the footsteps of approximately one hundred and fifty ancient Israelite Samaritan and households and families mentioned in Samaritan sources" and tracks this history, detailing that the vast majority "disappeared from the historical stage due to slaughter, conversion into another religion or biological reduction" (222). From the biblical period to the sixteenth century, the cumulative effects of millennia of war, forced conversion, and assimilation into other groups facilitated the steady extinction of dozens of ancient Samaritan communities from Alexandria to Damascus. As exhibited in map 1, Tsedaka's data in "Samaritan Israelite Families and Households that Disappeared" is presented as a Google map.[38]

In the nineteenth century, the Samaritans like many Ottoman subjects endured economic and political difficulties in the late age of Ottoman rule in Palestine. However, the Samaritans were a small minority and had less of a population than other groups to bear their portion of the Ottoman and later British tax burdens. In some cases, Samaritan minority status also meant that the Samaritans faced an undue burden. For example, in his 1862 "The Handwriting of God in Egypt, Sinai and the Holy Land," David Austin Randall discusses one moment of hardship in which the Samaritans were forced into selling one of their ancient manuscripts:

A lordly merchant Turk from Damascus visited Nabulous, and dealing with a Samaritan trader there, accused him of robbing him of a large sum of money, and had him and many of his connections arrested and cast into prison, and there seemed no way of satisfying the avarice of their oppressor. At the expiration of a few months the priest made a visit to the Russian missionaries at Jerusalem, and told the story of their wrongs. "What shall we do? My people are in prison. I have no means to help them. Appeals to the British and American Consuls have been in vain; has the Russian Consul no power with the Turkish authorities to interfere for us?" "How much," said Dr. Levishon, "is the claim against the imprisoned parties?" "The whole sum now demanded, including costs, is six thousand piasters." "Can you not in some way raise the money?" "We have no money; my people are all poor." "Go home," said the Doctor, "and bring me that old copy of your scriptures, and you shall have the money." Three days after the claim of the persecuting Turk was paid, the imprisoned persons were at liberty, and the missionaries were rejoicing over the possession of the most ancient copy of the Samaritan Pentateuch a Christian had ever been allowed to handle. (158)

In Randall's account, the Samaritans are in one of their most vulnerable moments in history. Their population has declined to well below two hundred,

Map 1. "Disappeared Samaritan Communities." This map is based on the data provided in Benyamim Tsedaka, "Samaritan Israelite Families and Households that Disappeared," in *Samaritans: Past and Present,* ed. Menchem Mor and Fredrich V. Reiterer (2010). It is important to note that many of the locations listed (Cairo, Damascus) were centers of Samaritan scribal production. Manuscripts from many of the communities listed on the map make up the diaspora of Samaritan manuscripts. (*See* http://goo.gl/fx1RpD *to interact with the map.*)

they are centralized now in Nablus, and they lack the means or influence to contest charges or corruption. In the Samaritans' moment of desperation, Westerners step in with wallet in hand, ready to make a deal first for one manuscript, then later for more. While the sale of this particular ancient manuscript to Westerners provides the crucial funds to free the imprisoned Samaritans in that moment, the Samaritans as a people parted with a piece of their cultural heritage, one that had been in their possession for hundreds of years. From the era of Randall's account in the 1860s and into the decade after the First World War, hundreds of complete manuscripts and thousands of fragments were sold to wealthy Westerners in order for the Samaritans to meet their basic survival needs.[39]

The First World War and the End of Ottoman Rule

While the entire Samaritan population declined to under two hundred in the nineteenth century, this was not the end of their descent into lower numbers. The first quarter of the twentieth century marked increased hardship for residents of Palestine, particularly during the last years of Ottoman rule and the First World War. On March 1, 1915, a census of the remaining Samaritan community reported that there were ninety-seven males and seventy-one females, and of those ninety-seven males twenty-four were soldiers in the Turkish army (Barton, "The War and the Samaritan Colony" 3).[40] Due to the Samaritans' position in Ottoman-ruled Nablus, the First World War took a heavy and disproportionate toll on their small community. In 1921, William E. Barton published a paper titled "The War and the Samaritan Community" that reported "the progress and vicissitudes of the little Samaritan colony at Nablus" (1) during and immediately after the First World War. Barton, a clergyman and scholar of Samaritan studies, had extensive contact with the Samaritans in Nablus from 1903 to 1926 and worked on a philanthropic foundation, the American Samaritan Committee with J.D. Whiting and Edward Warren, among others (Pentek). In "The War and the Samaritan Colony," Barton's article includes correspondence from Samaritan Abu-l Hassan Ben Yacop of Nablus. He writes on May 12, 1919, that the impact of the First World War on the Samaritan community was particularly severe in terms of loss of life, economic status, and Samaritan manuscripts:

> You asked to be informed of the work of business affairs, the members of our congregation after the war, and how they are able to obtain the needful food. I am very sorry to have to tell you that they are without employment, and that there is not found among them one who has a position or business. For they who were in business lost it during the war, and now they have resorted for their subsistence to the sale of the ancient books transmitted to them from their fathers, and held by them to be beyond price. Cast thy regard upon this lowly nation, and thou wilt see it upon the brink of death by total extinction, if you do not set a bound thereto by assistance in its business affairs. And if not, then, as I see and as every intelligent man sees, lo, after a little while you will be able to read in history that there once existed a Samaritan nation in the world. As for the priestly family they have been kept barely alive by the income of the synagogue and from the sale of books which they copied with their hands. And now with sor-

row I must tell you that they are in a pitiful condition, and that the nation cannot remain alive for lack of employment. (13–14)

The impact of the First World War, its death, and related economic hardships continued to have a significant impact on future generations of Samaritans.

In January of 1920, *National Geographic* magazine published the lead story "The Last Israelitish Blood Sacrifice: How the Vanishing Samaritans Celebrate the Passover on Sacred Mount Gerizim," by John D. Whiting. Whiting, a colleague of Barton, was active with him in the American Samaritan Committee,[41] and together they worked with Edward Warren to provide financial assistance to the Samaritans of Nablus in the early twentieth century.[42] In addition to his work with the American Samaritan Committee, Whiting served as deputy American consul for Jerusalem, and he conducted census data on the community from 1915 to 1919, the year after the First World War had come to an end. In the January 31, 1944, issue of the *Palestine Post*, Samaritan priest Yaakov Ben Uri HaCohen recounts that during the First World War "Samaritan soldiers had fought and fallen in foreign lands while at home families had starved. The war had cost the community over a quarter of its number, including the then High Priest" ("Good Samaritans in Jerusalem Join in Prayers for Persecuted Jews of Europe," *Palestine Post*, January 31, 1944, p. 3). Benyamim Tsedaka, remarking on Abu-l Hassan's letter and Yaakov Ben Uri HaCohen's reflection, said, "A whole generation of 24 Samaritans died during Ottoman military service in the First World War. In 1915 there were 168 Samaritans living in Nablus and Jaffa, and in 1919, the year after the end of the First World War, only 141 remained" (Tsedaka, "Personal interview in Holon, Israel, 28 Feb. 2012").

In Whiting's *National Geographic* article, he makes the dark prediction that he had witnessed one of the last Samaritan Passover sacrifices on Mount Gerizim:

As we turn for one last glance at the moon-lit camp and the redder glow of the flame with the pillar of smoke, we cannot but realize that here we have seen the last Hebrew blood sacrifice, and there comes the thought that it may never be seen again, for the Samaritans are a dying people. (46)

Thankfully for the Samaritans, Whiting's prediction turned out to be inaccurate. Perhaps thanks in part to the negative publicity and assistance from philanthropists such as Barton, Whiting, Warren, and the American Samaritan Committee. However, the Samaritans continued to remain in a vulnerable geopolitical position during the remainder of the twentieth century. Additionally, Samaritan manuscripts, sold and often produced to feed the community, were now dispersed around the globe.

Writing for Tourists

In the late nineteenth and first half of the twentieth century, the Samaritans wrote entire manuscripts for sale to tourists, largely on paper and not parchment. In 1903, William Barton details how he was worried he was in fact purchasing "a book made to sell to tourists" ("The Samaritan Pentateuch" 11). In 1904, the Palestine Exploration Fund published an analysis of a manuscript adorned with "clean sacrificial leather, of the congregation of the Samaritans at Shechem," which they describe as evidence of "an attraction to possible buyers among tourists" (Cowley 72).[43] In a 1913 edition of The Advocate: America's Jewish Journal, Dr. S. Weissenberg from Elisabethgrad[44] writes that copying and selling manuscripts to tourists has become one of the few ways that the Samaritans are able to earn a living:

> What are the means of support of the Samaritans? Some earn a living by copying their holy books for sale at extravagant prices to tourists and scholars. A few are clerks in the administration offices of the government. Some are artisans, but only earn a meagre income as they are dependent on Samaritan local traffic exclusively. (279)

The process of copying manuscripts continued after the First World War and into the British Mandate period. Henry Morgenthau's 1922 autobiography provides an account of how the Samaritans' production of manuscripts for sale to tourists even touched the Samaritans' High Priest,[45] who himself made a living "copying the Pentateuch in Samaritan" for sale to Westerners:

> The High Priest explained to us that the material condition of the tribes was very bad . . . He, himself, was supposed to live on a tithe of the income of the tribe, but he said that this amount would not suffice to keep him for more than one month of the twelve, so that although he was more than seventy-four years of age, he used most of his time in copying the Pentateuch in Samaritan, and selling it whenever he could. Upon this hint, I bought a copy. (70)[46]

Into the 1950s, when the economic situation of the Samaritan community finally began to improve, the Samaritans in Nablus continued to copy manuscripts for sale as part of their means of survival (Tsedaka, "Interview with Benyamim Tsedaka on April 19, 2012").

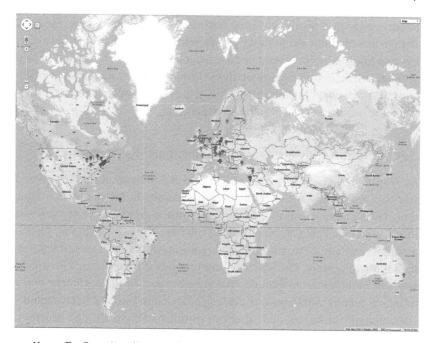

Map 2. The Samaritan diaspora of manuscripts. This map, based on three sources listed at the link, is not a complete or exhaustive description of Samaritan manuscripts abroad. Many manuscripts exist in the hands of private collectors. However, in addition to listing what's known abroad based on the sources, the geocoded resource includes hyperlinks to known online finding aids at the time of publication. (*To interact with the map, see* https://batchgeo.com/map/9882ff095531b419f b087a080b497b0f.) The objective of this map is to convey a sense of scope about the diaspora and all resources are plotted in relationship to their distance from the Samaritan community in Nablus. As Presner, Shepard, and Kawano write in *Hypercities: Thick Mapping in the Digital Humanities*, "Mapping is not a one-time thing, and maps are not stable objects that reference, reflect, or correspond to an external reality. Mapping is a verb and bespeaks to an on-going process of picturing, narrating, symbolizing, contesting, re-picturing, re-narrating, re-symbolizing, erasing, and re-inscribing a set of relations" (15). This map especially is not stable and is meant to represent only what's known at a given time about the location of some Samaritan manuscripts. Over time, this specific mapping resource will change and evolve.

By the 1950s, an estimated four thousand Samaritan manuscripts were no longer in the hands of Samaritans. Instead, they were spread out across four continents in the libraries, museums, archives, and private collections of Europe, North America, Australia, and South America. Given what the Samaritans have survived in the last several centuries, and especially the first half of the twentieth century, there is a shift in Samaritan attitudes about their manuscripts brought forward by the parallel economic and political circumstances the Samaritans have weathered and the role of their writing in their ability to survive those difficulties. These historical circumstances have caused a change in Samaritan attitudes not only toward the sale of their manuscripts but also toward the circulation of their manuscripts. This change has in turn prompted Samaritan reflection on their current scribal work and its connection to the diaspora of manuscripts around the world, and the rhetorical work that these manuscripts do or don't do in diaspora.

Zionism, Arab Nationalism, and the Samaritans: 1907–1949

As Whiting's *National Geographic* article conveys, the end of the First World War was a dire time for the Samaritan community in Nablus. At the same time, Jewish nationalism in the form of Zionist aspirations in Ottoman and then British Mandate Palestine were on the rise. The two situations, the Samaritans' existential circumstance and Zionism, would meet several times in the twentieth century. The first such meeting was through Yitzhak Ben-Zvi's *aliyah* or immigration to Ottoman Palestine in 1907. In the beginning of the twentieth century, Abraham Tsedaka, son of Malchim Tsedaka, left his impoverished family in Nablus and, after two or three attempts in 1897 and 1901, settled in the port city of Jaffa in 1905, where he sought out a better economic future for his family. Benyamim Tsedaka[47] recounts that

> The community normally criticized everybody that left Nablus because they felt so few and united. But of course, he just left because of the distress in Nablus, the financial stress. So he went to Jaffa, which was free of disease because it was very close to the open air and the sea. He himself had some fortunes that he inherited from his father, and with this money he bought the place for the shop in the market and a house surrounded by big garden in old Jaffa, just some meters from the sea. So he had two daughters, Rashia and Zena, Arabic names, and then he had also six sons. The first called Marchiv, following his own father's name, because Abraham was the son of Marchiv, first born, which is very common to call the first born the name of the grandfather. Marchiv, but also, he was called in Arabic Fabis, which is the same. And then the second son was Tsedaka, the third was Nor, or in Arabic Musbah, the fourth was Yefet, and his name in Arabic was Hosni, and the fifth was Goyl, which in Arabic is Badih, and the sixth Gamiel and the Arabic Jamel. His wife was Yarcha, or in Arabic Amra, which means moon. So these were the names. He raised them; he educated them. He slaughtered animals for food and conducted all the religious duties because he was the only Samaritan family in Jaffa and all the rest were in Nablus.

And first there was a lot of criticism about him leaving. But when he was successful, he invited priests from Nablus to come and stay with him for a couple of days and even to direct the prayer on Shabbat instead of him. He admired the priests and loved them, and they loved him. And step-by-step, the community changed their mind about him and they started to live with the fact that he moved to Jaffa. His success attracted other Samaritans to come and work in Jaffa, and at the end of the week they would return to Nablus. This was Abraham Tsedaka's own contribution to the community, because even at that time in the early 1900s, the community was still in a process of deterioration. But he never lost his hope that the future of the Samaritans will be better. (Tsedaka, "Personal Interview in Holon, Israel, 28 Feb. 2012")[48]

From 1904 to 1914, the second Aliyah or wave of Zionist immigration to Ottoman Palestine arrived from predominately Eastern Europe and Russia. Many of these immigrants (*Halutzim*) settled in the area around the port city of Jaffa in the settlement of Ahuzat Bayit or what would become the city of Tel Aviv. In 1907, Israel's future second president, Yitzhak Ben-Zvi, then twenty-three years old, emigrated to Palestine and was looking for an apartment in Jaffa.[49] It is here that the Samaritans first crossed paths with someone that would become a significant Zionist leader and future president of Israel, Yitzhak Ben-Zvi:

So in 1907, this gentleman, a young Jew from Russia immigrated to Palestine, and he started to work as a clerk at the Port of Jaffa. His name was Yitzhak Ben-Zvi. Ben-Zvi was searching for someone to teach him Arabic in order to understand and find common language with the Arab community. So he went to the market in Jaffa to search for someone to teach him Arabic. And when he entered the market he was attracted to the image of Abraham Tsedaka, sitting in the gate of his shop announcing his products.
  Ben-Zvi was already a very active Zionist, and he was part of a movement to help Jews settle in Palestine. Ben-Zvi asked Abraham who he is, and he told Ben-Zvi that he is a Samaritan. Who are the Samaritans? Ben-Zvi had never heard about the Samaritans. And Abraham asked him, "Where are you working?" And Ben-Zvi said that he was working in the Port of Jaffa that's why he needed to know Arabic. And Abraham Asked Ben-Zvi, "Where do you live?" Ben-Zvi replied, "I have one room in the attic of a house near the port." Abraham said in response, "One room? Why do you have to stay there? I have a big house. Come and stay with me. I know that you have no money to pay me so just, come and be my guest."

And Abraham took him to his house, but Ben-Zvi became more interested in learning all about the Samaritans. Especially when he saw how Abraham made every Shabbat with his children, making the prayer and singing with pride.

So Yitzhak Ben-Zvi came to the decision that whatever will be in Palestine, he would dedicate some time to rescue this old [Samaritan] tribe. They are the only descendants of the Kingdom of Israel, and the Jewish people are the descendants of the Kingdom of Judah. And this is what he did, all his life, until he died in 1963. He helped the Samaritans on individual and public matters. His home was always open to the Samaritans, and they came to him with every problem. So very soon he became a father to the whole Samaritan community in Jaffa and Nablus. (Tsedaka, "Personal interview in Holon, Israel, 28 Feb. 2012")

Ben-Zvi's involvement with the Samaritans ranged from a "thorough and comprehensive study of the Samaritans, their faith, literature and settlements" to what Israel Sedaka described in "Itzhak Ben-Zvi, David Ben-Gurion and the Samaritans" as a "love and admiration" from a "descendant of the tribe of Judah, perhaps even Benjamin, to the sons of his brother Joseph, the descendants of Ephraim and Manasseh" (241). As a Zionist focused on emigrating Jews to Ottoman and Mandate Palestine, Ben-Zvi saw in the Samaritans a biblical link to the land. While the historical Samaritans had an uneasy relationship with the biblical kingdom of Judah, the state of Israel would have a more favorable view of their estranged cousins, the descendants of the lost northern tribes (241). Speaking at an event in Jerusalem for the persecuted Jews of Europe in 1944, which a Samaritan delegation from Nablus attended, Ben-Zvi "emphasized their [Samaritan] link with the land of Israel, their faith in monotheism, and their literature. Their one difference from the Jews was their belief in Mount Gerizim as the site of the rebuilding of the Temple" ("Good Samaritans in Jerusalem Join in Prayers for Persecuted Jews of Europe," 3).[50] The Samaritans, according to Ben-Zvi, were part of the family of Israel. This new relationship, however, was not entirely without political ramifications, and the Samaritans were increasingly referenced in political arguments between Zionists and Arab Nationalists from 1932 to 1947.

The politicization of the Samaritan population of Nablus and Jaffa came at a time when the Samaritans disproportionately suffered from considerable political tensions, crime, and general social chaos during the latter half of the British Mandate. From 1935 to 1945, the Samaritan community incurred a number of losses during this era of social unrest, including the murder of a Samaritan in Haifa in 1939;[51] shootings and stone throwing in the Samaritan Quarter in Nablus in 1936 during the Arab Revolt;[52] a shooting, stabbing, and robbery in Jaffa;[53] destruction of a holy artifact in Nablus; and instances where the Samaritans were unable to worship on Mount Gerizim due to violence such as during the Samaritans' Sukkot in 1938.[54] In October 1936, angered at the loss of British military casualties in the area around Nablus, the British Mandate government imposed a collective fine of £5000 on the entire city under the Emergency Regulations provisions. As residents of Nablus, the Samaritans were thus required to contribute a proportionate share of their collective punishment to the British, £50. When they could not pay the large fee, the British "distrained [seized] upon their property"[55] ("Reflections," October 5, 1936, 4).[56] In 1938, the *Palestine Post* published a column commenting on the Samaritans' political situation:

In the hills of Nablus, between Gerizim and Ebal live the few Samaritans who are left remnant of townsfolk. It is not surprising that they have tried to win tolerance from their Arab neighbours by flattering them. But that has placed them in an awkward position. For the Jews of Palestine can hardly acquiesce in a Samaritan testament which is not true to fact. Hence, the poor community is to be pitied, liable to lose the sympathy of the Jews, and to attract the hostility of the Arabs. Such is the price of lawlessness in Palestine. ("Reflector," *Palestine Post*, August 5, 1938, p. 6)

This column seemed to point to the uncertain predicament of the Samaritans and their need to "walk between the raindrops" of the Zionist movement and a rising sense of Arab nationalism. In the next decade leading up to the end of partition, both political forces, Arab nationalism and Zionism, would make political reference to the Samaritans.

For example, in "Izhak Ben Zvi, David Ben Gurion and the Samaritans,"[57] the late Israel Sedaka provides an account that during a meeting of the 1945–1946 Anglo-American commission charged with investigating the Palestine question, the Palestinian representative Ony Abd el-Hady used the Samaritans as an argument against a Jewish state: "Let the Jews live with us in peace, as do the Samaritans in Nablus (Shechem)." The representative of the National Council (*Vaad Leumi*), Ben-Zvi, responded, "Historical truth does not bear out the Arab claims as to the status of Jews in Arab countries. At the time of the Arab conquest the Samaritans numbered approximately 135,000 individuals. Some 13000 years later their number has been reduced to 200 people in Shechem [Nablus] and some 60 people in Tel Aviv" (Sedaka 241).[58] In the above example, the condition of Samaritan and other minorities under Muslim rule was referenced as a defense of Zionist aspirations in Palestine. According to the logic of Ben-Zvi, if the Samaritan population were reduced to the edge of extinction under Muslim rule, could they be expected to fare any better in a majority-Muslim state of Palestine?[59] In response to Zionist state-ments on the Samaritans, in December 1947 the Arab Committee of Nablus called on the local residents "to consider the 200 Samaritans living here as the 'Arabs' brothers" ("Mercy for the Samaritans").[60] According to the *Palestine Post* article, the Arab Committee of Nablus's 1847 statement on the Samari-tans "followed an announcement that the Samaritans supported Arabs' aims on the Palestine issue" ("Mercy for the Samaritans").

By the beginning of the 1948 war, the Samaritans were at the heart of over-lapping identity claims. Arab Nationalists in Nablus were claiming them as Arab brothers and Zionist leaders such as Ben-Zvi were calling the Samaritans their biblical cousins from the tribes of northern Israel. For the Samaritans, a new political reality was developing.[61] The April 3, 1949, Armistice Agreement with Jordan would posit a new geopolitical reality for the Samaritans: they were to be divided by a new border, the 1949 Armistice Line, or Green Line.

Geographic Divisions: 1949–1967

The 1949 Armistice Agreement with Jordan meant that the Samaritan commu-nities of Tel Aviv and Mount Gerizim were effectively cut off from each other. On September 15, 1949, the Samaritan High Priest Yitzhak Amram crossed through the Mandelbaum Gate from East Jerusalem to West "on a four-day visit ... to meet Mr. I. Ben Zvi, member of the Knesset" ("Samaritans to Visit").[62] Amram's visit coincided with the recent immigration of one-sixth of the total Samaritan population from Nablus to Israel. According to an article in the September 15, 1949, *Jewish Telegraph Agency*, "Minister of Immigration Moshe Shapira informed the group that the Israel Government regards the Samaritans as Jews" ("One-sixth of 160 Surviving Samaritan Jews Enter Israel for Permanent Resettlement").[63] Over the next eighteen years, access between the two communities was largely limited to a select few visits and Passover festivities.[64] In Israel, through the support of Ben-Zvi, Samaritans were af-forded coverage under the July 5, 1950, Law of Return (*Hok Hashevuth*), "which states that every Jew is entitled to come to Israel ... [and the Samaritans] were given immigrant rights and were classified in the population registry as 'Sa-maritan Jews'" (Amit 256).

While the Green Line separated the two communities from 1948 to 1967, on both sides of the Green Line Samaritans saw improvement in their stan-dard of living, and the communities began to grow.[65] For example, in 1954, the Samaritan neighborhood in Holon, Israel, was established with support from David Ben Gurion and Yitzhak Ben-Zvi.[66] While the Samaritan community in Holon was doing well, the Samaritan community in Transjordan, on the other side of the Green Line, was doing better, benefitting from the Hashemite leadership in Amman. In the Jordanian West Bank, this lead to increased employment opportunities for Samaritans in the Hashemite government.[67]

For the first time in two centuries, Samaritan population began to increase; however, the Samaritans in Holon were cut off from daily interactions with their family in Nablus and, perhaps more importantly, the High Priest. Benyamim Tsedaka recounts how the Samaritans of Holon had to rely on a radio to communicate with their High Priest in Nablus for religious matters. For the Samaritans, one result of the June 5–10 1967 Six-Day War, the conquest and occupation of the West Bank by Israel, meant that the two communities of Holon and Mount Gerizim could once again have regular contact, relations, and resume a life together; however, the reunification of the two communities also came with a new political reality and, over the next forty years, new political pressures. What emerges in the midst of these new political pressures is greater efforts to assert Samaritan sovereignty in the midst of the political fray. The diaspora of manuscripts, their history of displacement, present locations around the world, and their potential future become more important as Samaritans argue for their sovereignty.

Post-1967: Between Raindrops and Two Fires and a Call for Samaritan Cultural Sovereignty

With the Israeli conquest of the West Bank came Israeli military and civil administration rule of Nablus. Similar to the years leading up to 1948, Samaritan life was complicated by the political reality of an Israeli-administered West Bank. According to Stephen Kaufman, "When news of the [1967] conquest reached Holon, the Samaritans there immediately arranged permits to travel to Mount Gerizim in order to celebrate the Pentecost with their newly accessible brethren. It was, as *A. B. Samaritan News* described, 'the warmest reunion on record'" (21). Future Israeli presidents would pledge that the Samaritans would never again be divided. In 1984, Israeli president Chaim Herzog visited Mount Gerizim and pledged to the Samaritans that "[w]hatever the nature of a political settlement between ourselves and our neighbors, I can promise you that never again will you be cut off from your brothers" ("Herzog Tells Samaritans They Will Never Again Be Separated from Their Brethren in Israel").[68] In the ensuing years, however, this reunion was followed by the First Intifada (1987–1993) and Second Intifada (2000–2004). During this time, the Samaritans worked hard to "walk between the raindrops" and the "two fires." But they encountered great difficulty. In 1989, a Samaritan woman was injured when a Bank Leumi (Israeli National Bank) branch in Nablus was firebombed (Sedan).[69] In 1993, a Samaritan store in Nablus was firebombed for selling liquor. The Samaritans were in an increasingly difficult situation, and they

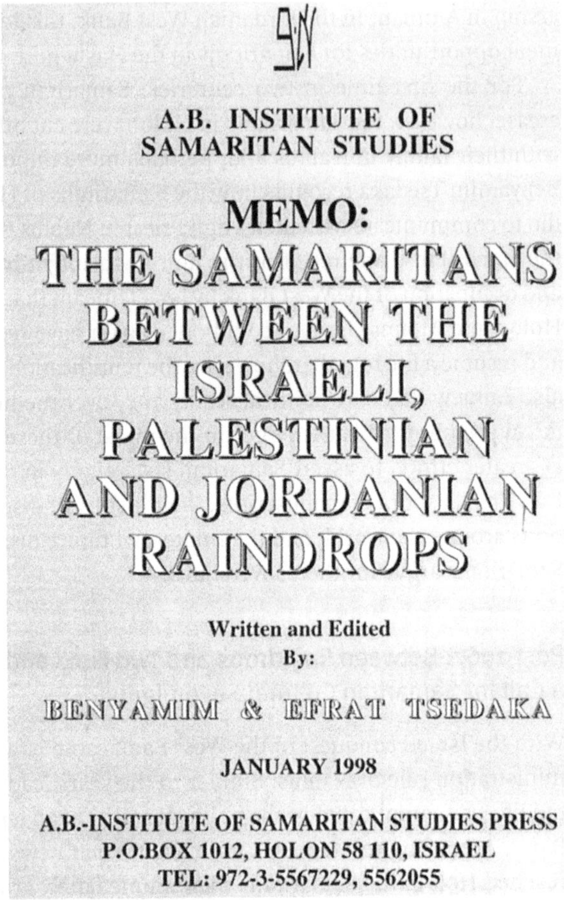

𝔚

A.B. INSTITUTE OF
SAMARITAN STUDIES

MEMO:

THE SAMARITANS
BETWEEN THE
ISRAELI,
PALESTINIAN
AND JORDANIAN
RAINDROPS

Written and Edited
By:

BENYAMIM & EFRAT TSEDAKA

JANUARY 1998

A.B.-INSTITUTE OF SAMARITAN STUDIES PRESS
P.O.BOX 1012, HOLON 58 110, ISRAEL
TEL: 972-3-5567229, 5562055

Fig. 7. Cover page of the 1998 "Memo: The Samaritans between the Israeli, Palestinian and Jordanian Raindrops."

needed to take proactive rhetorical action in order to safeguard the contiguity and peace of their two communities.

Oslo Accords and the Interim Agreement on the West Bank and Gaza Strip (Oslo 2)

For the Samaritans, the Oslo Accords represented the real danger that the Mount Gerizim community would once again be cut off from the Samaritans of Holon. For a population as small as the Samaritans, their future as a people would be in jeopardy if the two communities could no longer meet.[70] In response to this crisis, in 1995 Samaritan leaders embarked on a successful diplomatic mission to lobby Palestinian, Israeli, American, and British diplomats to adopt "Seven Principles" to safeguard the Samaritans' future:

> We, a selected group of leading personalities in the present-day Samaritan Community, leaders of the Community, editors of A.B.—The Samaritan News and directors of A.B.—Institute of Samaritan Studies, hereby set forth the seven principles which guide our efforts to ensure the future of the Samaritan Community, in the Middle East, in any political reality.[71]

Their efforts to lobby the Israelis and Palestinians were successful. According to a news report in September of 1995, "State Department officials have promised to intervene with Israeli and Palestinian officials—who, say Samaritan leaders, have accepted the principle of free-passage documents" (Klein).[72] In chapter 3, the "Seven Principles" document will be discussed in more detail. However, it's important to know that in the decade following the signing of the Oslo Accords, Samaritans continued to suffer difficulties during the Second Intifada. In 2001, Joseph Cohen, then fifty-six years old, was driving up the mountain from Nablus to Kiryat Luza:

> "When I was almost home, I came across two Palestinian boys and they shot me," he says. "The blood ran from me like water."
>
> He lost control of his car and drove into an Israeli roadblock. The Israeli soldiers shouted at him to stop.
>
> "But I couldn't stop the car. And so they also shot me."

Cohen[73] describes the Samaritan predicament in the region as to be "between two fires":

> "The Palestinians know we live with Arabic people, but inside their mind, they think we're Jewish," Mr. Cohen says.
>
> "And because we also speak Arabic, the Jewish people think we're Arab."
>
> "So we have a big problem—we're between two fires."[74]

For an example of how the Samaritans are described as being between Israeli and Palestinian societies, in the 2004 *Journal of Palestine Studies* article "Dispatches from Daily Life: The View from Nablus" Beshara Doumani writes that "the size of this historically small community of a few hundred is growing slowly and the material well-being of its members has visibly improved. This is happening precisely at the time that Nabulsis are suffering from a dramatic decline in living standards" (39). Doumani hypothesizes that if "this trend continues, the next generation of this most native of native communities may come to seem more like the colonial settlers from Brooklyn, Los Angeles, and Moscow than their fellow Nabulsis" (40).

In the July 2014 conflict between Israel and Hamas, the Samaritan community in Holon was inadvertently under rocket fire and one shell landed in the community playground. As Tsedaka and Tsedaka write at the conclusion of "A Journey to England to Ensure the Samaritan's Political Future," "still in question is . . . the uncertainty which tomorrow may bring . . . Precisely in an area so politically sensitive, we must keep our eyes open and check each day how to prepare for the new situation" (43).

In the next chapter, I explore the complexities of this contemporary political reality in relationship to their diaspora of manuscripts with a focus on what Samaritans want from their books in the future. Emergent from Samaritan narratives is the idea that preparing "for the new situation" also means communicating to neighbors and the outside world about Samaritan culture and heritage. This is not only a problem for the digital humanities but is also of concern for rhetoric. By examining the historical connections between the Samaritans' evolving contemporary rhetorical situation and their present-day diaspora of manuscripts, rhetoric and the digital humanities converge in Samaritan interests for the digitization of cultural heritage in libraries and institutions abroad. Just as the Samaritans' diaspora of manuscripts and its historical root causes of colonialism and poverty are interrelated, the rhetorical futures of both the diaspora of manuscripts and the Samaritans' communication of their identity to the outside world are also rhetorically intertwined.

THREE

From Parchment to Bytes: Digital Delivery as a Rhetorical Strategy

As long as [the manuscripts are] with foreign libraries [and] not Samaritan libraries it [digitization] will be easier to do . . . when you come to the Samaritans every manuscript has many partners to it.
—Menashe Altif

The place for the many findings that were found on Mount Gerizim should be in a museum that will be built on Mount Gerizim, on the top the mountain of our life and glory, with all means of secured display.
—Benyamim Tsedaka

In this chapter, I trace the recent history of the Samaritan diplomatic response to Oslo and argue that Samaritan diplomatic efforts require them to communicate their history and culture to their neighbors. Ever since the signing of Oslo, the Samaritans are increasingly "between the raindrops" or "two fires" in the Israeli-Palestinian conflict. A key factor in Samaritan lobbying efforts is their ability to leverage and reference knowledge, cultural heritage, and scholarship about their existence in international debates. Building on archival materials and oral histories with nine Samaritans from Holon and Mount Gerizim, I frame the Samaritan case for sovereignty as rhetorical work at the intersection of rhetoric and the digital humanities.

Oslo, Rhetorical Sovereignty, and Rhetorical Delivery

On July 12, 1995, eight Samaritans authored a position paper entitled "The Seven Principles Document" that was distributed to the government of Israel, the Palestinian Authority, the United States, and the United Kingdom in light of the Oslo Accords and the potential difficulties the Samaritans might face in the event of a new geopolitical reality and border. The document calls on the Israelis, Palestinians, and Jordanians to respect Samaritan cultural sovereignty and to allow free passage for Samaritans between Holon and Mount Gerizim:

> We wish to ensure that in any political situation and irrespective of any political development, even in case of deterioration in the relations between parties to the peace agreement, free and unlimited passage shall be given at all times to every Samaritan, from any place where he/she may live, to the centers of Samaritans on Mt. Gerizim and in Nablus, to the Samaritan Holy sites on Mt. Gerizim in particular and in Judea and Samaria (otherwise known as "The West Bank of the Jordan River") in general, and from there to any place within or outside the State of Israel. (Tsedaka and Tsedaka 33)

In their own words, the Samaritans "did not remain passive" during Oslo ("Memo: Between the Raindrops" 31), and Stephen Kaufman argues that the "Seven Principles" is significant because the Samaritans make a written case for their "extra-territorial rights, regardless of whether the individual holds the citizenship of the State of Israel or that of a future Palestinian state. It seeks recognition that the Samaritans in Holon and Qiryat Luza [Mount Gerizim] constitute one people, exempt from whatever political and territorial divisions that might occur around them" (Kaufman 54). As the "Seven Principles" document shows, Samaritan culture and history are inextricably bound to Samaritan arguments for cultural sovereignty in the Oslo era, and they connect with rhetorical sovereignty in two ways. First, the Samaritans engaged in direct rhetorical advocacy on their own behalf. Second, they made the case for their own cultural sovereignty based on their unique liturgical languages and history. These two points may seem removed from the digital humanities, but they are not. The Samaritans are "between the raindrops" or "two fires" in the Israeli-Palestinian conflict, and as I argue below the mission that emerges from being "between the raindrops" is connected to the Samaritan textual diaspora, the digital humanities, and rhetorical studies.

In *Shared Land/Conflicting Identity: Trajectories of Israeli & Palestinian Symbol Use*, Robert Rowland and David Frank argue that the Oslo agreement is as much a symbolic conflict as one rooted in the land: "The Oslo negotiations, the peace process more broadly, and all aspects of the conflict between Israelis and Palestinians have been shaped by the symbol systems used by Israelis and Palestinians to interpret the world" (15). Rowland and Frank examine symbolic practices in the conflict by sketching trajectories of symbol use by Palestinians and Israelis as a "sort of symbolic journey in which the rhetorics, ideologies, and myths of the Palestinian and Israeli groups have evolved over time" (19). They note that the "journey is not yet complete, and it is by no means clear that the movement toward peace reflected in the Oslo Accords will continue" (19). For the Samaritans, this lack of clarity regarding the future is also a lived reality. Their religious life and livelihood are attached to Nablus, the geographic heart of the Northern West Bank/Samaria. The drive between the two communities from Holon, Israel, to Mount Gerizim traverses languages and politics. The Samaritans increasingly find themselves in need of ways to convey their history and culture to their neighbors who, as we will see, continue to be of significance well into the years following the signing of the Oslo Accords.

In conjunction with the writing of the "Seven Principles," the Samaritans also undertook an active international lobbying effort in Washington, DC, the United Kingdom, and before human rights organizations to deliver the document, and their efforts included prompting internationals to advocate on their behalf. For example, On 22 August 1995, MP Jeremy Hanley writes to Lord Avebury on behalf of the British government that he agrees "that both parties to the peace process should be aware of the Samaritans' interests and that their concerns should be addressed," and that the British "Embassy in Tel Aviv and Consulate-General in Jerusalem have been asked to look for suitable opportunities to raise the Samaritans' case with their Israeli and Palestinian interlocutors" (40). On 12 January 1998, a similar letter was written by Simon Leaver stating that "[t]he British government agrees that both parties to the peace process should be aware of the Samaritans' interests and that their concerns should be addressed" (50). On 14 January 1998, Lord Avebury writes a letter to the UK Minute Room requesting "a written agreement be made between the parties confirming that the Samaritans may pass freely across the boundary in either direction, without waiting for an agreement on a comprehensive settlement of all outstanding matters" (58).[1] Direct lobbying is important to the Samaritans because as Tsedaka and Tsedaka say, they've survived because they know how "to walk between the raindrops" without getting wet, and it's important for them to continue to preserve their cultural heritage "in any political crisis" (38). They don't want to sit back and get "shuffled around or crushed between the political millstones" (Tsedaka and Tsedaka 38). For the Samaritans, their lobbying efforts address "an existential question which has arisen, in all its gravity," about their future survival as a people (44). To this end, Samaritan diplomatic work during Oslo was not in vain.

In "A Journey to England to Ensure the Samaritan's Political Future," Tsedaka and Tsedaka write that what was achieved from meetings with the British and the Americans was joint backing from both to help establish agreements with the Israelis and Palestinians to ensure Samaritan free passage between Mount Gerizim and Holon. Tsedaka and Tsedaka write that "[t]he US and Britain have raised, and continue to raise, the Samaritan issue in their contacts with the Israelis and the Palestinians" ("Memo: Between the Raindrops" 42). On the surface, these meetings may seem to be another bureaucratic footnote to Oslo. However, these meetings are representative of Samaritan efforts to lobby on their own behalf and make the case for their own sovereignty and freedom of movement.

Samaritan efforts in the mid-1990s were successful. Tsedaka and Tsedaka report that the Samaritan delegation to the United Kingdom "ended with political meetings in London, the results of which were akin to those in the U.S., thanks to the cooperation achieved between the two superpowers in the matter of the Samaritans," and in the years since the Samaritans have had freedom of movement between Holon and Mount Gerizim (52). The Seven Principles document helps to set the stage for why the digital amplification of Samaritans' textual diaspora is a desirable outcome for Samaritans such as late High Priest Elazar, Benyamim Tsedaka, and others. In addressing High Priest Elazar's 2009 call for the broad digitization of Samaritan manuscripts, such digitization and future repository-building work also calls for theorizing the future rhetorical potential of texts to communicate Samaritan cultural histories, specifically manuscripts dispersed in textual diaspora, by investigating their history of removal or how they became dispersed, as well as their future access potential (i.e., how they will be accessed and utilized in future digital environments).

As I will argue in chapter 4, the pursuit of these questions from the perspective of *research* may also be done in conjunction with work that's reciprocal and beneficial to stakeholder groups. Through engagement, especially the kind of engagement the digital humanities era affords, researchers can then identify and locate ways in which past and future delivery is *talked* or *written* about in relationship to questions of rhetorical sovereignty and circulation. For now, however, I will focus on a brief overview of recent scholarship in rhetorical delivery in order to provide the necessary framework for understanding how delivery matters for the digital humanities and also how both delivery and digital humanities helped the Samaritans in their efforts to achieve and sustain cultural sovereignty in one of the most complicated conflict zones in the world.

Looking back to Richard Enos's 1994 review of *Rhetorical Memory and Delivery* there is another significant but overlooked point to be made about delivery research: "we may choose to discuss the implications of memory and delivery among ourselves . . . and thereby elect to remain insular" or we can enrich our conversations of delivery with the work of other academic disciplines (609). Enos argues that such a focus on extra-disciplinary engagement is a potentially important "basis for helping us to a more thorough knowledge of memory and delivery." In my 2012 *Rhetoric Review* article "Rhetorical

Delivery as Strategy: Rebuilding the Fifth Canon from Practitioner Stories," I argued that rhetorical studies "needs to engage in delivery research in order to maintain a stake in studying the movement of texts. Other disciplines such as computer science, information sciences, and sociology are increasingly interested in the movement of texts, including recent work by Clay Shirky, Antonio Casilli, Henry Jenkins, Jure Leskovec, and Takis Metaxas, to name a few" (127–28) As Jenkins, Ford, and Green note, digital participation is not in itself neutral space:

> ... even if we get our messages through, there is often a question of whether anyone is listening. None of this allows us to be complacent about the current conditions of networked communications, even if the expanded opportunities for participation give us reasons for hope and optimism. (194)

For example, examinations of how digitized manuscripts in diaspora may be leveraged by cultural stakeholders to advance their cultural sovereignty, in tandem with developing the questions driving primary investigator decisions made about each digital humanities project, should be deeply rooted in a rhetorical understanding of the stakeholders' audience and rhetorical situation: what are these cultural values for a particular situation?

In the last twenty-five years, there has been a considerable amount of scholarship on the fifth canon such as Connors; Dragga; K. Welch; Helsley; Skinner-Linnenberg; Trimbur; Rude; DeVoss and Porter; Ridolfo and DeVoss; and Porter, to name a few. These scholars reconfigure how classical Greek and Roman rhetoric's definition of delivery as the "appropriate management of the voice, gestures and appearance" applies to print and digital texts (Crowley and Hawhee 29). The field quickly moved from thinking about delivery as print document design (Connors) to digital document design (Helsley; Dragga) to the movement of texts (Trimbur). In his 1983 *Rhetoric Review* piece "Actio: A Rhetoric of Manuscripts," Robert Connors contends that delivery for written manuscripts is equivalent to "the format and conventions of the final manuscript, as it is sent in, handed in, or given up" (64). Ten years later in the 1993 collection *Rhetorical Memory and Delivery: Classical Concepts for Contemporary Composition and Communication*, Sheri Helsley argues for the importance of rhetorical delivery in the digital age but limits her discussion to document design and not the strategic movement of texts:

> Rhetorical delivery is enormously important in an electronic age. Word processing and desktop publishing, for example, are now readily available to student writers, and classical rhetoric prompts us to address the use

and adaptation of these powerful post-typewriter presentation technologies. (158)

Rhetorical Memory and Delivery is also noteworthy because it includes one of the first empirical studies of delivery, Sam Dragga's 1992 chapter titled "The Ethics of Delivery." Dragga "decided to survey practicing technical communicators as well as technical communication majors and minors regarding their opinion of various delivery situations" (82). He asked his participants "to determine the ethical principles that guide their design decisions" and respond to the ethics of seven document, image, and page-design scenarios (82), but his definition or understanding of delivery is still synonymous with document design and an "ethics of visual and typographical display." Although it was nearly twenty years ago that Dragga discussed the ethics of delivery (94), only in the last ten years have scholars followed up on his research (see also DeVoss and Porter; Porter).

Since the publication of *Rhetorical Memory and Delivery* more than twenty years ago, there have been a number of additional discussions on rhetorical delivery, including an increased focus on rhetorical delivery in the age of the digital and an expanded, renewed discussion of corporeal delivery and written texts, including considerations of delivery, pedagogy, public space and the law (see N. Welch), race and identity (see Powell), and the gendered body (see Skinner-Linnenberg; Mountford; Buchanan). For example, Trimbur's 2000 *College Composition and Communication* article "Composition and the Circulation of Writing" marks a conceptual shift from scholarship that considers delivery as desktop publishing (Connors; Helsley; Dragga) to considering "the material conditions of producing writing and getting it delivered where it needs to go" (189). In contemporary rhetoric and composition studies, Trimbur is one of the first to articulate delivery as a consideration of the available means of delivery (the rhetorical movement of a text) and distribution, the passage of text from one point to another. Carolyn Rude points out in her 2004 *Technical Communication Quarterly* article that "rhetorical theory is robust enough to accommodate a long-term process of change and not just the single instance" of delivery (273). But Rude's conceptualization of delivery poses a challenge for researchers of rhetorical delivery: how should the field study a strategy of delivery spread out across time and place? For example, how might one study the *kairos* of the Seven Principles document in relationship to how the document was delivered and circulated? While in chapter 2 I examined the diaspora of Samaritan manuscripts from a political and historical perspective, in this chapter I analyze Samaritans' responses to semi-structured oral history questions to show that one approach to studying rhetorical delivery over time and place is to research how the historical and (potential) future circulation of text(s) matter to cultural stakeholders.[2] In order to understand what some Samaritans want from their diaspora of manuscripts, I conducted oral histories with members of the community about the diaspora of manuscripts and what they want from them in the future. These questions aimed to illuminate what Samaritans hope this diaspora will help them to accomplish in the future, to discover what informs their positions, and to elucidate the relationship of digitized manuscripts to the manuscript's present location, history of removal, and objectives on the part of the Samaritans to communicate their cultural sovereignty.[3] Their responses not only ground my theory of textual diaspora but also shed light on the relationship of rhetorical studies to the digital humanities.

The Past and Future of the Samaritan Diaspora of Manuscripts

To further my research and understanding of the textual diaspora and the implications of digitizing Samaritan manuscripts, in 2012 I received a Middle East and North Africa Regional Research Fulbright to return to the Samaritan communities on Mount Gerizim and Holon and conduct open-ended oral history interviews with Samaritans on what their diaspora of manuscripts means to them. With the help of Benyamim Tsedaka,[4] in 2012 I interviewed seven additional Samaritans about their diaspora of manuscripts, and one more in 2014.[5] In my oral history interviews, I was interested specifically in what Samaritans thought about the history and present-day circumstances of the Samaritan diaspora of manuscripts, and what they wanted from these manuscripts in the future.[6] I pursued these research questions about the relationship of the past manuscript dispersal to future digital delivery of manuscripts as research topics in their own right for this book project, but also as questions whose responses were especially important to informing the construction of future digital repositories of Samaritan manuscripts.[7] In the next section, I present situated responses from nine Samaritans:[8]—Benyamim Tsedaka, Yacop Cohen, Menashe Altif, Zolovon Altif, Ovadia Cohen, Raqheb Fara, Ghayth Cohen, Sameer Yousef Sarrawi, and Osher Sassoni[9]—on topics related to the diaspora of Samaritan manuscripts; what Samaritans want from this diaspora of manuscripts;[10] the return of Samaritan manuscripts; digitization of Samaritan manuscripts; and the importance of spreading knowledge about the Samaritans' history, present-day existence, and culture.[11] Following this section, I make connections between their responses, digital rhetorical delivery, and what Scott Lyons calls rhetorical sovereignty:

The inherent right and ability of peoples to determine their own communicative needs and desires in [the attempt to revive not their past, but their possibilities], to decide for themselves the goals, modes, styles, and languages of public discourse. (449–50)

Rhetorical sovereignty is very similar to the Samaritans' call for cultural sovereignty in the "Seven Principles" Oslo document, and throughout this chapter and the manuscript the terms are close in meaning. However, my conception of cultural sovereignty also refers to the Samaritans making the argument for contiguity of travel between the two communities of Holon and Mount Gerizim. I contend that such arguments for their freedom of movement are aided by practices very similar to what Scott Lyons terms rhetorical sovereignty. As the Samaritans argue their case for their unique cultural history, lobby on their own behalf, and communicate their identity to their neighbors and the world, they are demonstrating rhetorical sovereignty and, in this chapter, extending its conception and implications to the digital realm by strategizing how to leverage their textual diaspora to achieve cultural sovereignty.

Samaritan Attitudes toward their Textual Diaspora

All nine Samaritans expressed an attitude that digitizing the diaspora of Samaritan manuscripts serves to forward the necessary and essential task of advancing global knowledge about the Samaritans' existence and culture. There is, however, a diversity of opinion about how the physical location of the manuscripts may relate to the interests of place, tactile experience, and digitization. For example, Benyamim Tsedaka is clear that even though the ways the manuscripts left Samaritan hands are disturbing, today the manuscripts are better off in terms of preservation and scholarly study if they remain in libraries, museums, and archives abroad: "I believe that the way the manuscripts escaped [from the Samaritans], this is better for the manuscripts. And you [researchers] can have access any time to see. In Michigan State's Library, I've visited maybe 10 times. . . . They are keeping the manuscripts so well" (Tsedaka, "Personal interview in Holon, Israel, 16 Feb. 2012"). Raqheb Fara agrees with Benyamim Tsedaka that the manuscripts "are kept better than if they would be in the hands of Samaritans today" because of the preservation resources available to overseas libraries and museums. In addition, Fara says that these libraries', especially university libraries', collections of Samaritan manuscripts increase access to these collections for researchers and the public, and that this access is carefully facilitated to preserve the manuscripts. He also argues that, from the other side, Samaritans can "see copies of them" and that, together, the possession of Samaritan manuscripts by universities and copies of these manuscripts "gives a lot of pride to members of the community. That they know their culture is seen all over the world. And it is contributing a lot to the good reputation of the Samaritan community" (Fara). However, as Benyamim Tsedaka's 2003 address to the Michigan State University Board of Trustees shows, it is not enough for him that the textual diaspora simply be preserved or *stored* in libraries and museums abroad; their cultural contents must be *amplified* through scholarship, public displays, and digitization. In regards to making Samaritan manuscripts more widely accessible through digitization, Tsedaka makes a point that I saw echoed in the transcripts of all nine interviewees: it's important for the world to know more about the Samaritans and access to Samaritan cultural heritage is an important rhetorical tool to help them achieve this objective.

While Benyamim Tsedaka's main tactic for textual diaspora focuses on amplification and access through digitization and other means, Yacop Cohen expresses a desire for material connection and centralization, as does Sameer Yousef Sarrawi, who teaches Samaritan children on Mount Gerizim how to write in the Samaritan script and composes new manuscripts using a combination of computer technology and handwriting. For Sarrawi, he does want some manuscripts back because, "Always, [if] you want to build the future, you must take from something that was in the past. If you don't look to the past, you aren't able to progress into the future. I need to know what my grandfather wrote and what my father wrote and what my uncle wrote and how they wrote literature and the Parashot [Torah portions] . . . How they wrote everything." But Sarrawi also does extensive work with digital composing in Samaritan.

Together, these three leaders share a desire to harness the power of textual diaspora maintained by the manuscripts abroad, but their ideal tactical use differs significantly. Specifically, Yacop Cohen thinks that 50 percent of the manuscripts abroad should return to Samaritan hands and be centralized on Mount Gerizim. In centralizing the manuscripts, Yacop Cohen hopes to one day create a destination for Samaritan learning, knowledge, and study. However he also agrees in part with Benyamim Tsedaka that it is important for some manuscripts to remain abroad in order for scholars to have access. Ghayth Cohen, one of the younger participants interviewed, had not heard the story of the manuscript removal. Upon hearing the story, he speculated that if the Samaritan diaspora of manuscripts never happened, "maybe all our lives would look different today." The manuscripts abroad are "not now in the hands of Samaritans and they don't know about them . . . they contain parts of the history and parts of the [Samaritan] literature that we don't have." Each of these four Samaritans reflects a diversity of views on what to do with the Samaritan diaspora of manuscripts. While Tsedaka and Yacop Cohen are aware of the diaspora of manuscripts and have different plans concerning repatriation, Ghayth Cohen's remarks reflect the insights of someone who has not had the opportunity to visit the manuscripts spread out across the world and who would benefit from their digitization in terms of broader access to Samaritan history, an outcome Tsedaka and Yacop Cohen support.

Menashe Altif, on the other hand, wishes "that all manuscripts will return back to the hands of the Samaritan community" for similar reasons to Yacop Cohen. However, he "knows that is . . . not possible because each manuscript costs a lot of money and the Samaritan community does not have the money in order to return[12] their manuscripts." In response to Yacop Cohen and Menashe Altif's idea for physical repatriation, Tsedaka argues that returning any large percentage of manuscripts and centralizing them on Mount Gerizim would limit the future potential for scholars to access and do work on the collections. In turn, this geographic concentration would curtail the growth of Samaritan studies abroad, a concern also expressed by Raqheb Fara. Although Tsedaka disagrees with repatriating the texts, this perspective does not prevent him from underscoring the responsibility that institutions in possession of Samaritan manuscripts bear to their collections and the Samaritan people. Samaritans such as Tsedaka trust institutions abroad to preserve, provide access to, and digitize Samaritan manuscripts in order to make these collections more widely accessible.

Echoing High Priest Elazar ben Tsedaka, the five Samaritans Yacop Cohen, Menashe Altif, Osher Sassoni, Ghayth Cohen, and Benyamim Tsedaka agree about the importance and need for digitizing their textual diaspora as a means to communicate knowledge about the Samaritans to the world. For example, Tsedaka argues that it's

> very good to digitize them—to preserve them—and also to present them in order to get interest from students [in order to prompt them to] to make research about the Samaritans, in order to spread the knowledge about the Samaritans. It's very important to me. Especially when there are so many prejudices about the Samaritans. So it will open the issue for serious scholars. (Tsedaka, "Personal interview in Holon, Israel, 16 Feb. 2012")

Raqheb Fara also agrees that it's important to digitize Samaritan manuscripts so long as it's not affecting "the holiness of the book" by not damaging the manuscripts via the process of digitization; however, he thinks it's important that people "make their PhD and MA degree by researching these manuscripts," particularly at An Najah University in Nablus, the main center of higher learning for the city of Nablus and the closest university to the Samaritans of Mount Gerizim. For Tsedaka, the Samaritan diaspora of manuscripts is valuable for its cultural and historical meaning to the Samaritans, as well as for its potential to aid in the growth of Samaritan studies and thus also to help counter the "many prejudices about the Samaritans" (Fara). As Osher Sassoni remarks, "There is a lot of disinformation about the Samaritans all over the world. Most of the people outside of Israel, if you ask them about the Samaritans all they know about is the Story of the Good Samaritan, without any relation to those Samaritans still living in Israel." Ghayth Cohen similarly emphasizes the lack of information available to those outside the community: "Although the reputation of the community is greater than its number . . . still there is a lot of room to know more about the Samaritans and their culture and their origin. And with the help of digitizing those manuscripts and giving access to the whole world, they [the world] will be aware of the importance of the community and its tradition and culture." Ghayth Cohen continues to hypothesize that the digitization of Samaritan manuscripts abroad may "tell more about our lives, make it clearer to people, Israelis or Palestinians, make it clear that we are a living people with a language, origin and we are [here] from ancient [times] till [the] present." Similarly, Ovadia Cohen remarks that "[h]ere in the area of Nablus we are brothers; however, there are people outside of Nablus" who don't know about the Samaritans. In this regard, it's also very important to Ovadia Cohen that knowledge about the Samaritans and their manuscripts become available on the Internet. To paraphrase Ovadia Cohen speaking in 2012, there's "no [Samaritan] book today to find on the Internet"—but it's important that there will be, because the Samaritans are separate from the Kingdom of Judah and have their own history and language.[13] What these diverging Samaritan opinions help scholars in rhetoric and the digital humanities to understand is the rich tapestry of rhetorical meaning and potential that cultural heritage resources in diaspora may offer for cultural stakeholders, especially by providing the means for invention and future rhetorical potential of these resources to communicate to audiences outside and inside communities. For Samaritans such as Tsedaka, the manuscripts in their current locations, dispersed under duress but, now, located in academically significant institutions, have a greater potential to be actualized into study where they are today. In addition, the benefit of Samaritan study across the world is a significant step for his people.

For example, Menashe Altif notes that while the manuscripts are abroad, there is a greater potential for digitization because there are fewer overlapping property claims to the manuscripts. To understand his insight, it's important to know more about Samaritan textual practices. For example, ownership questions that exist are created because of Samaritan cultural practice, the sharing of manuscripts among families and the dividing of ownership as manuscripts are passed down from one generation to the next. Consequently, determining who has the authority to sell or grant access to a particular "shared manuscript" is difficult if not impossible in some circumstances. But if the manuscripts are abroad and located in a single institution, these competing ownership claims of Samaritan family members have less of an impact, as Menashe Altif points out: "As long as [the manuscripts are] with foreign libraries [and] not Samaritan libraries it [digitization] will be easier to do . . . when you come to the Samaritans every manuscript has many partners to it." For Osher Sassoni, "it's nice to have them back" but he wants "to be realistic" and knows that repatriation is "an issue of money," but he says he "want[s] to get [access to] them . . . to have them" when he searches "for a word [inside the manuscripts] or an issue that someone wrote about years ago." He wants to know that he can access them whenever he wishes, in order to search and compare different manuscripts.

Sassoni himself has been digitizing his grandfather's scribal works in order to make them available to scholars abroad and members of his own community, but also to preserve them because he wants future generations to have access to his grandfather's words. Similar to Sarrawi's idea that one must know their past in order to create a future, Sassoni argues that digitization is important because it aids in Samaritan manuscript preservation and makes Samaritan manuscripts available for the next generation. Many of his grandfather's manuscripts, including a book of philosophy and the book of Joshua, were written on inexpensive paper and digitization provides an additional safeguard that his grandfather's words will be preserved for Samaritan generations to come: "You cannot touch them even . . . the paper is lost . . . it's a cheap paper." For Sassoni, digitization of his grandfather's paper manuscripts "must be done," otherwise they will be lost. Sassoni proactively began to "digitize some. It's a lot of work, and to serve it [them] on the net" at http:// www.the-samaritans.com. If he did not do this digitization work, he says, "No one will have the opportunity to read them [his grandfather's books]" in the future. For Sassoni, libraries "have the facilities" to store and preserve their manuscripts so the potential of the manuscripts to be actualized does not change. He's focused his efforts on preserving and making available the manuscripts closest to him, manuscripts which are in a delicate circumstance. By digitizing his grandfather's manuscripts, he's increasing the potential reach of the manuscripts over time and increasing the manuscripts' ability to be accessed by the Samaritan community and researchers, to be actualized over time.

While Yacop Cohen, Benyamim Tsedaka, Menashe Altif, and Osher Sassoni have different ideas about repatriation, all three of them see the manuscripts' future potential to communicate knowledge about Samaritan culture in person and online. However, transmitting Samaritan culture is not simply about digitization and academic study. Textual diaspora has practical implications that move beyond researching Samaritan culture. According to Tse-

Fig. 8. Still from a video with Yacop Cohen, talking about the Samaritan Legends Association, 9 March 2012. (*Video available at* https://www.youtube.com/watch?v=sRhp1DqqPBI. *A full video transcript is available in Appendix A.*)

daka and Yacop Cohen, two Samaritans regularly involved in communicating knowledge about the Samaritans' culture, traditions, and history to outsiders, a key cornerstone of their work is the ability to reference and share their written cultural heritage with Palestinians, Israelis, and internationals. Benyamim Tsedaka's and Yacop Cohen's views are not without historical precedent. In an 1875 issue of the *Sunday Magazine for Family Reading*, there's a story written by James Finn, the former British Consul for Jerusalem and Palestine. Finn recounts a dialogue with Samaritan priest Amram, in which the priest "said that forty-two [Samaritan] volumes, large or small, had been stolen and sold." According to Finn,

He [Amram], being most desirous of conciliating the favour of our Government, then said that he *had no objection to the books being placed in public libraries for the advantage of our learned men*, but thought he ought to have the price of them given on behalf of the community, which was well known to be in a condition of extreme poverty. (229, emphasis added)

In the nineteenth century, the distribution of Samaritan manuscripts had the adverse effect of enabling a kind of Western awareness about the Samaritans in the halls of Western power, and now, in the twenty-first century, digitization has the potential to capitalize on perceived Western prestige (or the perception of Western ethos) and re-appropriate it to serve Samaritan interests and not only, or at least not exclusively, for Western scholarly and religious ends.

Writing for Themselves

While it's still too early to see the long term impact of how the circulation of Samaritan manuscripts in digital environments may help the Samaritans to leverage arguments for their cultural and rhetorical sovereignty, there are indications about how the Samaritan diaspora of manuscripts may be utilized by Samaritans in physical and digital form. For example, for over thirty years Samaritan scribe Raqheb Fara[14] from Mount Gerizim has been writing ritual manuscripts for himself and his community. Sitting with a strong quill that he dips in his ink over and over again, Benyamim Tsedaka describes Fara's work as a "talent" that is almost like "painting not writing" or an "art of writing" (Fara, "Personal interview on Mount Gerizim, 23 May 2012"). Fara learned to write Samaritan script and copy Samaritan books as a "pupil of the previous generation" but especially from his father, who he imitated in writing. His uncle, too, was also a talented scribe and "cried for joy that there is still a successor to the important work" of copying Samaritan manuscripts. Fara also walks in the footsteps of tradition by copying and retransmitting classic Samaritan manuscripts such as "Books of prayers, books of Midrash," and the Samaritan Torah. Fara's work as a copyist and writer is time-consuming. A single Samaritan Pentateuch (five books of Moses) may take "four to five months to copy," or as much as "six hundred hours" of work.

In doing the work of a copyist, however, Fara does not just copy Samaritan manuscripts word for word. Fara invents and creates new textual arrangements and shapes by creatively arranging the letters of words in centuries-old manuscripts, forming entirely new designs. The new designs, or new arrangements of letters in the text, are called tashkil in Arabic or acrostics in English. They are created when Fara copies a Samaritan book from right to left and, simultaneously, aligns the letters in rows from the top down via elaborate spacing patterns.

In doing so, he is able to encode and compose new sentences in the top down acrostic. However, his inventiveness does not only end with form. He's also produced original compositions including a poem about the birth of Moses, which he wrote in Samaritan Hebrew "and translated it into Arabic." Fara's works circulate as both individual handwritten manuscripts and as books that are photocopied and circulated among the Samaritan community for ritual use and study. While Samaritans in the "previous generation had no choice but to sell the books because they were very poor," the new generation has more economic means and options and does not have to "see what they have for manuscripts and to sell them for bread." As a result, Fara is able to write in order to "do something for the community . . . to encourage the religion and to encourage the reading of the law" (Fara). Today, because the com-

Fig. 9. Late Samaritan High Priest Aharon ben Ab-Chisda ben Yaacob displaying the *Ketubah* (wedding contract) he is writing for the wedding of Barry Tsedaka and Reoot Sassoni, May 2012. (Photograph by Jim Ridolfo.)

Fig. 10. Late Samaritan High Priest Aharon ben Ab-Chisda ben Yaacob chanting the *Ketubah* (wedding contract) he wrote for the wedding of Barry Tsedaka and Reoot Sassoni, July 2012. (Photograph by Jim Ridolfo.)

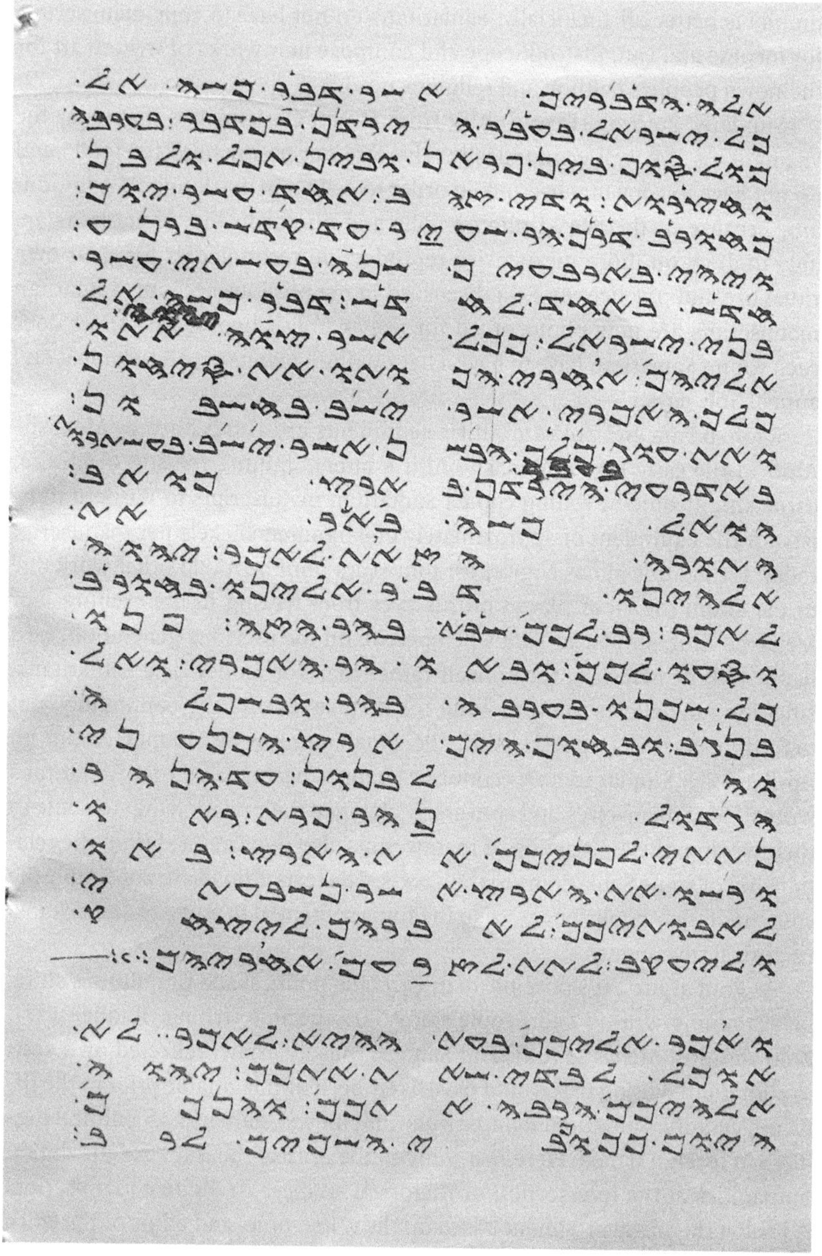

Fig. 11. Image of a *tashkil* from a Samaritan book in the home of Zolovon Altif, August, 2014.

munity is better off financially, Samaritans do not have to copy manuscripts for income and can, instead, copy and compose new works of written art for their own people's cultural and religious needs.

Similarly, Zolovon (Fayyad) Altif from Mount Gerizim says that today the "Samaritans live well economically. They are not in any need for food" and do not have to copy manuscripts in order to sell them any longer.[15] Additionally, because of the use of photography and photocopying, Samaritans are able to draw on more inexpensive reproduction technologies for their own ritual use and practice. As Fara discussed in the previous account, Samaritan manuscripts are now photocopied for use as prayer books. No longer does each young Samaritan have to have a handwritten manuscript on Shabbat and annual holy days.

Raqheb Fara and Zolovon Altif's sentiments are also echoed by Menashe Altif. In the early 1950s, Menashe Altif's father, Tamim, the son of Efraim, earned an income by selling copied Samaritan manuscripts to Western tourists for the equivalent of approximately one hundred shekels per manuscript today. He did this job as copyist for four years until he found other work due to the strain the labor placed on his eyes from writing in the evening. For Menashe Altif, similar to Fara's perspective on the previous generation, he's happy that he can write for himself rather than for money. The Samaritans' situation now allows them to write for themselves and the community, not to feed themselves (Menashe Altif, "Personal interview on Mount Gerizim, 19 April 2012"). Similar to how economic changes necessitated that Samaritans write to feed themselves and conversely changed their relationship to some of their writing, the digitization of manuscripts also indicates a shift in the relationship of some Samaritans to their texts. The texts abroad are not simply the content of their books but are also the future potential to advance Samaritans' rhetorical sovereignty.

As Pratt argues, it's possible to understand political and tumultuous shifts by examining writing and people's attitudes towards writing. Raqheb Fara, Zolovon Altif, Menashe Altif, and Sameer Yousef Sarrawi reflected on a shift in Samaritan writing that would have likely been unimaginable prior to the fifteenth century: Samaritan manuscripts and, indeed, Samaritans' cultural heritage in foreign hands. Here, we come to the crux of the issue for the digital humanities at the intersection of rhetorical studies. To digitize manuscripts is itself a rhetorical argument based on the value, time, and ethos of the work imbued in the act of digitizing manuscripts. In digital environments, the texts take on a new potential to be referred to and circulated. While it's still too early to see the long-term impact of how the circulation of Samaritan manuscripts in digital environments may help the Samaritans leverage arguments for their cultural and rhetorical sovereignty, we see an early example of how such work might be leveraged in other electronic publics by examining the Wikipedia edit wars about the indigenous peoples of Israel/Palestine.

Between the Two Fires: Wikipedia and Edit Wars

Why might a Samaritan book on the Internet matter? One of the ways in which the Samaritans have safeguarded their identity is to communicate their existence to the world, as is argued in the 1995 "Seven Points" document where the Samaritans make their case for their historical and contemporary cultural sovereignty. From Tsedaka's and Yacop Cohen's perspectives in the interviews above, we saw how the historic dispersal of Samaritan manuscripts in the nineteenth and early twentieth centuries creates a opportunity to educate the world about Samaritan cultural sovereignty through their re-transmission in the digital sphere.

For one example of the way digital arguments about identity circulate, consider the case of the English Wikipedia page for "List of Indigenous Peoples" (LOIP). On the LOIP, a curious rhetorical phenomenon has emerged regarding how Samaritans are discussed in relationship to Jews and Palestinians. As part of the electronic iteration of the Arab-Israeli conflict, years of "edit wars" and talk or discussion page threads have occurred on the LOIP page over who should be listed as indigenous to "Western Asia . . . the region of Dead Sea Transform, the Arabian peninsula, the Levant, Asia Minor, the Caucasus region and extending to the southern Caspian coast, Kopet Dag mountains and the eastern Dasht-e Lut desert," and why. The most recent result of the edit wars is that neither Jews nor Palestinians are listed as indigenous to the region on the main page. In fact, only three groups are currently listed as indigenous to the region:

> Assyrians—Aramaic-speaking people mostly found in northern Iraq. They are also found in Syria, Turkey, Iran, and Armenia.
> Marsh Dwellers (Ma'dan)—Arabic-speaking group in the Tigris-Euphrates marshlands of southern Iraq/Iranian border.
> Samaritans—An ethno-religious group of the Levant, closely related genetically and culturally to the Jewish diaspora and are understood [sic] to have branched off from the latter around the time of the Assyrian exile. Religiously, the Samaritans are adherents of Samaritanism, an Abrahamic religion closely related to Judaism. Their sole norm of religious observance is the Pentateuch.

On the LOIP, Samaritans are represented on the list while Jews and Palestinians are not. Why? How did the smallest religious and ethnic minority in the region become the only indigenous group on the Wikipedia page? The answer is in how the Samaritans have largely been left to the side of the English Wikipedia Arab-Israeli conflict edit wars. Wikipedia pages are, first and foremost, records of interest, argument, and activity at a particular moment in time. Going back to Rude, it's difficult to research what the relative impact or *kairos* of such material is, but there's some evidence to support the idea that the availability of such documents is important, because they are ready made, easily accessible, and thus also searchable for a future kairotic moment. In the case of the English LOIP page, the page edits about Jews and Palestinians were locked down in November 2010 as part of the settlement to the 2008 Request for arbitration/Palestine-Israel articles,[16] in which English Wikipedia editors arbitrated terms for how pages relating to the Arab-Israeli conflict may be edited. On the "Talk" page, there's a foregrounded "Arab-Israel Arbitration Enforcement" statement at the top with a bold header about how the Arab-Israeli conflict on Wikipedia has impacted page edits on the LOIP:

WARNING: ACTIVE ARBITRATION REMEDIES

The article List of indigenous peoples, along with other articles relating to the Arab–Israeli conflict, is currently subject to active arbitration remedies, as laid out during a 2008 Arbitration case, and supplemented by community consensus in November 2010. The current restrictions are:

All articles related to the Arab-Israeli conflict broadly construed are under WP:1RR (one revert per editor per article per 24 hour period). When in doubt, assume it is related.

Clear vandalism of whatever origin may be reverted without restriction. Reverts of edits made by anonymous IP editors that are not vandalism are exempt from 1RR but are subject to the usual rules on edit warring.

Editors who otherwise violate this 1RR restriction may be blocked without warning by any uninvolved administrator, even on a first offence.[17]

As we saw in chapter 2, in the twentieth and early twenty-first centuries the Samaritans have been navigating the "two fires" and have been walking "between the raindrops" of the conflict around them. In the twenty-first century, this delicate dance also extends to the digital world. The Samaritans cannot take it for granted that they necessarily will be counted in any given database about the region or Israelite faith: rather, they make their voice heard through speaking and publishing, such as Tsedaka's recent English translation of the Israelite Samaritan Pentateuch or in this Wikipedia page. To be counted in databases is not necessarily a given, but rather an ongoing task of rhetorical invention, composition, and engagement that's essential for the Samaritans to accomplish. To be counted in databases and finding aids is to place materials in strategic research locations to help enable future arguments, to be counted in the international community, and to help safeguard and communicate Samaritans' cultural sovereignty. Consequently, this rhetorical creation has important rhetorical and political implications.

Leveraging Rhetorical Velocity: Textual Diaspora

In my previous work on rhetorical delivery, I have written extensively about strategically theorizing the future recomposition of texts. I've called this concept "rhetorical velocity" (see Ridolfo 2009; Ridolfo and DeVoss 2009; Ridolfo and Rife 2011; Ridolfo 2012; Sheridan, Ridolfo, and Michel 2012) or the way rhetors strategize about the potential recomposition and redistribution of a text (Ridolfo and DeVoss). Rhetorical velocity draws attention to considerations for how the text may be recomposed and/or redistributed and the text's potential for becoming actualized in future cycles of recomposition and/or redistribution (Sheridan, Ridolfo, and Michel 80).

As an outsider to the Samaritan community, I find it difficult to discern what the potentiality of Samaritan manuscripts ought to be; however, the range of potentialities shows the significance of the Samaritan diaspora to the Samaritan people and their place in rhetorical theory as a textual diaspora. As I discussed in chapter 1, I use the term textual diaspora to refer to the way manuscripts, spread out across the world in the collections of influential museums and educational institutions, become strategic in relationship to their location and value to these institutions, and the potential of these institutions to study, conserve, put on display, digitize, and amplify the cultural content of these manuscripts.[18] While the diaspora's location is not predetermined or chosen by the Samaritans, the location is nonetheless a strategic rhetorical asset in the Samaritans' work to communicate their cultural identity to other audiences. Thinking about these resources as rhetorical and strategic speaks to Scott Lyon's notion of rhetorical sovereignty, in that they have the potential to be actualized in ways that will further help the Samaritans determine their cultural, religious, and political representation to "the two fires" and beyond. Furthermore, these potentialities of the *texts* speak to concerns regarding the future location and likelihood of study and digitization of the manuscripts.

As the interviews discussed earlier in this chapter acknowledge, manuscripts in museums, libraries, and archives abroad offer a different rhetorical *potential* than manuscripts centralized in a library on Mount Gerizim. This is not to say that one possibility is more ethical than another; however, it does mean that the manuscripts have several potential rhetorical futures. If, as Tsedaka argues, the manuscripts are utilized and digitized by institutions abroad, then that will lead to certain rhetorical outcomes such as greater knowledge about the Samaritans, increased digital reference to the Samaritan cultural materials by members of the community and scholars, and the potential recomposition of some of the digitized materials in Photoshop by members of the community (see Ridolfo and DeVoss). If, as Yacop Cohen argues, some of the manuscripts are returned to Mount Gerizim and centralized in a library or house of study, then that will set the stage for a different set of outcomes, such as physical access to the manuscripts, the potential creation of a house of community/scholarly study, and the above benefits of some digitized content. These differences are what I call *rhetorical potentialities*, building upon Aristotle's notion in the *Metaphysics*. The likelihood of these possibilities to be realized are what Aristotle would call actualities. In many ways, the diaspora of manuscripts presents Samaritans with a wide range of possible rhetorical options, all of which are theorized along the lines of rhetorical sovereignty; however, members of the Samaritan community differ in regards to what they think may happen *next* in regards to the future of the textual diaspora. For example, the acorn has the potential to receive sunlight and water and be actualized into a tree, or to not receive those resources and be actualized back into soil without blossoming and growing into a tree. Both of these two possibilities (potentialities) clearly exist for acorns. For writing and ideas, the outcomes are less clear; however, each of the nine Samaritans talked about the past and future circulation of Samaritan texts in relationship to what may potentially be actualized. For Yacop Cohen, some of the manuscripts have the potential to fill a Samaritan library of study on Mount Gerizim and promote learning among his people and their village of Kiryat Luza as a destination for textual Samaritan studies.

While Benyamim Tsedaka wants Samaritan manuscripts to remain in diaspora but be actualized by institutions to advance Samaritan studies and knowledge about Samaritans, he has a very different understanding on dispersed archaeological findings, including stone carvings and elaborate mosaics:

> As it is unimaginable that archaeological findings that symbolize the luxurious past of the Jewish People, found in Jerusalem will be displayed outside of Jerusalem, it is also unimaginable that the tens of thousands of findings that Magen exposed in his excavation on Mount Gerizim that represent the luxurious past of our nation from its Mount Gerizim centrality, will be taken and wander on display in various places outside of Mount Gerizim . . . The place for the many findings that were found on Mount Gerizim should be in a museum that will be built on Mount Gerizim, on the top the mountain of our life and glory, with all means of secured

Fig. 12. Museum of the Good Samaritan, April 2012. (Photograph by Jim Ridolfo.)

Fig. 13. Samaritan mosaics in the Museum of the Good Samaritan, April 2012. (Photograph by Jim Ridolfo.)

Fig. 14. Samaritan mosaics in the Museum of the Good Samaritan, April 2012. (Photograph by Jim Ridolfo.)

display. The place should not be at a Christian site nor in the Rockefeller Museum storages in East Jerusalem but in their most natural place of our luxurious culture of our forefathers—In Mount Gerizim. (Benyamim Tsedaka, "Why Are Samaritan Antiquities That Belong to the Samaritans in the Good Samaritan Inn Museum?")[19]

As Benyamim Tsedaka argues, the archaeological findings removed from Mount Gerizim and largely centralized at Israeli museums more than an hour away from Mount Gerizim have little potentiality in their present locations to benefit the Samaritan people as "an integral part" of their new uprightness. It's worth considering why Tsedaka wants the stone and archaeological findings repatriated to Mount Gerizim but not the manuscripts. One possibility is that the stone and archaeological findings at the Israeli Museum of the Good Samaritan or Israeli Antiquities Authority Museum at the Rockefeller Museum in East Jerusalem have very little rhetorical potential due to the media of stone and their current locations in areas with very little tourist or Academic traffic. On the days when I have visited both places, there is a low volume of visitors.[20] The media of stone, furthermore, is not as easily circulated in a digital context as is a text or manuscript. Furthermore, while the Samaritans have their own copies of many texts abroad, such as copies of Pentateuchs, the stone and mosaic work is unique and is imbued with the cultural context of place and space. These stone objects do not have as much potential to be recast into knowledge in diaspora. Furthermore, their palatial importance to Tsedaka and the community is valued over their minimal potential to spark future Samaritan studies in locations beyond Mount Gerizim.

Together, these nine Samaritans engage in *theorizing textual diaspora*, or strategizing the future rhetorical potential of a large diaspora of manuscripts to advance specific cultural and communicative goals or objectives. Strategizing textual diaspora simultaneously considers the past histories of manuscript dispersal, the present political and cultural pressures, and the imagined future potential of these texts to be conserved, studied, and placed on display in brick and mortar institutions and recast and redelivered in digital repositories. While these Samaritans' opinions may differ in terms of rhetorical strategy and implementation related to the physical future of the textual diaspora, the three share a deep understanding of the textual diaspora's importance to contemporary Samaritan identity, culture, and social-political circumstances. Samaritans' relationship to their manuscripts abroad differs from Samaritan to Samaritan; these responses from these nine Samaritans should not be understood as monolithic or ahistorical but rather as conversations situated in place and time; as such, I suggest that they provide insight into how some Samaritans are talking about their diaspora of manuscripts in strategic rhetorical ways. These insights, in turn, are important to conversations about digitization because they represent a range of strategic thinking about how the textual diaspora of manuscripts may physically and digitally benefit the Samaritan people in the future.[21] There has not, though, yet been a great deal of crossover work between rhetorical studies and the digital humanities that shows how work with a foot in both fields may prompt new histories and theories for rhetorical studies.

As the Samaritan example illustrates, rhetorical research into the history of diasporic collections, combined with current cultural stakeholder attitudes toward the past, present, and future removal, delivery, and circulation is crucial for digital humanities projects. In the next chapter, I examine how the digital delivery of cultural heritage has the potential to help cultural stakeholders advance their heritage through broader circulation. I analyze the Samaritan case example as one instance of what cultural stakeholder engagement might look like in the digital sphere. Drawing on what Jeffrey Grabill describes as "engagement as a form of intellectual work" (15), the next chapter proposes that rhetorical studies and the digital humanities can benefit from implementing collaborative models of engaged rhetorical scholarship with diverse stakeholder groups. This engaged scholarship may consider the rhetorical impact of communicating texts as they relate to the desired goals or objectives of cultural stakeholders. In turn, this scholarship may inform or enrich the construction of digital humanities projects. By participating in engaged research, digital humanities and rhetoric scholars alike benefit from not only long-term collaboration but also the rich insights that develop over time. Such an approach both deepens and thickens the rhetorical historiography of our field.

FOUR

Leveraging Textual Diaspora: Rhetoric and the Digital Humanities as Engaged Scholarship

I call that we . . . critically reflect on struggles for and engage with discussions about digital and visual rhetorical sovereignty, or the inherent right for indigenous communities to claim and shape their own communication needs (as well as rhetoric of their identities) in digital and visual spaces.
—Angela Haas, "Wampum as Hypertext: An American Indian Intellectual Tradition of Multimedia Theory and Practice"

As Angela Haas argues in her seminal article "Wampum as Hypertext," rhetorical studies and digital rhetoric intersect at the moment stakeholders—what Hart-Davidson and I refer to as groups with overlapping interests in the same resources—consider how best to shape their digital communication needs. In thinking about how digital technologies may help to amplify indigenous self-representation, Haas builds on Scott Lyons's work by arguing that "digital and visual rhetorical sovereignty, or the inherent right for indigenous communities to claim and shape their own communication needs" is an important area of rhetorical theory and engagement (Haas 96). In this chapter, I discuss the Samaritan repository project as engaged rhetorical work that helps the Samaritans attain greater rhetorical sovereignty based on ideas of tribal engagement (Howe; Cushman) and strategies for enacting digital rhetorical sovereignty (Howe; Haas) through collaborative community-based work (Howe; Grabill). This engaged work with textual diaspora provides an example of one of many possible ways rhetorical studies may intersect with conversations in the digital humanities (DH). In this specific case, the work of amplifying a textual diaspora requires multi-institution collaboration, teams of specialists, and fieldwork. At the heart of such work is a core rhetorical question: what do communities want to do with their texts? In providing a method for answering this question, rhetorical studies earns a seat at the larger DH table.[1]

In the last five years, digital humanities has grown as an area of research and engagement in the disciplines of literature, history, and library sciences.[2] While DH may be the most commonly accepted cross-disciplinary umbrella term for digital work in the humanities and social sciences, the term DH continues to (re)produce disciplinary silos. In the broader scope of DH scholarship, procedural and methodological conversations are based largely on the work of history and literature scholars. While scholars in computers and writing (C&W) have been doing digital work for over thirty years, research in C&W was not typically visible by scholars in literature and history before Gold's 2012 *Debates in the Digital Humanities*. Furthermore, the NEH Office of Digital Humanities (ODH) only funded a small number of projects based in rhetorical studies each year.[3] Not surprisingly, scholars from literature or history who talk about digital work in rhetorical studies are few and far between. Since the work of rhetorical scholars receives neither a significant share of ODH funding proportionate to literature nor significant attention from scholars in other areas of DH, where do computers and writing, rhetorical studies, and its related fields fit into the current DH conversation? In this chapter, I propose rhetorical delivery as a heuristic for thinking about engagement in and between rhetoric and the digital humanities. What do different stakeholder groups want to *do* with texts? How do these groups differ about what they want from the future of their texts? This chapter not only clarifies the methods for thinking through these questions, it also introduces several portals or tailored entrances to texts that I designed with William Hart-Davidson and Michael McLeod to enable scholars, the public, and the Samaritan community to see how the other groups view the texts. How might we develop unique portals to texts that are tailored to specific stakeholder groups, and then how might stakeholders learn about the differences between these groups by viewing other portals? By providing rhetorical ways of seeing circulation and discourse around texts, rhetorical studies may positively influence discussions in the digital humanities.

As I noted in chapter 1, a rhetorical lens for the digital humanities has been largely absent until the last few years, and there is still much work to do to inform digital humanities scholars about the potential benefits of a rhetorical heuristic for project planning, user-centered design, and study of impact for specific stakeholder groups. For example, the "big tent" of DH can benefit from rhetorical studies' documented focus on collaborative and engaged work with community and cultural stakeholders, and our resulting theory grounded in practice or engaged praxis (Haas; Cushman;[4] Grabill; Powell) through cross-cultural inquiry (Flower) and literacy practices (Grabill; Flower). As Jessica Enoch and David Gold argue in the introduction to their November 2013 *College English* special issue on digital humanities and rhetorical historiography:

There is collaboration among and extensive conversation with scholars inside and outside rhetoric and composition, stakeholder groups, and digital experts. We want to highlight the significant part collaboration plays in these projects, and we want to encourage these and other scholars to continue to discuss the nature of their collaborations. We are confident that as scholars become more involved in complex digital historiography projects, collaboration will become increasingly important. (109)

In the same special issue of *College English*, Ellen Cushman argues, "Digital archives, such as the Cherokee Stories and Songs DVD, have captured the imagination of humanities scholars and rhetoric and composition scholars alike for good reason" (115); however, Cushman warns that "[t]he ways knowledge is imparted—through what media, by whom, and for what ends—remain central, though unresolved issues in developing this curriculum, and speak to the troubled and troubling history of archiving" (119).[5] Cushman's warning about who is in charge of imparting knowledge and why knowledge is disseminated intersects with conversations between rhetoric, the digital humanities, and postcolonial studies in which power and knowledge are examined through digital resources.

At the intersection of postcolonial digital humanities and rhetorical studies, scholars Tarez Samra Graban, Alexis Ramsey-Tobienne, and Whitney Myers argue in their chapter "In, Through, and About the Archive: What Digitization (Dis)Allows" that "the most compelling aspects of digitization for rhetoric may come not from building electronic exhibits but from observing how various dilemmas surrounding location, migration, and access inspire new methodologies at the intersection of rhetorical and digital work" (233). Graban, Ramsey-Tobienne, and Myers persuasively argue for a new lens to view digital archives as rhetorical by viewing "the archive as a critical rhetorical space that demands equally of its creators and users" and as a "site for testing theories about how texts migrate among discourse communities" (233). In their chapter, Graban, Ramsey-Tobienne, and Myers also point to a rhetoric of engagement as related to the demands the archive places on creators and user communities. In order to understand what user communities want from digital archives and resources, stakeholder communities must have a role in the creation and circulation of digital resources: in other words, there is a need for engagement. For scholars interested in engaged collaboration with other communities, collaborative relationships must be built, maintained, and nourished.

The process Benyamim Tsedaka used to catalogue the Hebrew Union College Jewish Institute of Religion's (HUC-JIR) Samaritan manuscript collection at the Cincinnati Klau Library underscores the importance of engagement and collaboration at the edge of post-colonial studies and the digital humanities. While HUC-JIR had institutional finding aids for their large collection of Samaritan manuscripts, Director of Libraries David Gilner encouraged Tsedaka to produce a library catalogue from a Samaritan perspective. Tsedaka's work was successful, and in 2011 he completed his 162-page English and Hebrew catalogue of HUC-JIR's collection. Tsedaka's accomplishment was the first library catalogue of manuscripts ever produced and published by a Samaritan and is an example of university-community engagement to include cultural stakeholder voices in the description of collections.[6]

Tsedaka's Hebrew and English catalogue descriptions not only resulted in the print catalogue published by HUC-JIR but were subsequently used in the online digital resource for the Samaritan community[7] (http://www.samar itanrepository.org). In her 2014 chapter, "Archive Experiences: A Vision for User-Centered Design in the Digital Humanities," Liza Potts argues that by producing "connections between rhetoric and the digital humanities, we can focus on engagement . . . both with the internal digital humanities communities as they exist today and with the external audiences for digital humanities projects" (258). Tsedaka's catalogue is part of the connection between an institution and a cultural stakeholder. By itself, the catalogue may not be easily viewed as the building blocks for future DH work. However, the catalogue is one important project in a web of engagement and collaboration between institutions such as HUC-JIR and the Samaritan community. Engagement in the digital humanities is not only limited to digital engagement but includes face to face engagement with people, institutions, communities, and brick and mortar resources. As rhetorician and professional communicator Jeff Grabill reminds us from his own university community work, engagement is intellectual work (15). For example, Tsedaka's work on the catalogue was not initially digital but it was later incorporated into the digital realm; therefore it's important for scholars to remember that in the digital humanities not all work that eventually becomes digitally accessible was initially created in the digital world. As Tsedaka's work illustrates, the cross-institution and community relationships enable the analog work of cataloguing to become more visible and accessible through digital repositories.

Just as HUC-JIR reached out to involve Benyamim Tsedaka in the creation of catalogues, in our initial ODH funded project, "Archive 2.0: Imagining the Michigan State University Israelite Samaritan Scroll Collection as a Thriving Social Network," William Hart-Davidson and I worked with the Samaritan community to develop portals to access portions of three digitized Samaritan manuscripts (which turned out to be codices from the collection and not scrolls) at Michigan State University. We worked with the Samaritan community to develop the protocol, test the prototypes, and develop a framework for future engagement. This chapter is a story about what engagement means for rhetoric at the intersection of the digital humanities, why rhetorical delivery and audience are two concepts I use to think about engagement ("What do stakeholder groups want to do with their texts? Why? For what audiences?), and why fieldwork is necessary for the future of the digital humanities.

Reflective Engagement: Rhetorical Delivery as DH Engagement

Recent conversations in the digital humanities have questioned the relationship of theory to practice,[8] or how scholars in the humanities create new digital projects that foster/inspire new theoretical and historical questions and thus also investigations. We are making digital projects more frequently, but what impact do the projects have beyond discipline-specific scholarly audiences? For digital humanists in literature and history, the focus has traditionally been on the meaning of texts. For example, the third edition of the renowned Beowulf project, is designed

> to meet the needs of general readers, who require a full, line by line, translation; of students, who want to understand the grammar and the meter and still have time in a semester to study and appreciate other important aspects of the poem; and of scholars, who want immediate access to a critical apparatus identifying the nearly 2000 eighteenth-century restorations, editorial emendations, and manuscript-based conjectural restorations. ("Studying Beowulf")

However, the idea of studying not only the *meaning* of the words in digitized texts but also what digitized texts *do* beyond the direct reception from students and scholars, is a core goal in rhetorical studies (see in particular Bazerman and Prior's *What Writing Does and How It Does It*). As Casey Boyle has recently stated in "Low Fidelity in High Definition: Speculations on Rhetorical Editions," "as rhetoricians we are not as interested in what a text *is* as we are in what a text *does*" (127). Similar to how David Barry in the introduction to *Understanding Digital Humanities* suggests that questions of code become "increasingly important for understanding in the new digital humanities" and serve as "a condition of possibility for the many new computational forms that mediate our experience of contemporary culture and society," *Digital Samaritans* demonstrates that rhetorical studies can serve as a "condition of possibility" for theorizing the past, present, and future possibilities for the invention, delivery, and circulation of digital humanities projects (17). As a media communications scholar, Barry emphasizes code's importance because for him it has the "condition of possibility," an ability to do more in future output than its immediate function might suggest. I argue that for scholars in rhetorical studies, all digital objects provide a "condition of possibility" because they may be potentially picked up, used, or circulated in new and surprising ways. While the potential of code receives a great deal of attention in the digital humanities, the everyday potential of digitized texts to circulate and do more than their initial upload, particularly for cultural stakeholders, has received very little attention outside of that from a handful of scholars. Scholars such as Huatong Sun and Hart-Davidson in Human-Computer Interaction (HCI) argue in their 2013 Computer Human Interaction (CHI) conference proceedings that "affordances as discursive relations in HCI design to approach contested issues such as identity, agency, voice, and social justice in design situations where culture and political economy are foregrounded and where the feelings, attitudes, and emotions of individual users may be shadowed in structures of power, ideology, history, dominance, and epistemology" (3534). Such a view of affordances is essential to understanding the value and development arc of digital projects for cultural stakeholder communities.

For researchers, the questions driving decisions made about each digital humanities project should be deeply rooted in a rhetorical understanding of audience and situation: What are these cultural values for a particular situation? Who are the intended and potentially unintended audiences for particular texts? Who will use these resources, and to what end? As Jenkins, Ford, and Green argue in *Convergence Culture*, "circulation constitutes one of the key forces shaping the media environment. It comes also from a belief that, if we can better understand the social and institutional factors that shape the nature of circulation, we may become more effective at putting alternative messages into circulation" (194). Understanding the social and institutional factors, however, requires fieldwork and engaged research with cultural communities. While there are still too few examples of digital humanities projects that explicitly engage with cultural heritage stakeholders, there is great potential for research between both fields. In the next two sections, I call attention to a specific Samaritan digitization project and the Samaritan keyboard I designed in collaboration with the community to demonstrate the importance of the type of reciprocal community engagement and to offer one generative framework for engagement in and around rhetorical studies and the digital humanities at the intersection of studying cultural attitudes toward the rhetorical delivery of texts. Building on Grabill's idea of engagement as intellectual activity, this engagement through delivery research may serve as a means to inform the creation and ongoing development of digital humanities projects.

Building a Samaritan Manuscript Repository as a Case Example for Engaged Work in Rhetoric and Digital Humanities

Rhetorical studies has the potential to transform digital repositories from a site of storage to a platform to make arguments in a variety of digital environments—a rhetorical platform. In developing materials with and for the Samaritans, we followed the methodological calls for engagement issued by Howe on indigenous protocols and Potts on design. This included working on an audience-based platform for screening manuscripts, an interactive digital map of the Samaritans' textual diaspora, and a Samaritan script keyboard that enables UNICODE typing and reading of Samaritan script. In 2014 Potts, building on work at the intersection of rhetoric and human-computer interaction (HCI), argues that rhetoric and DH may complement each other at the intersection of engagement and HCI. Similarly, Native American scholars such as Craig Howe call for engaging with tribal stakeholders based on "the inherent expertise, value, and rights of tribal communities" (171). For the Samaritans, then a group of approximately seven hundred Samaritans in 2008, the manuscripts in libraries abroad represented a significant chapter of their cultural history and we proceeded as best we could to acknowledge and respect that tribal histories are "complex and require considerable thought to develop and present in a respectful and meaningful manner" (Howe 171). Here, Howe makes a compelling case for engagement as a complex and iterative process, and we followed his principles when establishing our protocol for HCI research with the Samaritan community. In what follows I theorize the way insights about textual diaspora and rhetorical sovereignty informed the engaged process I used to develop these materials. I also emphasize the way that this engaged process helped to facilitate a reciprocal relationship with the Samaritans and to enhance their cultural sovereignty and leverage their textual diaspora.

In developing the platform that would enable the digitization of Samaritan manuscripts so that they would be useful for multiple audiences, Hart-Davidson and I assembled a broad team of stakeholders that included Tsedaka, MSU Special Collections staff, Samaritan and biblical scholars, the MSU university archivist, and programming talent from the Writing in Digital Environments (WIDE) Research Center. For stage one of the project, our goal as rhetoricians working at the intersection of DH was to enhance access to the MSU collection through engagement with a wide range of stakeholders, especially the cultural stakeholder community, in order to work toward understanding issues surrounding Samaritan rhetorical sovereignty. In early 2008, William Hart-Davidson and I met with two local Samaritan and biblical scholars, Professor Robert Anderson and Associate Professor of Hebrew and Israeli Culture Marc Bernstein, as well as the director of MSU Special Collections, Peter Berg, and communicated with the university archivist, Cynthia Ghering. While other academic digitization projects may default to a scholarly or public audience, we based our project on the rhetorical notion that the repository should appeal to and be accessible by multiple audiences. While a primary audience includes the Samaritans themselves, we also recognized that such a repository would be useful for stakeholders beyond the Samaritan community.

In the Samaritan case example, fieldwork, engagement, and site visits were essential to learning more about what Samaritans want to do with manuscripts in diaspora, especially in relationship to the manuscripts they have in their own possession. Since 2008, Tsedaka has traveled to visit the United States for his yearly lecture tour and has been available for face-to-face meetings in Michigan in 2008 and 2010, and in Cincinnati in 2009, 2011, 2012, 2013, and 2014. Similarly, I have traveled to Israel and the West Bank to meet with Tsedaka and members of the community in 2009, 2010, 2012, and 2014. Maintaining regular contact with cultural stakeholders and face-to-face reporting on project updates is an important component of engaged research. While one might think that the digital humanities may mean less face-to-face meetings and the traveling they necessitate, in the case of engaging with cultural stakeholder communities, I strongly argue that more face-to-face time is better, and such contact cannot be replaced with digital meetings facilitated by communications tools such as e-mail and Skype. Relationships between institutions and communities must be built and maintained, and this requires face-time, fieldwork, and presence.

At the beginning of the project in 2008, we identified a total of three distinct stakeholder communities, each with different sets of interests in the collection. This stakeholder-based approach differs from a project such as Google's popular Dead Sea Scrolls initiative, which aims to digitize and make available the contents of the Dead Sea Scrolls from Qumran to a general public audience. While the Dead Sea Scrolls may have specific Jewish and Samaritan cultural stakeholder groups—Google's project goals were to provide the broadest form of access to as large a public as possible—our project aimed to tailor access in regards to what specific stakeholder groups want to do with these texts.[9] Rather than providing one way to access the texts suitable for the broadest possible audience, our work differs from Google's because we are interested in tailoring cultural digital repositories to the needs of specific stakeholder groups.[10]

Unlike the Dead Sea Scrolls exhibition, Hart-Davidson and I envisioned the Samaritan repository project from a technical and rhetorical perspective to allow for a plurality of descriptive metadata for each digitized manuscript. In

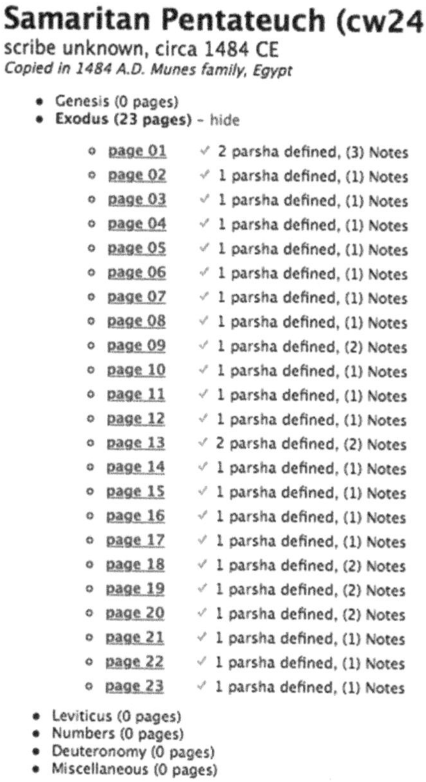

Samaritan Pentateuch (cw2478a)

scribe unknown, circa 1484 CE
Copied in 1484 A.D. Munes family, Egypt

- Genesis (0 pages)
- Exodus (23 pages) - hide

  - page 01 ✓ 2 parsha defined, (3) Notes
  - page 02 ✓ 1 parsha defined, (1) Notes
  - page 03 ✓ 1 parsha defined, (1) Notes
  - page 04 ✓ 1 parsha defined, (1) Notes
  - page 05 ✓ 1 parsha defined, (1) Notes
  - page 06 ✓ 1 parsha defined, (1) Notes
  - page 07 ✓ 1 parsha defined, (1) Notes
  - page 08 ✓ 1 parsha defined, (1) Notes
  - page 09 ✓ 1 parsha defined, (2) Notes
  - page 10 ✓ 1 parsha defined, (1) Notes
  - page 11 ✓ 1 parsha defined, (1) Notes
  - page 12 ✓ 1 parsha defined, (1) Notes
  - page 13 ✓ 2 parsha defined, (2) Notes
  - page 14 ✓ 1 parsha defined, (1) Notes
  - page 15 ✓ 1 parsha defined, (1) Notes
  - page 16 ✓ 1 parsha defined, (1) Notes
  - page 17 ✓ 1 parsha defined, (1) Notes
  - page 18 ✓ 1 parsha defined, (2) Notes
  - page 19 ✓ 1 parsha defined, (2) Notes
  - page 20 ✓ 1 parsha defined, (2) Notes
  - page 21 ✓ 1 parsha defined, (1) Notes
  - page 22 ✓ 1 parsha defined, (1) Notes
  - page 23 ✓ 1 parsha defined, (1) Notes

- Leviticus (0 pages)
- Numbers (0 pages)
- Deuteronomy (0 pages)
- Miscellaneous (0 pages)

Fig. 15. A screenshot of the CCMAT tool in use (2012).

this regard, each manuscript could exist in a digital environment with multiple portals, or narrative windows or portals to the manuscript. Later, it would be possible for metadata to be added to the site by multiple stakeholder communities and either be made visible to other groups if desired by the cultural stakeholder group or remain private just for the cultural stakeholders (for images of the prototype, see Ridolfo, Hart-Davidson, and McLeod, "Balancing Stakeholder Needs: Archive 2.0 As Community-centred Design"). The concept of thinking about stakeholders' digital access and privacy needs for cultural heritage resources is similar to the approach of Kimberly Christen's project with Mukurtu to set up intellectual property access controls and restrictions for digital materials as I discussed in chapter 1, but it is tailored to the idea of audience and the idea that texts are used in different ways by different stakeholder groups. In digital environments, there is no longer a spatial constraint to provide other narrative perspectives on materials as there may be in the space of physical notecards at a brick and mortar exhibit. As is the case with the Samaritan project, there's the possibility of providing multiple metadata windows to the same texts.

The Samaritan project is different from (although not opposed to) projects such as Mukurtu in that the digital archive is designed to be a rhetorical platform for multiple stakeholder groups with different interests. A rhetorical platform makes possible, for example, a means to enable Samaritans' access to the archive through mobile applications because they're already using such mobile platforms to share cultural content. Such an approach differs from many other digitization projects because of its focus on cultural stakeholders. For example, in a more broad survey of digital archive projects, the 2012 edited collection *Digitization in the Real World: Lessons Learned from Small and Medium-Sized Digitization Projects* provides case examples from over thirty small and medium library, archive, and museum digitization projects. The vast majority of these case examples call attention to issues of expanding access, not tailoring access to multiple groups with different interests in the collection. In the case of the Samaritan repository project, we engaged in extensive fieldwork to allow us to tailor future iterations of the repository to the needs of particular stakeholder groups such as the Samaritan community, scholars, and the public. This tailored approach provided a new method for designing and implementing the collaborative work of helping stakeholders to rhetorically leverage textual diaspora.

In early 2008, Hart-Davidson and I worked on an application for a NEH Office of the Digital Humanities Start-up Grant. This process included multiple meetings with then US representative of the A.B. Samaritan Institute, Sharon Sullivan, and identifying stakeholder audiences. Our particular angle was less about the content of the texts themselves and more about how different groups wanted to *use* the texts. In other words, to best design the interface, we first had to discover what each group wanted to do with the Chamberlain Warren Collection. While the Samaritans still have several hundred manuscripts in their possession for weekly ritual religious purposes and print photocopies for ritual use, an estimated four thousand of their manuscripts are abroad in more than seventy libraries, archives, museums, and private collections in Europe, North America, South America, and Australia.[11]

The first stakeholder group includes the Samaritans as cultural stakeholders. The second group includes over seventy Samaritan and many more biblical scholars interested in the collection. The website for the Société d'Études Samaritaines records that the organization "has 70 members, who work in academic institutions from Australia to Canada, from Israel to Scandinavia" and study "Samaritan literature, languages, history, religion, theology, rites, calendar, music, and more" ("About"). Some of these scholars are interested in access to help advance their work studying textual differences between manuscripts, while others are more interested in the colophons for books spread out across the world. The third and last group of initial stakeholders included MSU librarians and archivists, or what we call institutional stakeholders. These stakeholders are interested in enhancing access to the collection as well as developing a metadata schema that may be useful for other university digitization efforts. For MSU, the project serves as a case example to develop metadata schemes for other collections.

Based on the interests of these three different stakeholder groups, Hart-Davidson and I submitted the NEH Office of Digital Humanities Start-up Grant with the following three project objectives (listed below) foregrounding issues of engagement and fieldwork. While we set out to work with multiple stakeholder groups, we focused especially on advancing Samaritans' rhetorical sovereignty by not only providing the community with access to all digital materials but also working to tailor access to online resources in the pilot grant. To this end, the goals we proposed to advance rhetorical sovereignty through engaged research included the following:

- To create a working model of a culturally sensitive repository of Samaritan texts that may support a variety of learning activities including online teaching, learning, and research for members of the Samaritan community as well as scholars.
- To follow a model of system development consistent with best practices of user-centered design and the movement toward community-oriented transformation of archival collections.
- To adapt innovative approaches in digital technology associated with Web 2.0—especially social networking, tagging, and social bookmarking—to embody a new perspective on humanities research.

Each of these goals is inextricably tied to engagement and thus also to a core rhetorical premise. It is impossible to achieve these stated goals without working directly with the community. Such integrated engagement offers rich potential results, not just for the cultural stakeholder community but also for the other stakeholder groups interested in the collection and for the researchers themselves. To this end, our team engaged in an iterative design project to understand how stakeholders use texts in order to help us tailor the electronic repository to the needs of each stakeholder group.

Early Engagement: Building for Community Use

If we had not conducted fieldwork for the pilot phase, we would not have known other community-valued practices associated with the texts. In the first phase of our project, our team showed how rhetoric and iterative design methods could be applied to the digital humanities. Working with members of the Samaritan community and biblical/Samaritan scholars, we studied how these two groups study and use these texts differently. We learned how members of the cultural community value acrostics in the texts, scribal techniques, and establishing their own familial connection to the scribe of a manuscript. We also learned of some usage goals they shared in common with biblical/ Samaritan scholars such as comparing manuscripts, which we wouldn't have known if we hadn't done the engaged fieldwork. Consequently, this example demonstrates how fieldwork and engagement influenced the first stage of the digital project and how we as researchers would have missed important points—points that have significant bearing on how we reconceptualized the information architecture—if we hadn't done the fieldwork. However, less obvious to the outsider is how our engagement in the pilot phase of the digitization project led to additional research trajectories and questions that ultimately resulted in the creation of new resources such as the Samaritan keyboard project I discuss in the next section. As community needs are realized through engaged work, new collaborative projects and research trajectories have a greater likelihood of coming to fruition. To this end, as Craig Howe (2002) has noted regarding university-indigenous collaborations, DH with cultural stakeholders must also move forward with fieldwork and engagement on a face-to-face level with stakeholder communities or risk producing or reproducing what Hart-Davidson called during the start-up phase of our project a "tacit cultural violence" ("WIDE project meeting with Bill Hart-Davidson").

When creating digital representations of cultural stakeholder community materials in the absence of engagement and cultural input, one runs the risk of transforming brick and mortar collections, already the gatekeepers of geographically distant cultural heritage materials, into digital misrepresentations of cultural heritage. While digital work bereft of engagement poses significant problems with potentially negative consequences for cultural stakeholders, engaged research offers researchers and cultural stakeholders more possibilities—positive and negative. For researchers working to be ethical and receptive to cultural stakeholder needs, long-term engagement on matters such as digitization has the potential to lead to other research trajectories, questions, and discoveries. Samaritan community members' feedback was crucial not only in shaping interface designs so that they would find the resources useful but also in helping us identify specific areas where our observations about the user community and their needs were incorrect or inaccurate. Based on our engaged user experience protocol, we gained two key insights about Samaritan literacy practices that fundamentally changed the way we structured the information architecture of the prototype. First, we learned

more about Samaritan literacy practices that deeply impacted how we conceived the prototype. For example, we learned that they don't use the same
system of chapter/verse to divvy up their texts but instead divide them based
on the weekly reading portion. Although this method of breaking up the text
is similar to the *Parasha* (Torah chapter portions) system in Judaism, the specifics of where and how one section begins and ends differ between the traditions. We also learned that since most Samaritan community members memorize the text from an early age, the "quick browse" feature we had imagined
as so important turned out to be irrelevant to their community needs. Second,
we also learned that members of the community, especially young people, saw
a use for mobile-Facebook integration. In what follows below, I elaborate our
protocol in more detail to show how our engaged approach allowed us to ar-
rive at these conclusions.

In May of 2009, I traveled with then Writing in Digital Environments software designer Michael McLeod to Holon, Israel, and Mount Gerizim, Palestinian Authority, to conduct the second round of research. We conducted
formal interviews over the course of two days, met with then-Samaritan High
Priest Elazar ben Tsedaka ben Yitzhaq, and attended meetings and ceremonial
functions with families in the community.[12] The meetings on the mountain,
in Holon, and elsewhere resembled what Howe (2002) suggests, in terms of
process, where "meetings punctuate the continuous process of fieldwork and
research that goes into developing a tribal history and represent moment of
decision making and work review. The locations of these meetings alternate
between the two partners: the first, third, and fifth are in the community, the
second and fourth are at the institution" (Howe 192). On Mount Gerizim we
conducted three individual usability sessions; interviews were conducted in
an apartment made available to us by the community on Mount Gerizim for
this purpose. Because our aim in the pilot study was to produce formative
feedback with the goal of developing better design prototypes, our sample
was a convenience sample made possible by our community partner and insider, Benyamim Tsedaka. In other words, the study drew participants from
whoever was closest at hand and available to talk.

On the mountain, we showed each participant images of the site design
that included sample digitized pages from the Michigan State University Pentateuchs. These images also included sketches and mock-ups of interfaces
based on earlier brainstorming sessions conducted with Tsedaka in Michigan. We then asked each participant questions about how the planned features intersected with his or her goals for accessing the texts in the archive.
In addition, we also asked individuals to perform some of the tasks (such as
browsing, zooming, reading, tagging) discussed in the group session using the prototype. We asked the following types of questions of participants:

How might you normally read this text? Under what circumstances would you read the text? Can you show us what you usually do with the text? How do you imagine using this text on a computer? We also asked them to help us see how they might perform such tasks. We anticipated that this second type of data gathering session would provide more detailed feedback on task sequences as well as specific types of interactions users wanted the archive system to support. In addition, we conducted a group "walkthrough" with members of the Samaritan community in Holon, Israel. This "walkthrough" functioned largely in the same manner as the individual interviews, but it provided us with the added benefit of listening to groups of participants discuss the various mock-up archive designs with each other, rather than only responding to and interacting with us, the researchers.

In response to our page detail mock-up, the Samaritans we interviewed told us that they do not use the chapter-and-verse method of dividing and navigating their Torah, the method most often used by biblical scholars. Since Samaritan children are required to memorize and orally chant the Torah from an early age, they are intimately familiar with the text. We learned from these interviews that our first prototype was based on scholarly rather than community-based reading and browsing patterns. In Holon, community members showed us a more modern version of a Pentateuch that includes the corresponding numbers at the beginning of each verse. To accommodate this different information architecture in our interfaces, participants suggested that each page be labeled according to its corresponding *Parasha* name, instead of simply Exodus 3:12, for example.

This information architecture would in turn make the digital archive more useful for any weekly Samaritan *Parasha* study leading up to the Friday night *Erev Shabbat*, when all use of electronics stops until after sunset on Saturday. Here Sun and Hart-Davidson's relational model of affordances coincides with our design process by enabling us to look "beyond program functions to inspect the social capabilities that certain communication technologies enable" and explore "social interactions surrounding (and giving rise to) affordances" (3536). We cannot simply learn everything about digital resources from texts. We must also talk to and engage with communities to learn about how these resources matter and work in their daily lives.

As Potts notes, "by realigning project teams across disciplines to build user-centered experiences, we can have a huge impact on how these systems are received by their audiences" (256). What we as designers didn't expect prior to doing our interviews was how much the participants valued the content contained within the unique *tashkil* (acrostic). (I provided an example of this textual feature in chapter 3.) By engaging with the cultural stakeholders about their texts, we learned more about what's important to them in develop-

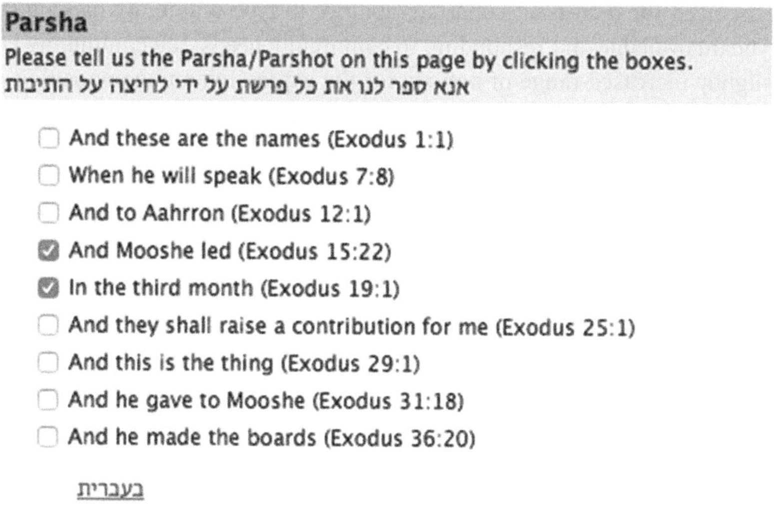

Parsha

Please tell us the Parsha/Parshot on this page by clicking the boxes.
אנא ספר לנו את כל פרשת על ידי לחיצה על התיבות

- ☐ And these are the names (Exodus 1:1)
- ☐ When he will speak (Exodus 7:8)
- ☐ And to Aahrron (Exodus 12:1)
- ☑ And Mooshe led (Exodus 15:22)
- ☑ In the third month (Exodus 19:1)
- ☐ And they shall raise a contribution for me (Exodus 25:1)
- ☐ And this is the thing (Exodus 29:1)
- ☐ And he gave to Mooshe (Exodus 31:18)
- ☐ And he made the boards (Exodus 36:20)

בעברית

Fig. 16. A screenshot from a demonstration of the *Parasha*-based information architecture of the Michigan State University pilot project.

ing new prototypes for navigation and metadata. Not only did such engagement lead to better, more usable design, it also uncovered the community's other rhetorical needs that would enable them to gain greater rhetorical sovereignty, for example the need to type in Samaritan in other contexts beyond word processing applications such as Dagesh or Microsoft Word. Consequently, this process also led to the development of the Samaritan script keyboard, which I detail in the next section.

Later Engagement: Building Beyond Digitization

The idea for a Samaritan keyboard layout emerged from a May 2013 Facebook conversation in which someone wrote a word in Samaritan characters on Benyamim Tsedaka's Facebook wall. In the process of continuing the digitization of Samaritan manuscripts, Tsedaka expressed to me a need for greater digital composing abilities in Samaritan UNICODE. To this end, I developed, with the help of Tsedaka, a Samaritan keyboard for Windows and OS X. My effort to create the keyboard with the help of Tsedaka, which I only learned about from our engaged interaction over time with the community, allowed me to leverage DH and rhetoric methods to create the prototype of a digital resource that might eventually aid in Samaritan aspects of circulating and exercising their cultural sovereignty. The keyboard was conceived as a response to the need for increased Samaritan abilities to type online. By making the keyboard available and responding to community needs, the community has a slightly increased range of options for the expression and composition of their digital texts in Samaritan. What does this slightly increased option *mean* in the long run and will the digital resource be leveraged in the future? How? That's exactly the provenance of rhetoric research. With engaged work in the digital humanities, only time will tell if resources are used or not, how they're used, and if they're built upon or leveraged to prompt or influence new projects. Engagement at the edge of digital humanities and rhetoric may not only be one activity or project deliverable but a constellation of activities and relationships at the crossroads of community needs and research.

In the NEH ODH pilot project, we had looked into utilizing Samaritan script in digital environments, but the UNICODE standard for Samaritan or Ancient Hebrew was still new. However, since 2008, and thanks to the work of Michael Everson and Mark Shoulson, there has been a UNICODE standard for Samaritan (Everson and Shoulson). With a UNICODE standard in place, if an individual has a Samaritan font installed on her computer, the font will be supported in any application that supports the UNICODE standard, including web pages, e-mail, Facebook messages, Photoshop, and more. As Everson and Shoulson identify in their UNICODE proposal, the technology is useful for "Ecclesiastical and cultural communities" (Everson and Shoulson 21).[13] As Samaritan Osher Sassoni states, the technology is also about rhetorical sovereignty. For Sassoni, he needs "to write in the Samaritan script" because he writes "poems, Samaritan poems. And Samaritan songs and Torah" for himself and friends in the community. Writing in Samaritan is meaningful and important for Sassoni, so much so that he spent six months converting and stabilizing the first Samaritan font created for the personal computer (created in 1988/1989 for the proprietary software Dagesh) to TrueType in the late 1990s. By converting the font to TrueType, he made the font more open and reliable.

According to Benyamim Tsedaka, the "first [Samaritans] to use computer fonts for Samaritan Hebrew was the Committee of the Samaritan Community in Holon, in 1989, in a publication of the SP [Samaritan Pentateuch] for the use of Samaritan readers" (Tsedaka, "Introduction" xxxii). In addition, "Israel Tsedaka published an excellent work utilizing computer fonts for the original text (SP), with all the notes and punctuations including the ten signs for reading found in ancient Samaritan manuscripts" (Tsedaka, "Introduction" xxxii). Thus, the keyboard is by no means the first or last effort to make use of computer technology, but what makes it unique is the circumstances that gave birth to it. Growing out of a larger project of engagement, it is imagined by me and the Samaritans as a stepping stone toward other future projects, such as full optical character recognition (OCR) support for Samaritan manuscripts, and as a key step to realizing a central goal for Sassoni, who desires the ability to search the contents of Samaritan manuscripts and look up words.

To this end, the keyboard I cocreated with Tsedaka builds off previous font and keyboard work while simultaneously laying the groundwork for future digital development and enhancement. I designed the keyboard based on the standard Hebrew and Arabic keyboard layouts. If you can type in Hebrew and understand Samaritan script, then the layout is intuitive. With twenty-two consonant forms, Samaritan Hebrew does not have the Biblical or Modern Hebrew's "final letters," and has a different set of diacritical markers, so these differences regarding keyboard letter placement, punctuation, and diacritical markers are very important. Samaritan UNICODE standard cocreator Mark Shoulson writes in the introduction to his book *The Torah Jewish and Samaritan Versions Compared: A Side-by-Side Comparison of the Two Versions with the Differences Highlighted* that in the Jewish tradition:

> The Talmudic name for the square Hebrew lettering we use today כתב אשורי katab asuri, literally means 'Assyrian script', and appears to be a derivative of an Aramaic form of the alphabet which the Jews adopted and developed into a national hand during their exile in Assyria. Technically, the only truly "Hebrew" script still in use is the Samaritan script. (xi)

The design of the keyboard was an iterative process of engaged work. At the risk of sounding repetitive, I cannot overemphasize the absolute necessity that such a project needs to develop out of reciprocal engagement with the community. Producing something such as a writing technology in a cultural vacuum could do more harm than good. For the Samaritans, there's even precedent of a kind of rhetorical harm relating to the far away production of their script. While the Samaritan script[14] has been scribed for millennia, it was first set to type in 1631 (Clair 227). As William Schniedewind notes in his 2013 *A Social History of Hebrew*, "The ideological value of Hebrew among the Samaritans is indicated, first of all, by the use of a Paleo-Hebrew script for Samaritan inscriptions" (171). According to Alan David Crown, "Samaritan type-faces made their appearance in the printing shops of the west at the time that the first Samaritan manuscripts were brought from Europe" (Crown, "Samaritan Scribes and Manuscripts" 266). Crown describes a dialectic of sorts between the circulation of Samaritan manuscripts in Europe, the production of Samaritan type to study those manuscripts, and the circulation of typeface back to the Samaritans. In describing this dialectic, Crown contends the movable type produced by Western scholars in the sixteenth and seventeenth centuries (based on texts procured under often questionable circumstances) were eventually circulated back to Samaritan communities via printed text:

It is important for the Samaritan palaeographer to be aware that the new Samaritan fonts became known to the Samaritans themselves through the polyglot bibles which they received from the hands of the Western savants and their agents. In turn, these printed works influenced the Samaritan calligraphic style, so there is a circulation in which the Samaritan scribes send manuscripts to the West which has been influenced by Western interpretations in cast type of Samaritan script. (Crown, "Samaritan Scribes and Manuscripts" 266).

This exchange, in turn, influenced Samaritans' own paleography and provides a case example for how the circulation of Samaritan paleography may be amplified by time, place, and institutions that have a later impact on the Samaritans. Crown's case example serves as an interesting model for scholars in the digital humanities to reflect upon and consider, because it shows how, ironically, the Samaritans had little efficacy in their own rhetorical sovereignty when it came to developing their own movable type for the printing press, at least initially. Rather, the typeface for their own unique script was designed by the same tradition of scholars who had deceptively worked to gain access to their cultural heritage and texts. While the technology Crown references is not digital, the argument for the necessity of reciprocal engagement becomes obvious because of the potential impact these printing technologies may have on the Samaritans through their adoption, proliferation, and influence.

In my iterative engagement with Tsedaka, he immediately told me to be sure to "[s]ee that all OTIOT SOFIOT [Samaritan final letter forms] will be in the same place. Don't leave the keys empty. See that any time it typed 'space' between word to word it will type a dot. Comma should be : [colon] End of sentence /:." (Tsedaka, "Response to Jim Ridolfo's post"). Tsedaka requested that in place of a space, the keyboard would produce a period as this is how Samaritan words are separated from each other. In addition, he asked that the final letters "repeat" in each place, allowing anyone familiar with the Hebrew keyboard layout to type on the Samaritan keyboard with ease. Unknown to me at the time, I had done work similar to what Moses Gaster, inventor of the Hebrew typewriter and later the first Samaritan typewriter, had done almost a century earlier in 1920 when he mapped the Samaritan character set onto his Hebrew typewriter layout ("Between the Raindrops" 53):

I ... had Samaritan letters cut to my specification and put onto the Hebrew typewriter in place of the upper case, so that I would have both alphabets together: with the upper case I write to the Samaritans in their script, while with the help of the lower case I transcribe Samaritan letters and writings. (Gaster 20)

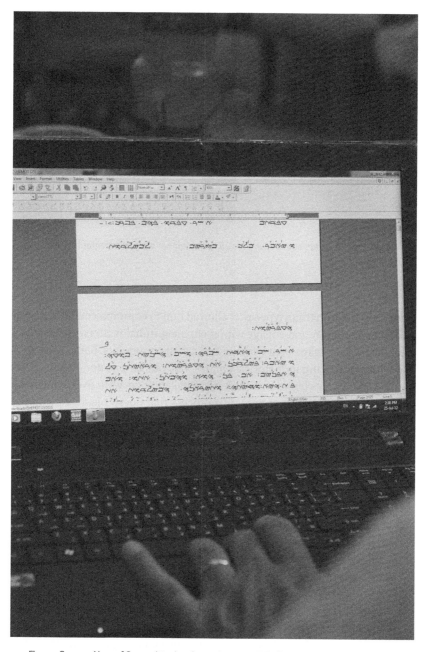

Fig. 17. Sameer Yousef Sarrawi typing Samaritan on a Windows computer. Mount Gerizim, West Bank, July 2012. (Photograph by Jim Ridolfo.)

Fig. 18. Samaritan keyboard layout for OS X. September 2013. (Photograph by Jim Ridolfo.)

Gaster's novel Samaritan typewriter allowed him to communicate with the Samaritan community and engage with them on spiritual matters. He created a mechanism for engagement with the Samaritan community, but to what end? For scholars working in rhetorical studies, one objective is not only to cocreate digital resources but to also study what stakeholders want to do with those resources. Engagement can become a process that doesn't just end with the creation of one resource, but begins as a process to understand not only what resources are useful but how and why they are rhetorically leveraged.

For researchers in rhetorical studies, engagement with the cultural stakeholder community into already existent, indigenous technological affordances helps to recognize, support, and ally with efforts already underway in the community. To this end, the keyboard, conservation efforts, digitization, and this book are all examples of rhetorical engagement with the Samaritans and their textual diaspora. Engagement is not only about the past and present work but also looking forward to the future potential of projects.[15]

What emerged from our pilot phase in the initial ODH project with the Samaritans and biblical/Samaritan scholars was a scholarly interest in a tool that could do algorithmic analysis of handwriting, as well as a mobile/Facebook application that would allow members of the Samaritan community to source images of these manuscripts in a social network environment. For each of these two future projects, the Samaritan keyboard is a useful tool that can be leveraged to advance Samaritan rhetorical sovereignty. As Osher Sassoni noted earlier, there's a desire among the Samaritans to type in Samaritan script. Helping to build on the Samaritan UNICODE standard and Samaritan font projects, the keyboard is one additional step forward to help advance those goals of rhetorical sovereignty.

What emerges from this chapter is a yet to be completed story of engagement, but one that is representative of Jeff Grabill's idea of rhetoric and community engagement as building resources with communities of practice. For the Samaritan cultural stakeholders, the work of extending the rhetorical use of their diaspora of manuscripts is work that must happen with the collaboration of institutions and faculty abroad, as evidenced by Tsedaka's 2003 exhortation to the MSU Board of Trustees to "do something" more with their Samaritan collection of manuscripts. In turn, what emerges from Tsedaka's 2003 request is a story of engagement and building with communities. The Samaritan specifics are limited to this stakeholder community, but the rhetorical principles may be extended to any type of DH work where engagement would serve stakeholder communities. Rather than thinking about research in the digital humanities in opposition to serving communities of practice beyond scholarly circles, there needs to be greater disciplinary space to cultivate reciprocal relationships (see Cushman's work). In turn, DH relationships based on engagement, informed by rhetorical studies, and guided by an ethos of reciprocity to stakeholder communities will, in turn, lead to even larger research questions, projects, and knowledge.

FIVE

The Good Samaritan: At the Crossroads of Rhetoric and the Digital Humanities

We want to tell people in the world that we are still alive. We have our
language, we have our culture, our heritage.
—Yacop Cohen

Every year, Benyamim Tsedaka makes a trip to Europe and North America to
visit Samaritan manuscript collections and speak about his people's culture
and heritage, to tell the world, as Yacop Cohen emphasizes, about the Samaritans. For each of the past six years, I have joined Tsedaka for a few days to
discuss projects and collaborate. On a recent November 2013 visit to Hebrew
Union College in Cincinnati, Tsedaka and I stopped at the Good Samaritan
Hospital next to the college and took the photograph above. This moment
is worth reflecting upon. Next to one of the largest collections of Samaritan
manuscripts in the Midwest (housed at Hebrew Union College) is the Good
Samaritan Hospital with a picture of a man wearing a kūfiyyah, or a traditional
Middle Eastern headdress.[1] What connection is there between the image of
the "Good Samaritan," the repository of Samaritans' cultural heritage just a
few hundred feet away, and the living cultural community in the West Bank
and Israel? Are the Samaritans a living people in the mind of the average driver
going past the "Good Samaritan" Hospital?

In North America and Europe, the word "Samaritan" is commonly associated with the Parable of the Good Samaritan from the New Testament Gospel
of Luke. Hospitals and clinics all across the United States are adorned with
references to the Samaritan of Luke. In the process of circulating as part of
one of the world's major religious texts, the parable has become a common-
place and has been rewritten onto the namesake of thousands of hospitals,
clinics, and crisis hotlines. Yet, these organizations and institutions that bear
the Samaritan namesake do so with little or no connection to today's living
Samaritan community. In fact, many Westerners are genuinely surprised to

Fig. 19. Benyamim Tsedaka stands in front of the Good Samaritan Hospital in Cincinnati, Ohio, December 2013. (Photograph by Jim Ridolfo.)

learn that the Samaritan people mentioned in Luke have continued to survive against great historical odds in their historical homeland. Since the time of Jesus, the Samaritans of today have survived countless wars, starvation, disease, and forced conversion; they remain Shomrim ("Keepers" in Hebrew) of a rich religious and cultural tradition. They have not only kept their traditions but have also continued them. They teach their children their two liturgical languages (Samaritan Hebrew, what Samaritans call "Ancient Hebrew," and Samaritan Aramaic), a system of writing, musical traditions, as well as their own foodways and recipes.[2]

The Parable of the Good Samaritan is an appropriate place to end, then, because like the Samaritans of today, the Samaritans of two millennia ago also found themselves in the midst of political fires. What's changed from first century Palestine to today, however, is that though the Samaritan population has gone from more than one hundred thousand to 770, the political fires around them are proportionally much larger. Because of this trend, the Samaritans have had to develop methods to "go between the raindrops." Today's Samaritans are a living, thriving people, and their more than three millennia-long story of survival has much to teach scholars in rhetorical studies. To better understand this connection, however, it is important to be familiar with the representation of the Good Samaritan found in Luke.

In the Parable of the Good Samaritan narrated by Jesus, a wounded traveler (possibly Jewish) on the road to Jericho receives compassion and aid from a Samaritan. What's most significant about the content of the story is that this kindness took place at a time when there was considerable sectarianism in first century Palestine. For the audience of the Christian Bible in the first few centuries after Jesus of Nazareth's death, it is significant that it was a Samaritan that assisted the needy traveler on the road from Jerusalem to Jericho because of the tensions in the first century between Jews and Samaritans:

[30] Jesus replied, "A man was going down from Jerusalem to Jericho, and he fell among robbers, who stripped him and beat him, and departed, leaving him half dead.

[31] Now by chance a priest was going down that road; and when he saw him he passed by on the other side.

[32] So likewise a Levite, when he came to the place and saw him, passed by on the other side.

[33] But a Samaritan, as he journeyed, came to where he was; and when he saw him, he had compassion,

[34] and went to him and bound up his wounds, pouring on oil and wine; then he set him on his own beast and brought him to an inn, and took care of him.

[35] And the next day he took out two denarii and gave them to the innkeeper, saying, `Take care of him; and whatever more you spend, I will repay you when I come back.'

[36] Which of these three, do you think, proved neighbor to the man who fell among the robbers?"

[37] He said, "The one who showed mercy on him." And Jesus said to him, "Go and do likewise."

—From the Parable of the Good Samaritan, Luke, chapter 10:30–37. 1901 Revised Standard Version of the Bible[3]

While the parable is a Christian story, it's a story that has circulated so widely in the West that, as the image of Tsedaka and the hospital at the beginning of the chapter demonstrates, it's become part of the everyday landscape of building and hospital names in North America and Europe. The parable is a story

that reflects favorably on the Samaritans, and it's a story whose circulation
has rhetorical benefits for today's Samaritan community.

For Benyamim Tsedaka, the parable's wide circulation serves as a com-
monplace to introduce the world to the living Samaritan community in Israel
and the Palestinian Authority. Tsedaka has done significant work not only to
explain the Samaritan community and its identity to his neighbors and the
world but also to draw on the Samaritans as a bridge for promoting peace and
mutual understanding. To this end, for the last five years Tsedaka has led a
group of Samaritan leaders to create The Samaritan Medal for Peace and Humanitarian Achievement in order to build on the ethos of the Good Samaritan
and to position the Samaritans as peace brokers in the region: "Many organizations offer 'Samaritan medals,' recognizing those who demonstrate the
behavior of the Good Samaritan in their lives. Few, if any, realize that 'Samaritan' is not merely an archaic term: it is the name of a living, vibrant people in
the heart of the Middle East, having the unique distinction of being on good
terms with all sides, in a region more commonly associated with conflict"
(Tsedaka, "Medal"). According to Benyamim Tsedaka, the medal serves as a
means to help "others to know about us more and more. In the 'Good Samaritan' spirit, we go and we give the Medal to prominent personalities all over the
world . . . [and] now every ceremony is doubling the interest in Samaritans"
(Tsedaka, "Personal interview in Holon, Israel, 28 Feb. 2012"). The Samaritan
Medal for Peace and Humanitarian Achievement may be seen as one way in
which the Samaritans position themselves to walk, as I discussed in chapters
2 and 3, between the fires and raindrops:

> Now the Samaritans themselves step forward to offer the first and only
> Samaritan medal awarded by the authentic historical Samaritan people of
> the Holy Land. As is the case with other "Samaritan" medals, its purpose
> is to recognize and reward service to humanity, especially in the cause of
> peace . . . The Samaritan Medal forms a bridge among all the People of the
> Book: the Children of Abraham; Samaritans, Jews, Christians and Mus-
> lims. The spirit of the "Good Samaritan" can live inside all people, even
> those who may be disparaged by others. (Tsedaka, "Medal")[4]

As the Samaritans position themselves as a "bridge among all the People of
the Book," they leverage the ethos of the Samaritan described in the parable
for their own rhetorical work to explain who they are to their neighbors. The
Samaritan Medal Foundation's example is an interesting one for scholars of
rhetorical delivery and cultural rhetorics, because the Samaritans connect another people's story about a Samaritan from long ago to the coexistence work
of today's Samaritan community, work that advances the Samaritans' long-

standing ability to live and work in peace with their neighbors and to communicate their existence to the world. As Yacop Cohen quoted at the beginning of this chapter suggests, they tell the world that the Samaritans exist and that the Samaritan people have a unique culture and history in the region.

Rhetoric and Digital Humanities at the Crossroads

In this book, I have looked beyond the digitization, keyboard, and maps project at http://samaritanrepository.org to explain why the communication of Samaritan cultural identity as an issue of rhetorical sovereignty matters, and matters differently in the digital age. Chapter 1 introduced the theory of textual diaspora or leveraging manuscripts spread out across the world for specific cultural-rhetorical ends. In chapter 2, I examined key historical events in recent Samaritan history: first, National Geographic's special issue on the Samaritans in 1920 where the author predicted the Samaritans' extinction by the end of the twentieth century. Second, the establishment of the Samaritan neighborhood in Holon by Israel's second president, Yitzhak Ben-Zvi, and his rhetorical move to claim the Samaritans as fellow Israelites. Third, the years of isolation, 1949–1967, when there was very little physical contact between the Samaritan communities in the West Bank and Israel. And fourth, Yasser Arafat's appointment of Saloum Cohen to the Palestinian Council in 1996 and his argument to claim the Samaritans as Palestinians. I contend that these recent events, the Palestinians' and Israelis' competing claims to the Samaritans' cultural heritage, the isolation between the two Samaritan communities as a result of the war of 1948, and National Geographic's yet-to-be recanted proclamation are important factors for understanding the historical context of the digital repository project and the rhetorical situation of the Samaritan diaspora of manuscripts. I argue that, together, the manuscripts and the Samaritans' work educating their neighbors about who they are constitutes a complex rhetorical strategy that's reflected in the title of the 1998 "Memo: Between the Israeli, Palestinian, and Jordanian Raindrops."

In chapter 3, I outlined some reasons that help to explain why delivering textual diaspora digitally matters for the Samaritans. First, it helps them to communicate their identity in a digital age, and second, this digital repository of textual diaspora may be more easily accessed and thus also leveraged to achieve greater rhetorical sovereignty. The implications for scholars of rhetorical delivery working at the intersection of the digital humanities are many, but in chapter 4 I argue that one of the more important lessons we learn from this case example is that long-term engaged work matters not only to the communities we work with but also the disciplines of both rhetoric and the digital humanities. Long-term, engaged work may assist not only scholars but also cultural stakeholders such as the Samaritans. I examined the complex history and relationship of the Samaritan diaspora of manuscripts to present-day Samaritan circumstances and desires for the material and digital future of those materials. I've shown how the very existence of the manuscripts and their unique record of Samaritan cultural practices, scattered in collections across the world, provide rhetorical tools Samaritans may use to communicate their identity to the world and to advance their own digital and scribal production, while also advancing knowledge about their textual history. To actualize the potential of these manuscripts, however, requires libraries, museums, archives, and private collectors to make their Samaritan collections available to the Samaritans through digitization. For material cultural heritage at the intersection of digital technology, there's a looming rhetorical crossroads on the horizon with many options for cultural communities about what to do. Cultural heritage content may be tailored to digital environments or may not be digitized at all; however, as I have tried to illustrate with the Samaritan case example, either path—doing something or choosing to do nothing—may have long-term rhetorical implications. While there are multiple paths to choose, there are no clear road signs about which path is preferable. On a case-by-case basis, only cultural stakeholders can make those kinds of decisions.

For example, as I write this last chapter during the summer of 2014, the Islamic State (*Dawlat al-Islamiyya* or *Daesh*) is engaged in a brutal military campaign in Iraq and Syria. On Mt. Sinjar of northern Iraq, *Daesh* has trapped thousands of Yazidis, members of an ancient religion with ties to Zoroastrianism, and a major humanitarian crisis is underway. In the week of August 15, dozens of news stories ran in papers throughout the West with a version of the same title: "Who are the Yazidis?"[5] As the West decided what sort of humanitarian response it would muster to help the trapped Yazidis in the Sinjar mountains, the media attempted to educate general publics about the Yazidis during the month of August 2014. The Yazidis, however, have a complicated history with the West, texts attributed to them, and the recent recording of their oral knowledge or *qawls*.[6] According to the *Encyclopedia Iranica*'s entry on the Yazidis,

> Most Yazidi religious texts have been passed on exclusively by oral tradition, and many features characteristic of oral literature can be seen in them. It is now generally accepted that the manuscripts of the Yazidi Sacred Books, the Maṣḥafā Reš and Ketēbā Jelwa, published in 1911 and 1913, were 'forgeries' in the sense that they were written by non-Yazidis in response to Western travelers' and scholars' interest in the Yazidi religion,

amid a general environment of trading in ancient manuscripts. ("Yazidis I. General")

Recently, however, members of the Yazidi community in Armenia and Germany appear to have begun to record and publish on Yazidi culture and religious traditions:

In 1979 two young Yazidi intellectuals published a number of the qawls, provoking considerable controversy within the community. (A few had been published in the Soviet Union the previous year, but were presented as part of a folklore anthology and largely ignored). By the beginning of the 21st century more had been published in Armenia and a research program in Germany was almost complete. With the assent of the community, this latter aimed to collect and transcribe the many unpublished qawls for use in academic research and the education of Yazidi children, especially in the diaspora. Yazidism is thus being transformed into a scriptural religion. ("Yazidis I. General")

While the Yazidis do not appear to have as large a textual diaspora as the Samaritans, there are two similarities. First, the Yazidis of northern Iraq are a minority in the midst of a dangerous conflict. Second, the Yazidis are trying to communicate their identity and culture to the world in order to safeguard their people on Mt. Sinjar.[7] In the time-sensitive popular news articles listed in the footnotes, there is very little online cultural heritage material available on the Yazidis. Should there be? How might have it impacted Western responses to their situation? Is any of the work referenced above available for digital work? What kind of digital communication would Yazidis in northern Iraq want to advance so that they may communicate their unique cultural heritage to the world audience as quickly and effectively as possible? I can't answer these questions for the Yazidis, and I shouldn't answer these questions as a researcher for any people. What I recommend is situated engagement at the intersection of rhetoric and the digital humanities. Why? So that the Yazidis, if they wish, might have the kairotic opportunity to maximize the communication of their cultural heritage to the world, and that scholars working at the intersection of rhetorical studies and the digital humanities may support, learn from, and help to advance their rhetorical strategy and delivery. While the Samaritan example may highlight some potential similarities with the Yazidis, textual diaspora and engagement are not limited to cultural, ethnic, and religious minorities living in the West Bank or Iraq. Rather, engagement, reciprocity, and fieldwork are relevant to any group with cultural heritage looking

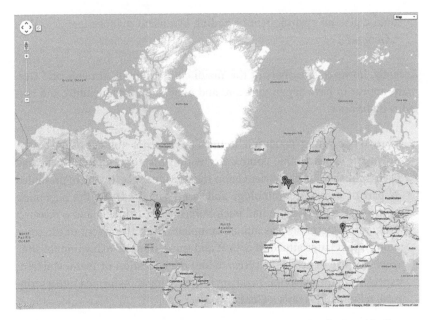

Map 3. A map of digitized Samaritan manuscripts and links to their finding aids. The map will be updated as new resources are made available: http://www.samaritanre pository.org/maps/manuscripts/).

to navigate the relationship between their traditions, heritage, and the opportunities and challenges digitization presents.

Engagement and reciprocity matter not just for digital humanities scholars' involvement with the Samaritans but also Samaritans' involvement with and beyond their local political circumstances. The Samaritans not only walk between the raindrops and two fires around them but also work to transcend them through their peace initiatives from Mount Gerizim. The Samaritan medal is another piece of the Samaritan textual diaspora; however, unlike other texts that might have arrived in diaspora via dubious means, the medals are Samaritan-authored texts given to those that advance cultural values the Samaritans wish to spread. In the Samaritan example, there's a dialectic between what others have said about the Samaritans (the Parable of the Good Samaritan) and the Samaritans' own reclamation of the "Good Samaritan" ethos not only to help members of the community conduct peace work but also to walk and thrive between the raindrops. Another factor is the manuscripts abroad, located in institutions whose locations and ethos may be capitalized on to advance the rhetorical goals of continuing to communicate Samaritan identity to their neighbors and the world. The relationship of reclaiming and recirculating materials for specific rhetorical goals or objectives is key to textual diaspora. Digital technology turns the possibility of recirculation into a much more likely potential while also increasing the reach and scope of media, formats, and options for tailoring cultural heritage resources to specific audiences.

The technological range of options for leveraging textual diaspora has increased from forty or fifty years ago. The current digital moment provides more opportunities to consider how stakeholders may leverage their textual diaspora to do rhetorical work, such as how some Samaritans want to utilize Facebook to share images of Samaritan manuscripts. In the case of the Samaritans, there's much more to learn as we see how their textual diaspora is digitized, delivered, and circulated over the next decade. When I first began to write this book in 2011, Michigan State University and Hebrew Union College Jewish Institute of Religion were the only two institutions working to digitize Samaritan manuscripts. Today in 2014, the University of Manchester and Cambridge University have digitized some of their Samaritan manuscripts. Additionally, within the Samaritan community some of the Sassoni manuscripts in Holon have been digitized as discussed in chapter 3.

The concept of textual diaspora along with the methods of engaged, reciprocal work with stakeholder communities offer a useful heuristic and model for research at the intersection of rhetorical studies and the digital humanities. Such a concept could prove strategically useful for the Yazidi people (if appropriate) or other cultural stakeholders. In the case of Benyamim Tsedaka's 2003 visit to the Michigan State University Board of Trustees meeting, requesting the university do something more with its collection of Samaritan manuscripts was the beginning of such a long-term collaboration (Tsedaka). As the digital humanities matures as a field and concentration in the university, digital projects too will mature and rhetoric scholars will have greater opportunity to study and understand how projects are referenced, leveraged, and circulated by stakeholder communities. This is one possible future for rhetorical studies at the intersection of rhetorical studies and the digital humanities.

Scholars in rhetoric might conduct the following types of work over the lifespan of a project:

- **Researching** the relationship of digital resources to stakeholder communities (see Potts; Sun and Hart-Davidson; Graban; Graban, Ramsey-Tobienne, and Myers).[8]
- **Theorizing** with stakeholders the relationship of digital projects to their communities. Work in cultural rhetoric such as that by Malea Powell,[9] Craig Howe, Ellen Cushman,[10] and especially Angela Haas[11] is essential for developing a deeper understanding of how rhetoric and cultural

heritage intersect in diverse indigenous community contexts. Work in community literacy (such as Grabill's book *Writing Community Change*) is also important for understanding practices surrounding digital resources as knowledge work. The goal or outcome of such work would not only be the development of relationships with stakeholders but also the beginning of an iterative process of research and engagement that could include building (or what many digital humanists call "making"), delivering, and studying.[12]

- **Building** digital resources with community members and also working with stakeholders to assess how building digital resources can serve their best interest, and what kind of access permissions they want with their cultural heritage materials (Christen's work).
- **Delivering** digital resources in rhetorically appropriate file formats (see Stolley's work). Consider how stakeholders may leverage diasporic texts and strategize future delivery (see Rude; DeVoss and Porter; Ridolfo and DeVoss; Sheridan, Ridolfo, and Michel; Ridolfo).
- **Studying** the long-term use (or lack thereof) of digital projects, especially the long-term conversation surrounding projects: for example, how are projects discussed or referenced by cultural stakeholders and outside communities? How are they referenced and cited? This latter work has yet to be done en masse but will be of increasing importance over the next twenty or thirty years.

The promise of work in rhetorical studies that researches, theorizes, builds, delivers, and studies digital projects alongside engaged research with communities is a multitude of rich case examples and relationships to co-create with, to learn from, and to extend our disciplinary knowledge about rhetoric and the digital humanities. In the future of the Samaritan textual diaspora, rhetorical delivery, the digital humanities, cultural, scholarly, and institutional stakeholders have practical and theoretical roles to play in assisting the Samaritan people to leverage textual diaspora in digital environments. The combination of disciplines, institutions, and stakeholders foregrounded is not uncommon to large humanities and social sciences grants, but I argue that researching the question of what stakeholders want to do with their digital texts is largely a question of rhetorical delivery and circulation, one that's not unique to this project but is not yet foregrounded in mainstream digital humanities conversations.

At the core of the question "what do stakeholders want from their digital texts" is an implicit call for engagement, reciprocity, and fieldwork in order to understand, contextualize, and actualize stakeholder concerns. This book is the byproduct of six years of engaged work to answer this core question as it pertains to members of the Samaritan community. This book is not an end in itself or an absolute representation of what all Samaritans think and want from their texts abroad until the end of time. Rather, it is one highly situated way of understanding the core issues of the last six years in light of field conversations in rhetoric and the digital humanities. As I write the conclusion to this chapter, the 2014 Israel-Gaza conflict (English Wikipedia title) has taken place and violence once again permeates the region. For the Samaritans, long-term safety and security is still a dream that must be supported through the community's seven principles and through international cooperation and engaged work. For scholars and institutions abroad, there is still much to be done to actualize the future rhetorical potential of Samaritan manuscripts abroad and to help the Samaritan people continue to make the strongest case possible to the world for their unique identity, heritage, and inalienable right to a future free of travel restrictions and geographic separation. For scholars abroad working not only with the Samaritans, we must do so in a way that the spirit of the Parable of the Good Samaritan (which the Samaritans have reappropriated) suggests: when possible and appropriate, help those that request assistance, learn from those actions, and do better in the future.[13] That is one vision of engaged rhetoric at the intersection of the digital humanities.

Appendix A: Transcripts

A1. Arutz Sheva Transcript

https://www.youtube.com/watch?v=P4fzcuLNBuY

Yoni Kempinski, Arutz Sheva TV
00:00:00.00
Shalom, we're here at a very special ceremony here on Mount Grizim. This is a very ancient archaeological site very important in terms of the history in terms of the story that is told here about the nation of Israel throughout the generations. And we are told here. Here you can see layer after layer the story of the nation of Israel in the land of Israel in this area and also other nations who passed here. We know many nations passed through the land of Israel. All can be found here on this very very mangnfiicant place that is here in the middle of the Shomron [Northern West Bank], near the community of Har Bracha.

Israeli tour guide on Mount Gerizim
00:01:07.20
Adi—So we are on Mount Grizim, this is one of the mountains in Samaria, a beautiful high mountain with amazing views abound. And the important thing in this place is there's an amazing archaeological site which has saved amazingly and we have here the most holy place to the Samaritans who live nearby, they had their temple here and around this temple grew a city, an enormous city which was here for about a thousand years. The temple was built and ruined a few times but we see the people which become later on to stay at this place.

Yoni Kempinski, Arutz Sheva TV
00:01:16.60
I understand that here we're seeing layer after layer of the Jewish history in the land of Israel.

Israeli tour guide on Mount Gerizim
00:01:21.90

Yeah definitely we're seeing very early history. If nearby here we have Abraham walks nearby here. Jacob. Joseph goes to look for his brothers over here by Shechem. When the Jewish nation, Jewish people walk into Israel they come to these mountains over here and have a ceremony here of entry into the land. And later on we have the Samaritans and we keep coming and Christians come so we definitely have layer after layer of history here.

Yoni Kempinski, Arutz Sheva TV
00:01:51.80

Now remind us who are the Samaritans?

Israeli tour guide on Mount Gerizim
00:02:00.90

The Samaritans are, well, depends who you ask. On the one hand there's one side which will say that they are the original Israelites. And they are the ones which have kept the Bible as it is meant to be. And on the other hand you will have people who say they were brought here by the Assyrians years later, about 700 BC.

A2. Yacop Cohen YouTube Video Transcript

https://www.youtube.com/watch?v=sRhp1DqqPBI

Yacop Cohen
00:00:00.00

Unknown
00:00:00.00

Interview is published on March 9, 2012. Participant is 43.

Yacop Cohen
00:00:00.30

Ok, for forty-three years me and my friends young girls or boys. We decided to do something for Samaritan. We opened our association. Why we open it, because we feel and we see that all the world they know nothing about the Samaritan[s]. Some, let's say, fifty percent or many more they know that there are no more Samaritans in the world. We say ok, we want to do something for the Samaritan. We want to tell people in the world that we are still alive. We have our language, we have our culture, our heritage, everything we have like a nation, a big nation. So we open our association. We begin to do lecture about Samaritan, exhibition about Samaritan, we do exhibition in all the universities in here and Palestine. Also we do lecture in Jordan and we hope to do more in all Europe the USA and Arab countries.

Yacop Cohen
00:00:00.50

We have many goals to achieve. This one of them is to tell the people that who are the Samaritan because some people know OK Jewish. Let's begin from the Palestinian that we live with them. They think OK well Samaritans are Jewish. We want to change this [idea] about Samaritans. No we are the Samaritan before lets say 6500 years. One nation, the people of Israel after it we separated into two nations the people of Israel and the Jewish people. One of our goals also is to be a bridge for peace between two peoples, the Palestinian and the Jewish. We can be a bridge for peace to tell them how we can cross this bridge and meet each other in the middle.

Appendix B: Images of Seven Principles Document

In the 1995 Seven Principles Document, Samaritans demand their cultural, economic, and political freedom. The Seven Principles emerged during the Oslo era. The Samaritans seek to maintain future contiguity and liberties for the Mount Gerizim and Holon communities.

꧁

A.B. INSTITUTE OF
SAMARITAN STUDIES

MEMO:
THE SAMARITANS BETWEEN THE ISRAELI, PALESTINIAN AND JORDANIAN RAINDROPS

Written and Edited
By:

BENYAMIM & EFRAT TSEDAKA

JANUARY 1998

A.B.-INSTITUTE OF SAMARITAN STUDIES PRESS
P.O.BOX 1012, HOLON 58 110, ISRAEL
TEL: 972-3-5567229, 5562055

D3: "The Seven Principles Document"

The directives, that were given to these delegates, were the result of the political activity of the Samaritans themselves. In July 1955 a Samaritan delegation, made up of Samaritans from Holon and Nablus, flew to Washington to meet the Americans, who specialized on the Middle East issue, in order to discuss with them their political future. The Samaritans brought with them the document - "Seven Guiding Principles", and here is what the document says:

"We, a selected group pf leading personalities in the present-day Samaritan Community, leaders of the Community, editors of *A.B.* - *The Samaritan News* and directors of *A.B.* - *Institute of Samaritan Studies*, hereby set forth the seven principles which guide our efforts to ensure the future of the Samaritan Community, in the Middle East, in any political reality.

Therefore, in view of the special status of the Samaritan Community:

1. We wish to ensure that in any political situation and irrespective of any political development, even in case of deterioration in the relations between parties to the peace agreement, free and unlimited passage shall be given at all times to every Samaritan, from any place where he/she may live, to the centers of Samaritans on Mt. Gerizim and in Nablus, to the Samaritan Holy sites on Mt. Gerizim in particular and in Judea and Samaria (otherwise known as "The West Bank of the Jorden River") in general, and from there to any place within or outside the State of Israel.

2. By virtue of the fact that the Samaritan Community is concentrated in population centers under different areas of administration, we request that each member of the Samaritan Community by given an identification document enabling him/her to move freely at all times among the various centers of the Community, irrespective of any political development and in any varying political situation. This document, which be issued in the from of a passport, a laissez-passer or any other identifying document shall be officially recognized by all political entities whose jurisdiction and/or control extends over the border checkpoints between the various areas of control.

3. we request that all members of the Samaritan Community by assured by all relevant political entities that, irrespective of any political developments in the area, no member of the Samaritan Community shall by economically disadvantaged as a result of the changes in the various areas of control.

4. We request with regard to all economic, educational and cultural matters, that each member of the Samaritan Community by assured of his/her right to the freedom to practice a profession and to acquire an education or a profession, without limitation and in accordance with his/her qualifications, at any appropriate instiution, wherever he/she desires to do so, in any political situation. The assurance of this right shall by recognized by all releant political entities.

5. We request that all entities involved in the peace agreement between Israel and its neighbors ensure their participation in the allocation of suitable material resources for strengthening the existence of the Samaritan Community and developing its holy sites on Mt. Gerizim.

6. We request that politicians and officials in the United States be aware of these requests and use their good and benefial influence with all entities involved in the peace agreement between Israel and its neighbors, so that those entities shall honor those requests in any political situation which may develop among them.

7. We insist that the right of free passage, the freedom to practice a profession and to scquire an education, and the need to assist in the development of the Samaritan Community in all areas, constitute an integral part of the peace agreement between Israel and its neighbors, and that all parties involved in that agreement consider it a duty and an honor to comply with these at all times and in all political situations. To this end, we propose the establishment of a follow-up committee, with the participation of all parties involved in the agreement, which will ensure complete implementation of all items concerned with the Samaritan Community.

whereto we hereby set out hands,
today, July 12,1995.

Priest Elazar (Abd El-Muin)
Zebulan (Fayyad) Altif
Peleg (Farouk) Altif
Batia b. Yefet Tsedaka
Miryam (Maryam) Altif
Benyamim b. Ratson Tsedaka
Yefet. Ratson Tsedaka
Ron (Ronny) Sassoni
Ratson (Radwan) Altif"

Appendix C: Benyamim Tsedaka's Call for the Repatriation of Artifacts

In this statement, published on Facebook and in the A.B. *Samaritan News*, Benyamim Tsedaka argues for the return to Mount Gerizim of stone artifacts dug up and removed by Israel Antiquities Authority over the last four decades. Note that these stone artifacts have a different rhetorical potentiality than the thousands of paper and parchment Samaritan manuscripts in diaspora around the world. For Tsedaka, these stone artifacts belong where they were discovered, in order to be appreciated as part of the physical and cultural landscape of Mount Gerizim.

Tsedaka writes:
Part of the findings belong to our Israelite Samaritan forefathers are displayed in the impressive museum in Ma'aleh Edomim, in the way from Jerico to Jerusalem, as said in the parable of "The Good Samaritan" alongside fancy mosaic tiles from Samaritan synagogues that Magen uncovered in various places in Samaria. The Samaritan findings include: tools, artifacts, mosaics and several inscriptions. There is a special big hall in "The Good Samaritan" Museum that contains the related Samaritan artifacts (just as there is a special hall of Jewish artifacts, and a hall for the Christian findings) that Dr. Yitzhaq Magen the Museum creator dedicated a big hall for display of each faith. In the process of establishing the museum Magen even published a special large volume called "The Samaritans and the Good Samaritan".

It is unpleasant for me to spoil the joy, by asking the troubling question: What do the Israelite Samaritans have to do with "The Good Samaritan"? If we insist upon historical accuracy, we will answer this question by saying that there was not anything common to the Israelite Samaritans and the parable of the "Good Samaritan" or the ancient Christian site that developed out of this parable. . . .

The site of "The Good Samaritan" as an outstanding Christian site with the relics of the Ancient Christian church within it, like other Christian sites in the region of Samaria, including the relics of the octagon Christian church on the top of Mount Gerizim—symbolize our historical frustrations, devastations and defeats.

An integral part of our new uprightness will be the eventual centralization of our luxurious past antiquities (of the Israelite Samaritan nation) in the place of our glory. As it is unimaginable that archaeological findings that symbolize the luxurious past of the Jewish People, found in Jerusalem will be displayed outside of Jerusalem, it is also unimaginable that the tens of thousands of findings that Magen exposed in his excavation on Mount Gerizim that represent the luxurious past of our nation from its Mount Gerizim centrality, will be taken and wander on display in various places outside of Mount Gerizim.

The place for the many findings that were found on Mount Gerizim should be in a museum that will be built on Mount Gerizim, on the top the mountain of our life and glory, with all means of secured display. The place should not be at a Christian site nor in the Rockefeller Museum storages in East Jerusalem but in their most natural place of our luxurious culture of our forefathers—In Mount Gerizim.

Reprinted from Benyamim Tsedaka, "Why Are Samaritan Antiquities That Belong to the Samaritans in the Good Samaritan Inn Museum?" Facebook. N.p., 23 April 2013. Web. 23 April 2013.

Notes

Preface

1. In my doctoral research, I was investigating rhetorical delivery through practitioner-activist stories, and in framing my project I became curious about fifteenth-century rabbi and rhetorician Judah Messer Leon, who wrote the first Hebrew treatment of rhetoric that, coincidentally enough, was the first book published on the Hebrew printing press in the life of the author. Because of my research into Messer Leon, I had taken several semesters of Modern Hebrew with Ellen Rothschild and Marc Bernstein. I remain indebted to them both for their excellent Hebrew instruction, which became essential to this project. For a careful study of Leon's connection to rhetorical delivery see my chapter in *Jewish Rhetorics*, edited by Michael Bernard-Donals and Janice W. Fernheimer.

2. The finding aid's brief and laconic description of how the collection moved from Ottoman Palestine to Three Oaks, Michigan, made me even more curious to learn the full story of these materials. In the next few hours I located two significant texts that would come to shape the next five years of my work. The first, a journal article referenced in the finding aid itself, was Professor Robert Anderson's 1984 "The Museum Trail: The Michigan State University Samaritan Collection." Anderson describes a complicated scenario where Warren was "impressed by their [Samaritan] poverty and disturbed by the abandon with which they were selling their precious religious artifacts, Warren . . . purchased many of the treasures to hold in safekeeping until the Samaritans could repurchase them." However, this plan where the Samaritans would repurchase the collection never came to fruition. After Warren's death in 1919, the collection remained in Three Oaks until 1950, when the family finally closed E. K. Warren's museum and donated much of its contents to then Michigan State College, or what's known today as Michigan State University.

As Anderson explains, Michigan State College did not have any biblical scholar at the time that could identify the collection, and appeals for help to other institutions, in the form of circulated photographs, went unanswered. With the exception of a few artifacts, the majority of the collection was "placed in cardboard boxes in a storage area under the bleachers of the football stadium until a renovation of the area led to their rediscovery in 1968." During the renovation, Robert Anderson, then an associate professor of religion at Michigan State University, was asked by the university to identify the contents of the cardboard boxes. Anderson discovered that the boxes under the football stadium bleachers contained three fifteenth-century Samaritan manuscripts, "a piece of bluish-streaked, white marble bearing an inscription (Exodus 15:13,11) dating between the third and sixth centuries" and more than two dozen other materials dating to a later time but "not without interest and even intrigue" (Anderson, "The

Museum Trail"). After identifying the contents of the collection as significant, the materials were moved to University Archives and Historical Collections.

3. Robert Anderson also authored two other important books on the Samaritans with coauthor Terry Giles: *The Keepers: An Introduction to the History and Culture of the Samaritans* (2005) and *A Tradition Kept* (2005). Aside from Anderson, few scholars have written about the collection. MSU has never had a doctoral program in religious studies, and, beyond the widespread circulation of Anderson's scholarship in Samaritan studies, few scholars beyond him and Benyamim Tsedaka have taken an interest in the collection.

4. After 2003, Tsedaka returned to Michigan State once a year from 2004 to 2010.

5. Nine years later, Tsedaka recalls that the November 2003 "[meeting] was fun. They were giving time for people to ask questions, so I utilized it to the best of my ability. Telling them about . . . [my idea for a] Samaritan corner . . . [that they should] have a Samaritan corner" in the main library" (Tsedaka, "Personal interview on 8 June 2012").

6. Related to this point of gaining consent from cultural stakeholders, Cushman in "Wampum, Sequoyan, and Story: Decolonizing the Digital Archive" reminds us that

> Though open access to digital archives is thought to be a good thing by scholars invested in the digital humanities, for some tribes creating digital materials and giving open access to them is controversial and, in some cases, even prohibited. For me, it is important to respect the views of tribes and Nations. Anything less is to impose, yet again, a Western epistemological understanding onto their practices, even if this perspective purports itself to be liberal and egalitarian. (132)

7. Coedited by Sharon Sullivan Eretz.

8. See Catherine Prendergast's *Buying into English: Language and Investment in the New Capitalist World* for her discussion of English and globalization.

9. As of September 9, 2014, Benyamim Tsedaka reports the Samaritan population as 770.

10. "Between the raindrops" and "two fires" are phrases Samaritans have used to describe their delicate geopolitical situation as the smallest religious and ethnic minority in the Middle East, and almost equally divided as a population between their two neighborhoods, one in Israel and the other in Palestinian Authority.

11. Stakeholders have a stake in the project. Multiple groups may have a stake or vested interest in the outcome of a digital humanities project. This does not necessarily mean that all stakeholders have an equal vested interest or expected outcome, but understanding the different interests of groups in a single project is as much a rhetorical understanding of what different audiences desire.

Chapter One

1. As of July 2014.

2. In my previous work on the strategic circulation of texts, I've looked at two forms of rhetorical velocity. First, rhetors intentionally circulate manuscripts with an idea for how those texts may be appropriated, recirculated, or recomposed in relation to the interests of the rhetors. In this idea of rhetorical velocity, the concept is useful for practitioners as a framework to think about what audiences will *do* with texts in

relationship to specific rhetorical goals or objectives. The concept of rhetorical velocity is also useful from the perspective of rhetorical analysis to study how texts circulate over time. For example, how a rhetor's press release contributes to another writer's newspaper story, and how that newspaper story benefits the rhetor's own interests. Rhetorical velocity is a theory that's useful for thinking about the circulation of texts over a foreseeable or forecastable amount of time; however, the concept is not useful for thinking about the circulation of commonplaces or ancient manuscripts. It was never intended to be applied to long ago instances of delivery where the texts were sold or stolen for the purposes of survival, as was the case with the Samaritan manuscripts. Rather, rhetorical velocity was intended to explain noncoerced acts of delivery.

3. I use the term stakeholder to identify groups by their interest and connection to the texts. This could include a scholarly, historical, cultural, and religious connection to the texts.

4. Israelite is a distinct identity from Israeli. Janice Fernheimer's book *Steppin' Into Zion* looks at how Israeli/Israelite identity functions in relationship to notions of Jewishness and blackness. The Samaritans offer another interesting case example to expand the work that she has done on Hebrew Israelite (Black Hebrew and Black Jewish) identity.

5. There is debate over the age of the manuscript. Benyamim Tsedaka has dated the scroll as 1145 CE. Robert Anderson has dated the scroll much later. The debate is ongoing; however, there is no doubt that the document is several hundred years old.

6. Mark Cohen explains in the Stanford Encyclopedia of Philosophy entry on "Actuality and Potentiality" in Aristotle's *Metaphysics* that

This last illustration is particularly illuminating. Consider, for example, a piece of wood, which can be carved or shaped into a table or into a bowl. In Aristotle's terminology, the wood has (at least) two different potentialities, since it is potentially a table and also potentially a bowl. The matter (in this case, wood) is linked with potentiality; the substance (in this case, the table or the bowl) is linked with actuality. The as yet uncarved wood is only potentially a table, and so it might seem that once it is carved the wood is actually a table. Perhaps this is what Aristotle means, but it is possible that he does not wish to consider the wood to be a table. His idea might be that not only can a piece of raw wood in the carpenter's workshop be considered a potential table (since it can be transformed into one), but the wood composing the completed table is also, in a sense, a potential table. The idea here is that it is not the wood qua wood that is actually a table, but the wood qua table. Considered as matter, it remains only potentially the thing that it is the matter of.

The important takeaway is to consider the brick and mortar archive's contents as something that has the *potential* to manifest (and not simply become, as the block of wood once carved is no longer a block of wood, but something else) as something else with a combination of human and economic resources, technology, and desire on the part of cultural and institutional stakeholders.

7. The over seventy libraries and collections are based on a list generated from Jean-Pierre Rothschild's 1989 article and recent correspondence with Benyamim Tsedaka. I discuss this more in the next chapter along with my visualization of the Samaritan diaspora of manuscripts; however, I want to note that this diaspora does not include manuscripts in private collections. There's no comprehensive way to track the

circulation of Samaritan manuscripts in private hands beyond monitoring the activity on auction houses such as Kedem in Jerusalem. Public Radio International reporter Daniel Estrin has been researching an investigative story on the private sale of Samaritan manuscripts for the last year.

8. The exact end of the Second Intifada is disputed. Some mark the end with the death of Yasser Arafat on November 11, 2004, while others consider Palestinian president Mahmoud Abbas's declaration to end the violence at the Sharm El-Sheikh Summit in February 2005 to mark the end.

9. The Israel Nature and Parks Authority was not mentioned in Levinson's 2010 article as an Israeli steward for the site: "The deputy head of the IDF Civil Administration, told those present that the Civil Administration was not interested in managing the archaeological site, but ordered that steps be taken to have the site operated by another entity. Sources at the Samaria Regional Council said that the council wished to do so."

10. Erdan continues and says, "Our answer is in our presence and our development . . . This is not the only site that will be opened in Judea and Samaria [West Bank]. We will formulate a clear plan for development of nature and Jewish heritage sites throughout Judea and Samaria, which emphasize the historical connection of the people of Israel to its land. We will do it without shame and without stuttering" (Benardi and Kempinski).

11. The Palestinian Authority had joined UNESCO as a full member in 2011. The UN executive board voted to admit the P.A. into UNESCO: forty were in favor, fourteen abstained, and four—the United States, Germany, Romania and Latvia—voted no. The United States was against P.A. admission into UNESCO and, as a consequence of the decision, has withheld funding for UNESCO. Secretary of State Hillary Clinton responded to the admission of the P.A. into UNESCO: "Unfortunately there are those who, in their enthusiasm to recognize the aspirations of the Palestinian people, are skipping over the most important step, which is determining what the state will look like, what its borders are, how it will deal with the myriad issues that states must address" (Sayare and Erlanger).

12. The Babylonian (Bavli) and Palestinian (Yerushalmi) Talmuds differ on the rabbinic status of the Samaritans. For a thorough breakdown of the Talmudic differences on the Samaritans, see Itzhak Hamitovsky's "Rabbi Meir and the Samaritans: The Differences between the Accounts in the Yerushalmi and the Bavli," in *Jewish Studies Internet Journal* Vol. 8 at http://www.biu.ac.il/js/JSIJ/sum8.html [Hebrew].

13. Samaritan Hebrew, or what the Samaritans would simply refer to as Ancient Hebrew.

Chapter Two

For the epigraphs at the beginning of this chapter: Faruk Rijan Samira, quoted in Franklin; Joseph Cohen, quoted in Merriman.

1. As Pratt is disturbed in her book by the idea that the more she studied travel writing, the more she "became of the participants whose voices" she wasn't hearing:

There was a huge gap in the archive. What had the people who received these visitors thought of them and the imperial designs they brought with them? How and in what forms of expression had they interpreted the historical process they were living? (5)

As was the case with Pratt's work I had similar questions about the lack of Samaritan in much of this travel writing. To begin to address this gap, I chose to talk with Samaritans about what the diaspora of manuscripts means to them. I am interested in the next two chapters, specifically, what Samaritans think about this diaspora of manuscripts, its origins, and future.

2. There is no doubt a larger project in examining Samaritan representation in these travel narratives; however, for the purpose of this book project, I focus exclusively on accounts regarding the acquisition or attempted acquisition of Samaritan manuscripts.

3. As Pratt argues, historical transitions "alter the way people write, because they alter people's experiences and the way people imagine, feel and think about the world they live in" (4).

4. The diaspora of Samaritan manuscripts matters not only historically, but also in the present and future rhetorically. The history of the Samaritan diaspora is important for further understanding the present-day rhetorical context of Samaritan manuscripts as they enter the digital age, and some Samaritan attitudes toward their diaspora of manuscripts, which is discussed in the end of this chapter and in chapter 4.

5. I note once again that I am not a biblical scholar or historian. I have nothing new to add to conversations in biblical or ancient/medieval Samaritan history and my purpose in providing this overview is to provide sufficient context in order to discuss the rhetorical circumstances of the Samaritan diaspora of manuscripts and, in later chapters, its future. Scholars in biblical Samaritan studies such as Anderson, Giles, Pummer, Crown, Knoppers, Kartveit, Schur, Shem Tov, Tal, and others should be consulted for their extensive work in this area.

6. From pages 14–21 of *The Samaritan Pentateuch*, Anderson and Giles provide a comprehensive overview of recent critical scholarship regarding Samaritan origins. Given that this book is less interested in origin stories and more focused on how the diaspora of manuscripts may be of rhetorical use for present and future Samaritans, I will refer interested readers to Anderson and Giles's comprehensive work in biblical studies.

7. While Talmudic Judaism came to praise the Samaritans for their "strictness in observing the commandments (Hul 4a). . . . they were considered lax in observing the law of the levirate and of marriage generally (ibid. 76a)" so that a Jew was forbidden to marry a Samaritan (*Jewish Encyclopedia*, "Samaritans"). In the *Masechtot Qetanot Kutim* or minor tractate *Kutim*, named after the Persian peoples Talmudic Judaism thought to have been transported to Samaria during the Asssyrian conquest, "The general principle is that they [Samaritans] are to be trusted in so far as their own practise [sic] agrees with that of the Jews: in other respects they count as non-Jews" (Ibid). While outside the Samaritan community, some scholars have debated Samaritan origins in regards to "whether the Samaritans originated as an offshoot of Judaism as it existed in the Hellenistic-Roman period or as a separate Yahwistic community that came into being long before that time" (Pummer 1), the "Samaritans consider themselves, and are considered by others, as members of an independent religion, albeit one that is closely akin to Judaism in its beliefs, sacred writings, and practices" (Pummer, "Samaritanism—a Jewish Sect or an Independent form of Yahwism?" 1). As an Yahwistic Israelite faith, the proximity of Samaritanism to Judaism has led to interest from Christians especially, as their biblical texts mention Samaritans by name several times, and their theology builds on the Masoretic Text, the authoritative Hebrew text of the Jewish Bible.

8. "This northern migration to Samaria led to the building of the temple on Mount Gerizim at the time of Alexander the Great. Ant. 11 302f., 306–312." (2).

9. Knoppers explains that choosing terminology to describe the Samaritans is difficult: "I am referring to the residents of Yehud and Samerina (Samaria) during the Neo-Babylonian, Persian, and Hellenistic periods as Judeans and Samarians to distinguish them from the later Jews and Samaritans of the later Roman period. In both cases, one can see lines of continuity from one period to the next. To be sure, traditional usage dies hard. Adopting one nomenclature and completely ignoring others is impossible, because the usage of Samaritan and Jew is longstanding and pervasive both in popular and in scholarly parlance (and hence is retained in the title of this book)" (17).

10. Beginning with the Assyrian conquest, Knoppers's book provides a careful argument for how Samarian-Judean relations may not have been so distinct or antagonistic in the Neo-Babylonian, Persian, and Hellenistic periods. As Knoppers posits, "The periods under view predate the consolidation of classically distinctive Samaritan and Jewish identities. Hence, one must come to grips with multiple stages in the history and development of both groups" (14).

11. Tapani Harviainen and Haseeb Shehadeh argue that in 1537 Guillaume Postel was probably the first European to acquire a Samaritan manuscript (167). As Moshe Florentin notes, the seventeenth century is when significant European acquisition of Samaritan manuscripts begins. (1)

12. According to Tapani Harviainen and Haseeb Shehadeh, French linguist Guillaume Postel was probably the first European to acquire a Samaritan manuscript in 1537 (167). Jean-Pierre Rothschild writes that Postel and Joseph Justus Scaliger are "known to have initiated the curiosity of religious (e.g. Jean Morin) and lay scholars or the curious (achille Harley de Sancy, Perisec) towards the Samaritan texts through their own gathering of manuscripts" (771–72). According to Tsedaka, In 1584 Joseph Scaliger

> wrote a letter to the Samaritans in Cairo. He asked them to send him a Torah and they didn't, but they agreed to send him the Samaritan book of Joshua—in Arabic. And [this book] was also a discovery for the Europeans especially when they took one of the manuscripts from the Vatican to be in the base two manuscripts, one of them is Samaritan Hebrew text and the other one Samaritan Aramaic. So they are in the base of the polyglot. (Benyamim Tsedaka, "Personal interview in Holon, Israel, 16 Feb. 2012")

13. According to Moshe Florentin, Western acquaintance with the Samaritan Pentateuch stoked Christian religious fires at a time of considerable transition: "The discovery gave rise to an argument which not only affected Jews and Samaritans, but also Catholics and Protestants. The discovery of the Samaritan text at the time of the Reformation proved an effective weapon in the hands of the Catholics. They argued that since there was more than one version, it was impossible to substantiate the principles of faith merely on the written word, as the Protestants believed; rather, they held, it was necessary to rely on the definitive authority of the Catholic Pope." (1)

14. For a comprehensive survey of European collectors, see Harvianen and Shehadeh's 1994 "How Did Abraham Firkovich Acquire the Great Collection of Samaritan Manuscripts in Nablus in 1864?" They write:

The transfer of Samaritan manuscripts from several Samaritan centres in the Middle East, such as Damascus, Gaza, Cairo and principally Nablus, to the West, has been carried out over the last four centuries. Guillaume Postel (1510–1581) was in 1537, as far as we know, the first European to acquire a Samaritan manuscript. Postel was followed by a long line of Western travellers and scholars who have attempted to acquire manuscripts either through the Samaritan centres or by correspondence with Samaritan priests. It suffices to mention the following sample names which are known in the history of Samaritan studies: Joseph Scaliger (1540–1609), Nicolaus Claude de Peiresc (1580- 1637), Archbishop James Ussher (1581–1656), Pietro della Valle (1586–1652), Edward Pococke (1604- 1691), Job Ludolf (1624–1704), John Usgate, Henri Gregorie, Bishop of Blois (1750–1831), R. Huntington (1637–1701), Ulrich Jaspers Seetzen (1767–1811), Thomas Marshall (1621–1685), M. Corancoz, S. De Sacy (1758–1838), B. Kennicott (1718–1783), J. H. Petermann (1801–1876), J. Mills, J. Rosenberg, P. Kahle, J. A. A. Montgomery, W. E. Barton, E. K. Warren, M. Gaster. The intensive quests for Samaritan manuscripts made by these scholars and others that we have not mentioned have merely resulted in sporadic acquisitions. (168)

15. I do consider this process to be one of European colonial appropriation, particularly in the case of della Valle, who was more or less operating on an official mandate. Without any official mandate, however, these practices of collection mirror European colonial dreams in North Africa and the Middle East. The tactics and strategies have been mirrored in other spheres of European colonial interest, particularly North and South America and the Indies. Indigenous scholars in my field of rhetorical studies (Powell; Howe, Haas, Driskill, etc.) speak in their work to some of these issues surrounding the politics of indigenous archives and collections in colonial hands.

16. Silvestre de Sacy writes about Huntington: "The interest which he appeared to take in their affairs, excited the astonishment of the Samaritans, and induced them to ask him whether there were any Israelites in his country. Upon his replying in the affirmative, they presented him with a sheet written in Samaritan characters; and when they found that he could read their characters, they were still more astonished, and then concluded that the Israelites settled in England, of whom Mr. Huntington spoke, must be their brethren. Mr. H. availed himself of that circumstance to propose then writing to these their supposed brethren, a brief statement of the principal points of their religion, and above all, of those particular points by which they are distinguished from the Jews, and to subjoin to their letter a copy of the law." (de Sacy, "On the Samaritans" 93–94).

17. As an article in the 1803 *Evangelical Magazine* proposes, Huntington's portrayal of the Samaritans of England appears to have been be "a mere artifice . . . to obtain a copy of the Pentateuch from the Samaritans at Sichem [Nablus], by imitating to them, that there were a people in England who worshipped the same god; and wished for a copy of their law" (S.C. 537).

18. Even after Huntington's death, the correspondence between the Samaritans was resumed by Dr. Thomas Marshall, Rector of Lincoln College, Oxford, who appears to have had no problem continuing the ruse.

19. According to Benyamim Tsedaka, Ludolph was one of the worst of the European deceivers because he provided further substantiation that there were Samaritan com-

munities in Europe. Based on his letters, the Samaritans of Nablus believed "that there were [Samaritan] communities in Europe" (Benyamim Tsedaka, "Personal interview in Holon, Israel, 16 Feb. 2012"). However, the Samaritans lacked the resources to "go and see" because the community in Nablus was too poor to visit. Because the Samaritans were in a position to continue to be deceived, in the seventeenth century Europeans were able to take forty manuscripts from the Samaritans (Benyamim Tsedaka, "Personal interview in Holon, Israel, 16 Feb. 2012").

20. Translated from Samaritan Hebrew.

21. For example, in an 1839 travel account by Dr. Bowring titled "Samaria and the Samaritans," he writes that community in Nablus

> had even been told that there were Samaritans in England, and in the English countries to the east (meaning British India), and were very curious to know whether I knew or had ever heard of such Samaras or Samaritans, and whether it would be possible to establish intercourse with them. They seemed much afflicted when I told them that I believed there was no reason to suppose that any of their race existed in any portion of the British empire. (815)

The following year in 1840, Lady Francis Egerton writes that the Samaritans of Nablus produced for her to see a letter from "Samaritan brethren in India about 160 years ago" (51). Both of these two accounts show that after Huntington and other European scholars' deceit in leading the Samaritans to believe that they had long lost brethren in Europe as a means to obtain copies of their manuscripts, this trickery continued to be discussed by Samaritans well into the nineteenth century. While early European instances such as these were successful in deceiving the Samaritans out of approximately forty manuscripts, the largest emigration of Samaritan manuscripts occurred in the second half of the nineteenth century when, through a series of unfortunate historical circumstances, the Samaritans' economic desperation coincided with American and European tourism to Palestine. According to Benyamim Tsedaka, "the big sale of Samaritan manuscripts started during the 19th century and the beginning of the 20th century. So now it's the case that we have over 4000 manuscripts all over the world" (Benyamim Tsedaka, "Personal interview in Holon, Israel, 16 Feb. 2012").

22. Morag Kersel's contemporary work on the Israeli antiquities trade examines some of the underlying motivations and desires of Holy Land antiquities. While her work speaks to contemporary markets, it's worth considering how or if Holy Land collecting has changed (or not) since the beginning of biblical tourism. See, specifically:

> Kersel, Morag M. "The Lure of the Relic: Collecting and Consuming Artifacts from the Holy Land." YouTube. University of Pennsylvania Museum of Archaeology and Anthropology, 14 Dec. 2011. Web. 10 Oct. 2013.
> Kersel, Morag M. "From the Ground to the Buyer: A Market Analysis of the Trade in Illegal Antiquities." *Archaeology, Cultural Heritage, and the Antiquities Trade.* Ed. Neil Brodie, Morag M. Kersel, Christina Luke, and Kathryn W. Tubb. Gainesville, FL: University of Florida, 2006. 188–205. Print.

23. At the beginning of the nineteenth century, there is evidence that the Samaritans remained reluctant to sell manuscripts, but some were sold. By the mid-nineteenth century, the Samaritans were selling views of manuscripts and later photographs. Af-

ter the 1850s, especially, there's documented accounts of Europeans purchasing Samaritan manuscripts and, by the 1860s, there are large sales of Samaritan manuscripts to collectors. In addition, the Samaritans begin to write manuscripts specifically for sale to tourists, and the sale of manuscripts and fragments, sale of photographs, and production of writing for the tourist economy continues well into the early twentieth century.

24. The *Christian Herald and Seaman's Magazine* introduces the piece by describing it as a conversation that "took place between Mr. Wolff, a Missionary in the employ of London's Jew's Society, and a Jew" and also describes Israel as a "Samaritan Jew" in the introduction to the article (238).

25. Wolff also writes that Israel then said that the Samaritans "have heard that some of our brethren lived in the desert of Moscovia" (239). Moscovia appears to be Moscow; however, it is not clear why Moscow is referenced. Perhaps Israel was trying to remember England or Paris, alluding to previous correspondence with Huntington and others.

26. Jowett's observation about how the Samaritans stored their manuscript remains true today for some families, where manuscripts are still wrapped in cloth. Samaritans still adhere to this practice.

27. In Andrew Alexander Bonar's 1839 account of traveling to Nablus, he writes that he visited the Samaritan synagogue where sacred manuscripts were stored: "After long delay, and the promise of a considerable sum (for he told us the sight was worth 150 piastres at any time,) the priest agreed to show us the copy of the Torah, or five books of Moses, which is so famed for its antiquity. They said that it was written by the hand of Abishua, the son of Phinehas, and is 3600 years old. It was taken out of its velvet cover, and part of it unrolled before us" (Bonar and M'cheyne 215).

28. Elliot writes first about an earlier failed attempt to acquire a Samaritan manuscript from Isaac Basire's *The Correspondence of Isaac Basire in the Reigns of Charles I. and Charles II*, where Basire writes that he "did solicite Paisius Ligaridius, the then Archbishop of Gaga . . . to purchase it for me, but he failed" (Basire and Darnell 291); however, while Basire was unable to procure a full manuscript in his own time, Elliot remarks about his own success.

29. In addition to telling the Samaritans to "take care," the traveler asserts his belief that one day the British will be in control of Nablus. The traveler then indicates that in order for the Samaritans to safeguard their future under British rule, they would do well to provide the traveler with a copy of their manuscript. The Samaritans refused the traveler's request. Wilson's narrative is also significant because he records that the Samaritans understood in the early nineteenth century that their manuscripts had previously been stolen.

30. Prime writes that the Samaritans were willing to sell more than just fragments to tourists: "They showed us some other manuscripts of the law, of which they had perhaps ten or twelve in the closet behind the curtain, which I opened and examined. They would sell moderns, but I could not get them to name a price for the old one" (335).

31. The story of how Firkovich acquired the Samaritan manuscripts is complex. I refer to professors Harviainen and Shehadeh's work "How did Abraham Firkovich acquire the great collection of Samaritan manuscripts in Nablus in 1864?" where they examine Firkovich's primary letters and explore in close detail the question of how Firkovich was able to buy such a massive collection of Samaritan manuscripts at that specific moment in history. They argue that Firkovich did not actually travel to Pal-

estine to purchase Samaritan manuscripts. Rather, Firkovich sent an agent of his to Nablus to see what was for sale, and received assistance from a Samaritan in the theft of one of the two Genizot Firkovich eventually purchased before he left Palestine for Russia.

32. After the fall of the Soviet Union, the St. Petersburg/Firkovich collection was so important that Samaritans such as Tsedaka were in Russia only a few weeks after the Soviet Union's dissolution. The collection, which had been off limits for almost the entire twentieth century, was once again made available to visitors.

33. Tsedaka recalls that after the fall of the Soviet Union in 1991, he and a group of Samaritans made a trip to view the St. Petersburg collection and the Firkovich manuscripts:

> made a delegation and we went to Leningrad and we stayed there two weeks and we saw all the manuscripts. We copied many compositions that we don't have. Over four or five hundred pages. We were a delegation of five and we worked from ten in the morning until ten in the evening. Even not making a break to eat something because we were so enthusiastic about the first meeting of this collection after 150 years. (Benyamim Tsedaka, "Personal interview in Holon, Israel, 16 Feb. 2012")

34. There's no shortage of travel narratives in this era regarding the purchase of Samaritan manuscripts. For example, in 1865, Henry Baker Tristram writes that for a "liberal backshish" he could see the synagogue rolls. Additionally, he was shown "several fragments of old rolls, and some ancient manuscript books—the former, portions of the law; the latter, service-books—which he offered for sale" (156–57). In 1867, Mark Twain writes that he himself purchased a Samaritan manuscript during his visit to Ottoman Palestine: "I procured from the high-priest of this ancient Samaritan community, at great expense, a secret document of still higher antiquity and far more extraordinary interest, which I propose to publish as soon as I have finished translating it" (177).

35. In the decades that followed, Samaritan poverty and economic desperation continued to rise. In Laurence Oilphant's 1887 travel account titled *Haifa, or, Life in modern Palestine* he tells the story of a Samaritan he met in Haifa that may exemplify the sale of manuscripts for survival that Altif and Fara reference. In the story below, a Samaritan youth sells one of his only possessions, an inheritance manuscript, for, in the end, a small sum of money:

> He handed me a document in Arabic, in which, after stating that for certain reasons, which he implied were by no means discreditable to him (he was an outcast from his own people), he implored charity, and requested me "to cast upon him a regard of compassion and benevolence." The document further said:

> "All that I have inherited from my parents and ancestors is a manuscript written in ancient Hebrew, nine hundred years old, containing two chapters of the Bible, including the commandments, which I beg to offer you, in the hope that you will recompense me in return by a sum which will relieve my distress."

> He signed himself "Shellabi, the son of Jacob, the Samaritan." . . . Anyhow, here was the son of a prince in distress, and here was an extremely ancient and curi-

ous manuscript for sale. The youth looked such a scamp, however, that he did not enlist my sympathies. I suspected that he had lost his money by gambling, which proved afterwards to be the case; so when he said he considered the manuscript worth ten dollars I offered him one dollar, on which he retired indignantly. A few days later, however, he reappeared, took his dollar thankfully, and I retain possession of the manuscript. (346)

In a matter of decades, the economic pressure to sell manuscripts combined with the limited work opportunities available to Samaritans prompted them to make a living off tourism. While in the early nineteenth century the Samaritans began to charge for manuscript viewings, in the late nineteenth century they began to sell photographs.

36. As Samaritans Raqheb Fara and Menashe Altif said in separate interviews, manuscripts were often sold to purchase bread ("Personal interview on Mount Gerizim, 23 May 2012"; "Personal interview on Mount Gerizim, 19 April 2012").

37. See also Schur's "The Modern Period (from 1516 AD)" in Crown's *The Samaritans*.

38. In pink are former large centers of Samaritan population, blue are former small centers of Samaritan population, and green are the two current centers of Samaritan population.

39. In *The Messianic Hope of the Samaritans* (1907), Samaritan High Priest Jacon Ben Aaron writes more directly about a change in Samaritan attitudes toward the sale of manuscripts, their market, and authenticity. He writes that the Samaritans

are now willing to sell to them accurate modern copies of the ancient books of the Samaritan religion. I think it well, however, to warn intending purchasers, that not all the copies offered for sale, even in Nablus, are accurate. Some people of little learning, relying on the ignorance of tourists, have made garbled copies of our Torah, and have sold them to tourists or correspondents. Manuscripts purchased at our Synagogue, from myself or my sons will be certified as complete and correct. Several recent purchasers have sent their manuscripts to me for inspection, and I have been sorry not to be able to certify to their correctness. It grieves us to have our Law incorrectly copied. I request my friend, Dr. Barton, to make this statement to intending purchasers. We desire that such copies of our sacred books, as go forth into Christian libraries shall be accurate. Any manuscript purchased in our Synagogue, and bearing my seal, is genuine and complete. (5)

40. The census was conducted by John D. Whiting in his capacity as then "United States Vice-Consul at Jerusalem, acting as the Palestine representative of the Samaritan Committee" (3). This is the same John D. Whiting that is referenced in the next few paragraphs, the author of the *National Geographic Magazine* story.

41. The American Samaritan Committee's agenda was a mix of providing direct aid with the eventual (unrealized) aspiration of converting the Samaritans to Christianity. Below, Barton describes the evangelical motivations of Edward Warren:

He [Warren] felt, and the Samaritan Committee was in entire accord with him, that it would be better for us as Christian Americans to go to this forlorn little community and endeavor to manifest a Christian spirit, than to undertake a campaign for their conversion. Mr. Warren said that the Lord had permitted this colony to remain under the influence of their own religion from the time of the Exile until now, we could afford to wait and be sure that we were not attempting to force the hand of Providence by a too sudden anxiety for their instantaneous conversion. (3)

42. Whiting was a resident of the American Colony in Jerusalem and took photographs for them. Whiting also served as deputy American consul for Jerusalem from 1908–1915, volunteered for the Turkish Red Crescent during the First World War, and served as an intelligence officer for the British (Library of Congress, "Biography of Whiting"). The Library of Congress has an extensive online collection of Whiting's photographic work: http://www.loc.gov/rr/print/coll/629_whiting.html.

43. On the sale of Samaritan manuscripts to the British museum (see also Ayers 123–34), American tourist Lydia D. Adler wrote the following racist screed in her 1912 travel narrative *The Holy Land:*

> These Samaritans possess the true Jewish instinct, for though they claim so much reverence for those ancient manuscripts, a committee of them from Nabulous have but recently offered them for sale in London. In speaking of this, the more devout claim that it was not the originals, but copies that were thus offered for so small a price. The Samaritans are desperately poor and despised by both Moslems and Jews. (201)

44. The article was "translated from the German for the Reform Advocate by J.H" (274).

45. In 1919, Isaac, son of Amram, wrote to William Barton on the well-being of the community after the First World War and notes that the Samaritans have resorted to selling more ancient books in order to sustain themselves in the difficult post-First World War moment:

> I am very sorry to have to tell you that they [Samaritans] are without employment, and that there is not found among them one who has a position or business. For they who were in business lost it during the war, and now they have resorted for their subsistence to the sale of the ancient books transmitted to them from their fathers, and held by them to be beyond price. (Barton, "The War and the Samaritan Colony" 14)

46. Benyamim Tsedaka says that most of the scribal work for tourists was "done by the Cohen Aphsda ben Yaakov the father of the current high priest, and his son was also a high priest, Joseph." In general, Tsedaka says that scribes at that time did not write a "whole scroll, just the 10 commandments" (Benyamim Tsedaka, "Personal interview on Mount Gerizim, 19 Apr. 2012").

47. In "Itzhak Ben Zvi, David Ben-Gurion and the Samaritans," the late Israel Sedaka gives a generally similar account (some differences include the date 1908 instead of 1907 and the duration of time Ben-Zvi spent at Abraham's house); Benyamim Tsedaka noted these differences in my interview with him.

48. See also pages 107–10 in Dan Ross's *Acts of Faith,* in which he recounts an interview with Tsedaka on Ben-Zvi's aliyah and support for the Samaritans.

49. See also Crown's entry on Yitzhak Ben-Zvi in the *Encyclopedia of Modern Jewish Culture,* Volume 2. See also Yitzhak Ben-Zvi's 1935 *Sefer Ha-Shomronim* or Book of Samaritans.

50. "Good Samaritans in Jerusalem Join in Prayers for Persecuted Jews of Europe." *The Palestine Post*. February 1, 1944. Page 3.

51. "Samaritan, not Arab. Haifa Victim Identified." *The Palestine Post*. July 4, 1939. Page 2.

52. For details on shootings near/around the Samaritan community in 1936, see "In Short." *The Palestine Post*. March 3, 1936. Page 5. "5 Arabs Arrested for Possessing Arms. Official Communique Sunday July 26." *The Palestine Post*. July 27, 1936. Page 5.

53. "Samaritan Shot and Robbed in Jaffa." *The Palestine Post*. November 1, 1945. Page 3.

54. "Samaritans Curtail Feast of Tabernacles." *The Palestine Post*. October 7, 1938. Page 2.

55. Seized their property.

56. "Reflections." *The Palestine Post*. October 5, 1936. Page 4.

57. Israel Sedaka transliterates Yitzhak Ben-Zvi's name as Izhak Ben-Zvi.

58. Israel Sedaka's account of the exchange is difficult to verify at this time. He doesn't provide a source for his quotations. I have however located a March 14, 1946, article in *The Palestine Post* confirming that Ben-Zvi brought up the Samaritans within the same hearing and context:

The President of the Vaad Leumi in his address had referred to the Assyrians of Iraq, who had been practically wiped out as a community, and of the Samaritans of Palestine, whose numbers had declined from 100,000 at the time of the Arab conquest to 200 today, as characteristic fates of minorities under Arab rule. ("Partition Raised at Inquiry: Vaad Leumi Replies to Questions")

Whether or not Ben Zvi's wording and figures are correct or not in either account, this corroboration does lend evidence that this is something Ben Zvi advanced in 1946. This would also correspond with his other writings in *Essays and Reminiscences* and *Book of the Samaritans*.

59. This argument has resurfaced over the last seventy years in relationship to Mizrachi Jews. The most recent iteration is from the Israeli deputy foreign minister, Danny Ayalon, and his campaign to raise awareness of Mizrachi Jews' emigration and expulsion from Middle Eastern/North African countries.

60. "Mercy for Samaritans." *The Palestine Post*. December 10, 1947. Page 3.

61. Palestinian scholars Hussein Ahmad Yousef and Iyad Barghouti argue that before 1948, Samaritans in Nablus were divided politically as well. "Before 1948, like other Palestinians, the Samaritans were divided politically into two factions. The first was led by al-Kahen Sadaqa, who supported the Palestinian leader al-Haj Amin al-Husseini, the leader of the Palestinian revolution against the British and the Zionist movement. While the second faction was led by al-Kahen Wasef, who supported another Palestinian Ragheb al-Nashashibi, who was supported by the British" (38). Yousef and Barghouti do not provide a source or reference for this political claim.

62. "Samaritan to Visit" *The Palestine Post*. September 15, 1949. Page 3.

63. "One-sixth of 160 Surviving Samaritan Jews Enter Israel for Permanent Resettlement." *Jewish Telegraphic Agency*. September 15, 1949.

64. Yearly *Maariv* stories from 1949–1967 focus on Samaritan Passover from Holon to Mount Gerizim. Some sample stories include "Samaritans Crossed to Jordan" (1953), "Samaritans Crossed for Passover to Nablus" (1954), "87 Samaritans Left For

Mount Gerizim" (1954). These stories continue up until 1967. In the last few years leading up to 1967 war, these annual stories included more descriptions of travel difficulty. See, for example, "100 Samaritans Exit to Jordan" (1966) and "Jordan Prohibits Entrance of 33 Samaritans from Israel for the Passover Festival" (1967).

65. In the twentieth century, Samaritan men also began to marry Jewish women. This added to the Samaritans' genetic diversity and health, and the ratio problem of more women to men. In 1937, for example, *The Palestine Post* reports "Thirty young men have been living in enforced celibacy because of the scarcity of girls of marriageable age. Although some of the girls reached the age of consent recently, hopes were dashed when the fathers demanded high dowries. Now, however, there are to be seven weddings, owing to the change of paternal hearts brought about by the High Priest. These will be the first marriages in many years. Since 1922, there have been only five or six weddings celebrated; including four with Jewesses of Oriental communities" ("Samaritan Plan." *The Palestine Post.* November 22, 1937. Page 5).

66. Israel Sedaka writes: "In Israel he [Yitzhak Ben-Zvi] assisted in moving the community to a single place and in the building of the Samaritan neighborhood in Holon. He was the one who planted the foundation stone to the Samaritan synagogue in Holon, as well as the one who, despite ill health and only two months prior to his death, opened that same synagogue. This had been his last public appearance, where he called for a reunion of Samaria and Judea, since all of the tribes of Israel are but one nation" (243).

67. Hussein Ahmad Yousef and Iyad Barghouti write, "During the 1936 revolution in Palestine, King Abdullah had warned of the consequences of attacking the Samaritans. After that, Samaritans started to have good relations with King Hussein. For example, after the earthquake in Nablus in the fifties, King Hussein himself compensated the Samaritan families whose homes were destroyed. Another example; when Jordanian Education Minister, Mr. Shankety, attempted to force Samaritan teachers to work on Saturday (Sabbath), King Hussein rejected the attempted the attempt. Also the King ruled for the Samaritan community in a case concerning land on Mt. Gerizim . . . [and] many of the Samaritans worked in governmental jobs during the Jordanian rule of the West Bank. The Samaritans who live in Nablus Jordanian [have] Passports and are treated as full Jordanian citizens . . . their situation in the West Bank was almost ideal" (39).

68. "Herzog Tells Samaritans They Will Never Again Be Separated from Their Brethren in Israel." *Jewish Telegraphic Agency.* May 2, 1984.

69. Sedan, Gil. "Bank Leumi Branch Firebombed." *Jewish Telegraphic Agency.* January 24, 1989.

70. In "The Anxious Samaritans," reporter Yossi Klein writes about 1995 that "the Samaritans fear that the tentative renewal of the last few decades may be at risk. With Nablus, and apparently Mt. Gerizim, about to be transferred to Yasser Arafat's control, the community could once again be torn apart. During the Jordanian occupation of the West Bank, Holon Samaritans were permitted to come to the mountain only once a year, on Passover. They were treated as virtual prisoners, kept under armed guard and subject to roll calls and interrogations. Sometimes the Jordanians forbade young Holonites from even attending the Passover sacrifice; one year, half the Holon community couldn't cross the border. If a future peace treaty collapses, they warn—with the bitter wisdom of an ancient minority that knows the Middle East—the pre-67 era could return. 'We can't afford to be apart from each other,' says Tsedaka. 'We are all we have.'"

"The Anxious Samaritans." *The Jerusalem Report.* September 21, 1995. 30. ProQuest Research Library. Web. 2 Nov. 2012.

71. The full text of the Seven Principles reads as follows (see also Appendix B for a scanned copy):

Therefore, in view of the special status of the Samaritan Community:

1. We wish to ensure that in any political situation and irrespective of any political development, even in case of deterioration in the relations between parties to the peace agreement, free and unlimited passage shall be given at all times to every Samaritan, from any place where he/she may live, to the centers of Samaritans on Mt. Gerizim in particular and Judea and Samaria (otherwise known as "The West Bank of the Jordan River") in general, and from there to any place within or outside the State of Israel.

2. By virtue of the fact that the Samaritan Community is concentrated in population centers under different areas of administration, we request that each member of the Samaritan Community be given an identification document enabling him/her to move freely at all times among the various centers of the Community, irrespective of any political development and in any varying political situation. This document, which be issued in the form of a passport, a laissez-passer or any other identifying document shall be officially recognized by all political entities whose jurisdiction and/or control extends over the border checkpoints between the various areas of control.

3. We request that all members of the Samaritan Community by assured by all relevant political entities that, irrespective of any political developments in the area, no member of the Samaritan Community shall be economically disadvantaged as a result of the changes in the various areas of control.

4. We request with regard to all economic, educational and cultural matters, that each member of the Samaritan Community by assured of his/her right to the freedom to practice a profession and to acquire an education or a profession, without limitation and in accordance with his/her qualifications, at any appropriate institution, wherever he/she desires to do so, in any political situation. The assurance of this right shall by recognized by all relevant political entities.

5. We request that all entities involved in the peace agreement between Israel and its neighbors ensure their participation in the allocation of suitable material resources for strengthening the existence of the Samaritan Community and developing its holy sites on Mt. Gerizim.

6. We request that politicians and officials in the United States be aware of these requests and use their good and beneficial influence with all entities involved in the peace agreement between Israel and its neighbors, so that those entities shall honor those requests in any political situation which may develop among them.

7. We insist that the right of free passage, the freedom to practice a profession and to acquire an education, and the need to assist in the development of the Samaritan Community in all areas, constitute an integral part of the peace agreement between Israel and its neighbors, and that all parties involved in that agreement consider it a duty and an honor to comply with these at all times, and in all political situations. To this end, we propose the establishment of a follow-up committee, with the participation of all parties involved in the agreement, which will ensure complete implementation of all items concerned with the Samaritan Community.

whereto we hereby set out hands,

today, July 12, 1995.
Priest Elazar (Abd Ei-Muin)
Zebulan (Fayyad) Altif
Peleg (Farouk) Altif
Batia b. Yefet Tsedaka
Miryam (Maryam) Altif
Benyamim b. Ratson Tsedaka
Yefet. Ratson Tsedaka
Ron (Ronny) Sassoni
Ratson (Radwan) Altif

72. Klein posits:

Arafat, sensing a public relations opportunity, has "adopted" the Samaritans as examples of Palestinian generosity toward minorities. During the Intifada, when some Samaritan houses in their old Nablus quarter were burned, Arafat ordered the PLO to pay compensation. He regularly meets in Gaza with Samaritan leaders; during his recent visit to Jericho, the Nablus community chartered a bus and went to pay their respects to the new boss. They are weary experts in accommodating power. In Kiryat Luza's community center, alongside framed drawings of the symbols of the Israelite tribes and posters of WWF [World Wrestling Federation] wrestlers, hang streamers in the colors of the Palestinian flag, taped to the wall by visiting Ramallah Scouts and prudently left hanging by the Samaritans.

"The Anxious Samaritans." *The Jerusalem Report*. September 21, 1995. Pages 31–32. Pro-Quest Research Library. Web. 2 Nov. 2012.
  73. There were additional incidents during the Second Intifada. In 2003, two Palestinian gunmen entered the Samaritan village of "Kiryat Luza closely pursued by the army. A brief gunfight broke out, in which two soldiers, and the gunmen, were killed" (Walter).
  74. Merriman, Helena. "The Modern Trials of the Ancient Samaritans." *BBC News*. January 3, 2011. Web. 16 Nov. 2012. http://www.bbc.co.uk/news/world-middle-east-12069728.

Chapter Three

  1. In regards to Palestinian lobbying efforts, Efrat and Benyamim Tsedaka remark that it was a stolen Samaritan Torah manuscript that helped break the diplomatic ice with Arafat. Tsedaka and Tsedaka argue that "This incident helped the Samaritans of Nablus to obtain an organized system of relations between them and Arafat and they used these meetings between them, in Gaza, and recently in Nablus, [to which Arafat came on December 15, 1995, two days after the IDF redeployment] in order to tell him their demands concerning their future political situation in this region. The Samaritans received a guarantee from the Israelis that they would take care of them in any political development," and this will be important for chapter 3. For example, on December 15, 1995, increased relations with Arafat also appear to have translated into a seat for a Sa-

maritan in Nablus for the eighty-three-member Palestinian Legislative Council ("Chronology: 16 November 1995–15 February 1996" 171). In 1996, Saloum Cohen (who would also serve as Samaritan High Priest from 2001–2004) ran against two other Samaritan candidates in the Palestinian general elections. Saloum Cohen kept his seat on the Palestinian Legislative Council until his death in 2004 ("The Palestinians: Arafat Rules"). Upon Saloum's death, "Palestinian leader Yasser Arafat and other Palestinian officials called the community to express their condolences for Cohen's death" and stated, "'He was a wise man and a friend to all the people of Nablus,' said Nablus Governor Mahmoud Alalouz, who called him a true friend of the Palestinian people and a dedicated parliamentarian" ("Samaritan High Priest Saloum Cohen Dies at 82"). In the 2006 election, the Palestinian National Authority did not have a seat reserved for the Samaritans in the Palestinian Legislative Council and the Samaritans chose to not run a candidate. See also "The Palestinians: Arafat Rules." *The Economist.* December 23, 1995. 52–. ABI/ INFORM Complete. ProQuest Research Library. Web. 2 Nov. 2012.

2. While Powell finds value in uncovering archival stories, Nancy Welch provides an example of studying contemporary practitioners in her 2005 *College Composition and Communication* piece "Living Room: Teaching Public Writing in a Post-Publicity Era." She provides a useful model for framing instances of practitioner delivery as a case example. In her article, she discusses the 2003 story of Katie, a student in her undergraduate rhetoric seminar who composed an antiwar poem for class and then wanted to distribute her poem around her town. As Nancy Welch describes, one evening Katie and a friend posted her poem on surfaces around downtown and eventually ran into trouble with a local police officer. From this single case example she is able to extract a number of significant and under-theorized aspects of distributing flyers: the rhetorician's consideration of public space, the law and corporeal risks inherent in certain kinds of delivery. From Katie's story, Nancy Welch is able to show how knowledge of rhetorical delivery often comprises additional knowledge about places, organizations, institutions, technologies, and people. Welch's telling of Katie's story challenges the field to think about the legal and corporeal risks as well as specific knowledge associated with certain forms of activist delivery. Given the valuable knowledge such activist stories are poised to reveal, the field needs more stories of practice. This need constitutes perspective that's largely absent from the field's research and literature on rhetorical delivery.

As Holmberg provoked the field to consider in 1980, delivery also obscures. The rhetorician's knowledge and strategy is not a metadata packet attached to texts or their movement. This work of uncovering such knowledge for students and the field requires research methods such as interviews and other human subject protocols. But these research methods are not without their own problems. For example, in my own study of political activist Maggie Corser in my *Rhetoric Review* article "Rhetorical Delivery as Strategy: Researching the Fifth Canon through Practitioner Stories," I interviewed her after-the-fact and introduced the problem of hindsight into the equation. In addition, she was also prompted by my instrument questions to think about the delivery of her text. While I think that her reflections are true to the spirit of events and tell a useful story for rethinking rhetorical delivery as strategy, we cannot rely on merely studying the location of texts at different points in time (movement and speed) as a means to understand delivery in the twenty-first century. The missing element, a rhetor's own perspective on her strategy, needs to be at the forefront of our delivery research.

3. Carolyn Rude's insights into an "expanded sense of delivery" raise several questions for researchers: What are some of the challenges to studying rhetorical delivery? Should researchers focus on the print or digital location of texts across time and place or should we engage with practitioners directly? Based on the work of Carl Holmberg, I would argue that both areas of delivery research are important. In his 1980 *Rhetoric Society Quarterly* piece "Some Available Conceptions of Rhetorical Experience," he considers Aristotelian oral delivery, *hypokrisis*, as the "concealing of motives" (138). Through a literal translation of the Greek *"hypo"* as under and *"krisis"* as judgment, he posits a definition of *hypokrisis* as "under-judgment." Holmberg hypothesizes that "perhaps the Greeks realized that delivery is also a matter of what is concealed by the overt delivery as well as what can be revealed by the concealment of the delivery" (138). If Holmerg's discussion of oral delivery has even the smallest application to print and digital delivery, what does this mean methodologically?

4. Prior to my 2012 Fulbright research trip to collect Samaritan stories and responses to questions about their manuscripts, I had four years of electronic contact with the Samaritan community through the digitization project through, largely Benyamim Tsedaka. My history of contact included 2009 fieldwork on Mount Gerizim and Holon for user-center design testing with Samaritan young people (see Ridolfo, Hart-Davidson, and McLeod 2010 and 2012), a second trip in the summer of 2010 to Holon, and Facebook/e-mail contact with members of the community during and after the first year of the NEH Office of Digital Humanities Start-up Grant project. While the Samaritans do not have any official ambassadors, Benyamim Tsedaka is an ambassador for his people. As Sameer Yousef Sarrawi explains, Tsedaka is "an Ambassador for the Samaritans" to the outside world because he goes abroad every year in order to maintain his "good connections with teachers and professors at universities abroad" interested in Samaritan studies through his lectures and his publication of the *A.B. Samaritan News*. Zolovon Altif agrees and remarks that the world knows about the Samaritans and studies their manuscripts thanks to "this Mr. Benny, [who] went all over the world to tell [the world about] the Samaritans" and who we are. Tsedaka is an important and recognized contact between the Samaritan community and the outside world, and I have primarily worked with him to gain access to community members for interviews related to this book project.

5. Starting at the beginning of my Fulbright in February 2012, Tsedaka helped me to identify a snowball sample, a sample in which I was assisted by a member of the group in forming the interview sample, of Samaritans that I should interview about the diaspora of Samaritan manuscripts. Tsedaka also wrote a letter of sponsorship for my Fulbright and his small research center in Holon, the A.B. Samaritan Institute, was my primary host institution for Israel. My snowball sample included Samaritans he felt had an interest in Samaritan scribal practices, codices, and scrolls. This informed convenience sample of Samaritan society included Samaritans active in cultural matters with broader Palestinian civil society, respected community members that still scribe Samaritan manuscripts in the ancient script, and members of families possessing rare manuscripts. Given that Samaritan ritual writing is historically a male practice, the snowball sample focused on male voices in the Samaritan community. It's important to note however that Samaritan women are also involved in Samaritan writing and cultural production. For example, in 2004 the late Batya Tsedaka published a Samaritan handwriting book for children. Miriam Tsedaka is the foremost painter in the commu-

nity and has won awards for her work on Samaritan life. Samaritan women also serve in a leadership capacity on the community councils.

6. While some scholars have studied delivery by examining archival examples (Powell; Buchannan; Mountford), others have examined contemporary examples of practice via documents and interviews (N. Welch). I'd argue that both approaches have something to tell the field. For example, Malea Powell's work has been particularly successful in uncovering and theorizing stories of native rhetorics from archival material. Her historiographic research is especially important because it helps to establish a historical record of native rhetorical practices that would have otherwise would have been erased and suppressed by European colonialists. As Powell argues, telling stories of practice has the power to challenge notions of a singular rhetorical canon or tradition. My approach works across archival, secondary literature, and interviews with Samaritans to develop a more comprehensive rhetorical picture. I say rhetorical picture both to describe the research topic and to identify that this work is itself not absent from a rhetorical situation in which I, as a researcher/collaborator with the community, pursue a convenience sample bounded in place, time, and situation. While I believe the results of my work have a valuable story to tell, I also equally believe in the limits of my own subject position as a researcher/collaborator from the West.

7. This includes the work that I've been doing at http://samaritanreposity.org as part of the ongoing digitization project. At the time of writing this chapter, samaritan-reposity.org includes manuscripts from Michigan State University Special Collections and Hebrew Union College—Jewish Institute of Religion Klau Library in Cincinnati. The server is hosted in the United Kingdom in order to provide an optimal mirror for the Samaritans in the West Bank and Israel, and biblical/Samaritan scholars in Europe and the United States. Prior to hosting the repository in the UK, I hosted the repository on a colocated server in Seattle, Washington. This location proved to be too slow to access across the transatlantic cable.

8. It is important to contextualize these interviews, then, as not representative of the entire Samaritan population but as individual case examples or what Julie Lindquist calls "socially situated acts of rhetoric" (9). Furthermore, these case examples represent a snapshot in time of a small portion of the population, a convenience sample, however, that's far more qualitatively significant to the subject matter than its statistical percentage of the overall population. This convenience sample of Samaritan insight, then, should be understood as rhetorics of time, place, and audience. While I have access through Tsedaka for interviews, I am not an insider to this community. As rhetorics and stories they are, however, highly informative and valuable not only to their own community but also to scholarly audiences in rhetorical studies and the digital humanities. Their stories, rather than presenting neat package of monolithic views, are valuable to both fields for their nuance and complexity on a number of issues related to access and delivery. It's also important to anticipate that the views expressed by Samaritan community leaders will continue to change. For example, on September 4, 2012, Benyamim Tsedaka published a public request on Facebook calling for the return of Samaritan artifacts from Israeli museums to Mount Gerizim:

The place for the many findings that were found on Mount Gerizim should be in a museum that will be built on Mount Gerizim, on the top the mountain of our life and glory, with all means of secured display. The place should not be at a Christian site nor in the Rockefeller Museum storages in East Jerusalem but in their most natural place of our luxurious culture of our forefathers—In Mount Gerizim. (Tsedaka, "Why Are the Samaritan Antiquities that belong to the Israelite Samaritans in the Good Samaritan Inn Museum?")

9. Samaritans in the 2012 snowball sample included everyone that Benyamim Tsedaka believed was still practicing the Samaritan scribal arts. The snowball sample includes Benyamim Tsedaka (b. 1944), Yacop Cohen (b. 1970), Menashe Altif (b. 1938), Ovadia Cohen (b. 1964), Zolovon (Fayyad) Altif (b. 1929), Raqheb Fara (b. 1940), Ghayth Cohen (b. 1967), Sameer Yousef Sarrawi (b. 1950), and Osher Sassoni (b. 1979). With the exception of Benyamim Tsedaka and Osher Sassoni who live in Holon (Tsedaka lives in his apartment on Mount Gerizim half the year and was also born in Nablus), all of the seven of the nine interviewed reside on Mount Gerizim all year. As Zolovon (Fayyad) Altif explains, "every Samaritan has two names. An Arab name and a Hebrew name. My Arab name is Fayyad (Overflowing). My Hebrew name is Zvolon Ben Yosef the Son of Zvloon and the son if Itzhak, from the tribe called Dinti" (Altif, Zolovon). To avoid confusion in this manuscript, I have listed interviewees by the name they used the most before and during our interviews. This 2012 snowball sample included eight participants, including Tsedaka, or just over 1 percent of the total Samaritan population of 750. In February 2012, Tsedaka estimated there were 750 Samaritans. 751 by April 2012 and 755 by October 2012. Osher Sassoni was interviewed in Tel Aviv during the summer of 2014. We came in contact after I published a Hebrew article on the digital repository and keyboard project for the *A.B. Samaritan Newspaper* earlier in 2014.

10. This question, "what do you want from your manuscripts?," is also a rhetorical question and leads to a productive theoretical connection between rhetoric and the digital humanities. In this sense, the Samaritan example provides an excellent case to more closely examine where rhetoric and the digital humanities intersect.

11. For the majority of these interviews, Tsedaka was present. In the case of two interviews carried out primarily in Arabic, Tsedaka served as a translator. He and I agreed that a member of the community who is familiar with cultural and familial nuances is preferable, and he was also my primary point of access to the community for the snowball sample. Interviews were recorded and later transcribed and translated, and in several cases I sought out a third opinion on the translation of specific passages. After interviews, I talked with Tsedaka about what I heard and we had conversations about themes I was noticing in the meetings. This engagement provided the space to reflect on my understanding of stories and to verify dates, facts, and spellings. In doing so, I was influenced by Cushman's (Cushman; Cushman and Green) ideas of reciprocity, or trying to understand how the resharing of stories might call attention to Samaritan interests in the conservation, preservation, and digitization of their manuscripts, and Sullivan and Porter's call for critical and reflexive research practices and Jeff Grabill's ideas about research stance. My background studying Modern Hebrew allowed me to carry out, transcribe, and translate interviews; however, there were only two interviews that were completely in Hebrew. For most, the interviews were a mixture of English and Hebrew. In some cases, I sought out an outside opinion on Hebrew translations. While I had in 2012 approximately two years of university Arabic study including several months of Palestinian dialect, I relied on the help of Benyamim Tsedaka to translate Arabic interviews in real-time. As Tsedaka is a member of the community, that made the most sense to me as a researcher. I also sought out outside interpretations

of Arabic responses and continued Arabic study, returning to the interviews over the next two years. By the time I returned in 2014, I had completed three years of university Arabic and four months of independent tutoring in Palestinian dialect.

12. He means the community does not have the money to purchase their books from abroad. Samaritan manuscripts regularly go up for auction/private sale. There are no estimated numbers about the private number of Samaritan manuscripts abroad, but based on recent trends from Kedem Auction House and the like, there are easily several thousand.

13. Beyond my own project, today there are a small but growing number of digitized manuscripts on the Internet. See http://samaritanrepository.org for a map of these new digital resources.

14. Raqheb Fara's last name in Hebrew is Marchiv—מרחיב.

15. Zolovon Altif describes the history of Samaritan manuscript acquisition as follows, focusing specifically on Firkovich as a turning point:

> Once the Samaritans were millions. Now the Samaritans are hundreds. And of course, when they were millions, they had many manuscripts. And because they suffered very much from tyranny and from wars, and from every other troubles. They were obliged to give or forget their manuscripts. And because all the people are interested in studying these manuscripts they were eager to have it. But to have it this began only about 150 years ago. Before that the Samaritans refused to give anybody one of their manuscripts. But after a Russian Priest (Firkovich), came from Russia and he was wealthy . . . and he was able to buy some of the Samaritans. How? He convinced a Samaritan to convince the Samaritan priests to sell them. The Samaritans at that time were very very poor. They don't have any one thing to eat. So he offered them 200 gold bans. Now the high priest took 100, and the man took another 50, and the rest was separated to all the other community. And during that week, all the Samaritans began to eat Mujadara . . . because they [finally] have money. Now after a month or two weeks even they . . . to the corner of the synagogue of that . . . was empty. Because they sold them [the manuscripts] to Firkovich! Now they [the Samaritans] were very angry. Where, where, where. Oh he [Firkovich] took them and [but] he was drowned in the sea. And because of that [Firkovich dying] they forgot everything about it [the manuscripts]. Time went on. The manuscripts went to Russia . . .

16. See http://en.wikipedia.org/wiki/Wikipedia:ARBPIA.

17. See   http://en.wikipedia.org/wiki/Template:Arab-Israeli_Arbitration_Enforcement.

18. Although throughout this book I discuss the Samaritan diaspora specifically, the term is more broadly applicable to other groups with similar circumstances.

19. The full text of Tsedaka's call for the repatriation of artifacts can be found in appendix C.

20. At the time of writing this manuscript, the contents of the Rockefeller museum in East Jerusalem may be moving to a new location.

21. By situated in time and place I mean that these responses do not constitute an absolute and unchanging position on these issues. Rather, responses on these topics may change over time.

Chapter Four

1. For more about the field intersections of rhetoric and the digital humanities, see my coauthored introduction to *Rhetoric and the Digital Humanities* (2015).

2. In Matthew Kirschenbaum's 2010 piece in the ADE bulletin "What Is Digital Humanities and What's It Doing in English Departments?," he defines the digital humanities as "a field of study, research, teaching, and invention concerned with the intersection of computing and the disciplines of the humanities. It is methodological by nature and interdisciplinary in scope. It involves investigation, analysis, synthesis and presentation of information in electronic form. It studies how these media affect the disciplines in which they are used, and what these disciplines have to contribute to our knowledge of computing" (Kirschenbaum 56).

3. Some ODH funding for scholars in R/C include Potts and Gossett 2012; Carter 2011; Ball, Eyman, and Gossett 2010; Hart-Davidson and Ridolfo 2008) and a NEH Digging into Data grant (Rehberger 2010).

4. Ellen Cushman's early work on rhetoric and social change, "The Rhetorician," and especially her ongoing collaborative new media work with the Cherokee Nation (Cushman and Green), has significantly influenced my work.

5. Cushman also raises the questions: "Why archive in the first place? What types of mediation and information make collecting and displaying possible? What types of knowledge work do archives make possible and limit? These questions point to the problems of imperialist archives that establish Western tradition by collecting and preserving artifacts from othered traditions" (119).

6. Hebrew Union College—Jewish Institute of Religion published several hundred print copies of Tsedaka's catalogue and hosted a release party at the Cincinnati Klau Library for Tsedaka's work. The director of HUC-JIR's libraries, Dr. David Gilner, has supported Tsedaka's project and values his insights into the HUC-JIR collection. For Gilner, helping Tsedaka conduct his catalogue work is valuable work. See HUC-JIR catalogue entry: Tsedaka, Benyamim. *Osef Kitve Ha-Yad Ha-Shomronim Be-Sifriyat Ḳla'u, Hiberu Yuniyon Ḳoleg', Sisinaṭt, Ohayo, Arh"b =: The Collection of Samaritan Manuscripts in the Klau Library of the Hebrew Union College–Jewish Institute of Religion, Cincinnati, Ohio, USA.* Cincinnati: Hebrew Union College—Jewish Institute of Religion. 2011. Print. Available at: CIN RBR (PJ 4860 T7.4 2011), CIN Reference (PJ 4860 T7.4 2011), LA Stacks folio (PJ 4860 T7.4 2011).

7. Tsedaka's catalogue descriptions may also be relevant to scholars interested in how Tsedaka describes the materials.

8. See Natalie Cesario and Adeline Koh for background on the "hack/yack" debates in DH, where "yack" is generally understood to be the critical/media theory necessary to explain acts of "hack" or practice and making.

9. The objective of the Samaritan repository to provide multiple portals may be viewed in contrast to the recent Dead Sea Scrolls exhibition where, as Norman Golb explains in "The Current Controversy Over The Dead Sea Scrolls, With Special Reference To The Exhibition At The Field Museum Of Chicago," the exhibit descriptions were locked down by the Israeli Antiquities Authority (IAA), leading scholars to question the "exhibition's overall equitability" (Golb).

10. The primary work of core team members on the 2008–2009 NEH ODH is inquiry-based design. William Hart-Davidson, Michael McLeod, and I researched as a set of writing and reading practices the interest of the three stakeholder groups: Samaritan community stakeholders, biblical/Samaritan scholars, and legacy stake-

holders. The features of both the main archive site and the proposed mobile application are representations of what individual stakeholder groups want to *do* with the manuscripts in digital environments, and theories about the way users' work can be productively transformed to meet shared goals. Our design work is research-based because we seek to carefully vet theories-made-manifest in our software by examining 1) when and how users use the systems' features and 2) if the outcome is successful for our stakeholder groups. We answer these questions by watching real users doing real tasks—sometimes presented in more controlled settings like a usability lab and sometimes out there in the field—and analyzing the results.

Our research methods are typical of user-centered design research and represent a range of naturalistic observation and follow-up interviewing techniques to controlled, lab-based testing. We work with representatives of each stakeholder group and each user role throughout the development process to refine the design. User-centered design (UCD) inquiry yields the best results when we have clear and realistic tasks for which we define success conditions that have clear, measurable indicators. But before we can run scenario-based tasks in a lab setting, we must understand the goal-oriented tasks and motivations of users in each of the three stakeholder roles. So our UCD questions begin at a high level, for example, what do community stakeholders wish to focus on when they access the online codices?

For these higher-level questions, we used a method known as "Contextual Inquiry" (CI) (Beyer and Holtzblatt 1995), which pairs direct user observations of users conducting work-related activity with interviews that elicit details from participants about goals, motives, and expectations as they relate to the operational details of a given task. CI methods typically produce "work models" at various levels of abstraction that represent the way work should proceed from users' point of view (Beyer and Holtzblatt 1993). In practice, CI interviews proceed like a play-by-play analysis, where the user provides commentary on a task either while it is going on or retrospectively in response to an activity log or recording. We also used CI methods to evaluate proposed solutions to issues that have been uncovered. Users are shown wireframes and mockups meant to address problems or enable actions mentioned in a previous CI interview. We then solicited feedback about the proposed solutions to refine them before committing resources to the development of new code.

Our mainstay for usability evaluation is the scenario-based test which involves asking users to perform a specific task with a known set of success conditions, usually in a semi-controlled environment so that we can monitor time on task, note errors or problems encountered, and measure success (Neilsen 1987; Carroll 2000). Pre- and post-test (and occasionally post-task) questionnaires are used with scenario-based tests to gather complimentary data regarding user satisfaction and confidence. If a user failed a task, for instance, but is confident that she completed it successfully, this tells us that we have a design problem to solve.

11. This diaspora of manuscripts is what initially motivated Benyamim Tsedaka to travel around Europe and North America.

12. Over the last six years, this has resembled what Howe suggests in terms of process:

Once formal contact between the head authorities of the mainstream institution and a partner community is established and agreement has been reached to proceed, a five-phase iterative process is set in motion. The five phases are characterized by an important meeting between representatives from both the tribal community and mainstream institution. These meetings punctuate the continuous process of fieldwork and research that goes into developing a tribal history and represent moment of decision making and work review. The locations of these meetings alternate between the two partners: the first, third, and fifth are in the community, the second and fourth are at the institution. (Howe 192)

13. Everson and Shoulson note that until 2008 there had not been a UNICODE proposal for Samaritan submitted to the Consortium:

C. Technical—Justification

1. Has this proposal for addition of character(s) been submitted before? If YES, explain.
   No.
2a. Has contact been made to members of the user community (for example: National Body, user groups of the script or characters, other experts, etc.)?
   Yes.
2b. If YES, with whom?
   Alan Crown, Osher Sassoni, Benny Tsedaka
2c. If YES, available relevant documents
3. Information on the user community for the proposed characters (for example: size, demographics, information technology use, or publishing use) is included?
   Ecclesiastical and cultural communities. (21)

14. The Samaritan script or simply "Ancient Hebrew script" as it is known in the Samaritan culture is a Paleo-Hebraic script that differs from the Aramaic script used by biblical and Modern Hebrew. While the UNICODE format calls this character set "Samaritan," Benyamim Tsedaka reminds us that "Samaritan" is a recent term for Ancient Hebrew, and that it's more appropriate to call this writing the "Ancient Hebrew used [and still used] by the Israelite Samaritans." As a parallel example, it would not be appropriate to call Ancient Hebrew in Aramaic script "Jewish Hebrew," as both Israelite groups have used the two character sets in their historical artifacts (Tsedaka, "Introductuon").

15. In the next phase of the project our team plans to iteratively research, design, and deliver both web and mobile versions of our repository project. Designed as single web service, the system will include an EAD compliant web-based repository of Samaritan manuscripts with interactive features specified in our Digital Start Up project including multiple information architectures for user-specific (i.e., "faceted") browsing and shared annotations. We also have plans to design an algorithmic tool to do handwriting analysis specific to the needs of Samaritan scholars.

Chapter Five

1. The *kūfiyyah* is also especially significant and meaningful for Palestinians. See Mohammed Assaf's winning performance of *ʒly al- kūfiyyah* (Raise the *kūfiyyah*) on Arab Idol.
2. The Samaritans have recently published a community cookbook of their recipes

in Hebrew. There's also a plan to translate the book into English as a means to more broadly convey the diversity of Samaritan culture.

3. http://quod.lib.umich.edu/cgi/r/rsv/rsv-idx?type=DIV1&byte=4782437.

4. From http://www.samaritanmedal.org. Some recent recipients of the Samaritan Medal for Peace and Humanitarian Achievement have included Israeli equal rights attorney Michael Corinaldi, Secretary-General of the Palestine General Federation of Trade Unions (PGFTU) Shaher A.F. Sa'ed, former mayor of Nablus Ghassan Al-Shaq'ah, Palestinian billionaire and philanthropist Munib al-Masri, and Israeli President Shimon Peres/The Peres Center for Peace.

5. See for example:

Hafiz, Yasmine. "Yazidi Religious Beliefs: History, Facts, and Traditions of Iraq's Persecuted Minority." *The Huffington Post*. HuffingtonPost.com, 13 Aug. 2014. Web. 8 Sept. 2014.

Jalabi, Raya. "Who Are the Yazidis and Why Is Isis Hunting Them?" Theguardian.com. Guardian News and Media, 11 Aug. 2014. Web. 8 Sept. 2014.

Miller, Jake. "Who Are the Yazidis Targeted by Militants in Iraq?" CBSNews. CBS Interactive, 10 Aug. 2014. Web. 8 Sept. 2014.

Tharoor, Ishaan. "Who Are the Yazidis?" *Washington Post*. WashingtonPost.com, 7 Aug. 2014. Web. 8 Sept. 2014.

6. According to the *Encyclopedia Iranica*, the Yazidi's "core religious texts are the qawls, hymns in Kurmanji which are often dedicated to a ḵāṣṣ and which make frequent allusions to events and persons not explained in the texts. These have, for most of their history, been orally transmitted" ("Yazidi").

7. See especially Dakhil, Vian. "Iraqi MP Breaks Down in Tears Pleading Parliament to Save Yazidis from Genocide." YouTube, 14 Aug. 2014. Web. 8 Sept. 2014. https://www.youtube.com/watch?v=5WBbIA20eE4.

8. See work by Sun, Hart-Davidson, Potts and Graban, Ramsey-Tobienne and Myers referenced in chapters 1 and 4.

9. See:

"Down By the River, or How Susan LaFlesche Can Teach Us About Alliance as a Practice of Survivance." *College English* 67.1 (September) 2004. 38–60.

"Rhetorics of Survivance: How American Indians Use Writing." *College Composition and Communication* 53.3 (February) 2002. 396–434.

10. See also:

Cushman, Ellen. *The Cherokee Syllabary: Writing The People's Perseverance.* Norman: University of Oklahoma Press, 2011.

11. See also:

Haas, Angela M. "Subject Matter Expert Meets Technical Communicator: Stories of Mestiza Consciousness in the Automotive Industry." In *Negotiating Cultural Encounters: Narrating Intercultural Engineering and Technical Communication.* Eds. Han Yu and Gerald Savage. IEEE Press, 2013. 227–45.

Haas, Angela M. Race, "Rhetoric, and Technology: A Case Study of Decolonial

Technical Communication Theory, Methodology, and Pedagogy." *Journal of Business and Technical Communication* 26.3 (June) 2012. 277–310.

12. My understanding of the conversation around "making" in the digital humanities is that for the time being, making is largely in relationship to relationship to scholarly audiences, and is not yet a response to the needs of external community stakeholders (see, for example, http://maker.uvic.ca. Such a turn for DH would be rhetorical, situated in UX/UCD, and would respond to community literacy needs. As I argue in chapter 4, such engaged work would require field research and relationship building with communities.

13. Arabic Wikipedia as of September 2014: *Al Harb 3la Gaza* or The war on Gaza; Hebrew Wikipedia: *Mivtsa Tsuk Eitan*, literally "strong cliff" but Israeli English title is Operation Protective Edge.

Bibliography

Aaron, Jacob ben. *The Messianic Hope of the Samaritans.* Trans. Abdullah Ben Kori. Reprinted from The Open Court, May and Sept, 1907. Print.

Abood, Jill. "Michigan State University Libraries." MSS 287 *Chamberlain Warren Samaritan Collection.* Michigan State University, 20 Nov. 2006. Web. 12 Jan. 2012.

"About Société D'Études Samaritaines." *Société D'Études Samaritaines.* N.p., n.d. Web. 08 July 2012.

Ackerman, John, and David Coogan. *The Public Work of Rhetoric: Citizen-Scholars and Civic Engagement.* Columbia: University of South Carolina, 2010. Print.

Adler, Lydia D. *The Holy Land.* Ed. Edward H. Anderson. N.p.: Desert News, 1912. Print.

Altif, Menashe. Personal interview on Mount Gerizim. 19 April 2012.

Altif, Zolovon. Personal interview on Mount Gerizim. 16 May 2012.

Anderson, Robert T. "The Museum Trail: The Michigan State University Samaritan Collection." *The Biblical Archaeologist* 47.1 (1984): 41–43. Print.

Anderson, Robert T. "Samaritan History During the Renaissance." *The Samaritans.* Ed. Alan D. Crown. Tübingen: Mohr Siebeck, 1989. 95–112. Print.

Anderson, Robert T., and Terry Giles. *The Keepers: An Introduction to the History and Culture of the Samaritans.* Peabody, MA: Hendrickson, 2002. Print.

Aristotle. *The Complete Works of Aristotle: The Revised Oxford Translation.* Ed. Jonathan Barnes. Princeton: Princeton UP, 1984. Print.

Aristotle. *The Basic Works of Aristotle.* Ed. Richard McKeon. New York: Modern Library, 2001. Print.

"Award Information—Fulbright Scholar Catalog of Awards." *Award Information—Fulbright Scholar Catalog of Awards.* Fulbright Scholar Program, 2011. Web. 18 June 2012.

Ayers, Daniel H. "Samaritan Annals and the Mystic Name." *The American Tyler-Keystone* 22.1 (1907): 123–25. Web. 08 Dec. 2013.

Barton, William E. *The Samaritan Pentateuch: The Story of a Survival Among the Sects.* Oberlin: The Bibliotheca Sacra Company, 1903. Print.

Barton, William E. "The War and the Samaritan Colony." *Bibliotheca Sacra: A Religious and Sociological Quarterly* 78 (1921): 1–22. Print.

Bazerman, Charles, and Paul A. Prior. *What Writing Does and How It Does It: An Introduction to Analyzing Texts and Textual Practices.* Mahwah, NJ: Lawrence Erlbaum Associates, 2004. Print.

Benardi, Elad, and Yoni Kempinski. "Mt. Gerizim Archaeological Site Reopens—Inside Israel—News—Israel National News." *Israel National News* 6 July 2012. Web. 10 July 2012.

Benjamin, Walter. 1968. "The Work of Art in the Age of Mechanical Reproduction." In

Illuminations. Eds. Walter Benjamin and Hannah Arendt. London: Fontana, 1968. 214–18. Print.

Ben-Zvi, Yitzhak. *Sefer Ha-Shomronim: Toldoṭehem, Moshavoṭehem, Daṭem Ve-Sifruṭehem.* Tel Aviv: A.J. Shtybel, 1935. Print.

Bodenhamer, David J., John Corrigan, and Trevor M. Harris. *The Spatial Humanities: Gis and the Future of Humanities Scholarship.* Bloomington: Indiana University Press, 2010. Print.

Bonar, Andrew A., and Robt. M. M'cheyne. *Narrative of a Mission of Inquiry to the Jews from The Church of Scotland in 1839.* Philadelphia: Presbyterian Board of Publication, 1839. Print.

Bowman, John. *The Samaritan Problem: Studies in the Relationships of Samaritanism, Judaism, and Early Christianity.* Pittsburgh: Pickwick, 1975. Print.

Bowring, Dr. *The Weekly Christian Teacher* 2 (1839): 815–16. Web. 08 Dec. 2013.

Boyle, Casey. "Low Fidelity in High Definition: Speculations on Rhetorical Education." In *Rhetoric and the Digital Humanities.* Eds. Jim Ridolfo and William Hart-Davidson. Chicago: University of Chicago Press, 2015. 127–39. Print.

Buchanan, Lindal. *Regendering Delivery: The Fifth Canon and Antebellum Women Rhetors.* Carbondale: Southern Illinois UP, 2005. Print.

C., S. "Enquiry Concerning the Samaritans." *The Evangelical Magazine* 11 (1803): 536–37. Print.

Cameron, Fiona, and Sarah Kenderine. "Introduction." In *Theorizing Digital Cultural Heritage: A Critical Discourse.* Cambridge, MA: MIT Press, 2007. Print.

"Campus Compact." *Campus Compact Research University Engaged Scholarship Toolkit.* Campus Compact, n.d. Web. 16 Oct. 2013.

Christen, Kimberly. "Does Information Really Want to Be Free? Indigenous Knowledge Systems and the Question of Openness." *International Journal of Communication* 6 (2012): 2870–93. Print.

"Chronology: 16 November 1995—15 February 1996." *Journal of Palestine Studies* 25, no. 3 (Spring 1996): 164–84. Print.

Clair, Colin. *A Chronology of Printing.* New York: Praeger, 1969. Print.

Cohen, Ghayth. Personal interview on Mount Gerizim. 23 May 2012.

Cohen, S. Marc. "Aristotle's Metaphysics." *The Stanford Encyclopedia of Philosophy (Summer 2012 Edition).* Ed. Edward N. Zalta. Stanford University, 8 Oct. 2000. Web. 08 Dec. 2013.

Cohen, Yacop. Personal interview in Holon, Israel. 28 Feb. 2012.

Connors, Robert J. "Actio: A Rhetoric of Manuscripts." *Rhetoric Review* 2.1 (1983): 64–73. Print.

Corbett, Edward P. J. *Classical Rhetoric for the Modern Student.* 1st ed. New York: Oxford UP, 1965. Print.

Cornhill Magazine. "The Pigeon as a War Messenger." *The Living Age* (Sept. 1887): 57–62. Print.

Cowley, Arthur E. "Descriptions of Four Samaritan Manuscripts Belonging to the Palestine Exploration Fund." *Quarterly Statement—Palestine Exploration Fund* (1904): 67–78. Web. 08 Dec. 2013.

Crown, Alan David. *A Catalogue of the Samaritan Manuscripts in the British Library.* London: Library, 1998. Print.

Crown, Alan David. "Ben-Zvi, Yitzhak [Yishak Shimshelevitz]." *Encyclopedia of Modern Jewish Culture.* Vol. 2. Ed. Glenda Abramson. London: Routledge, 2005. 129–30. Print.

Crown, Alan D. *The Samaritans*. Tübingen: J.C.B. Mohr (Paul Siebeck), 1989. Print.

Crown, Alan David. *Samaritan Scribes and Manuscripts*. Tübingen: Mohr Siebeck, 2001. Print.

Crown, Alan David., Reinhard Pummer, and Abraham Tal. *A Companion to Samaritan Studies*. Tübingen: J. C. B. Mohr, 1993. Print.

Cushman, Ellen. "The Rhetorician as an Agent of Social Change." *CCC* 47.1 (1996): 7–28. Print.

Cushman, Ellen. "Wampum, Sequoyan, and Story: Decolonizing the Digital Archive." *College English* 76.2 (2013): 115–35. Print.

Cushman, Ellen., and Erik Green. "Knowledge Work with the Cherokee Nation: Engaging Publics in a Praxis of New Media." *Public Work of Rhetoric*. Eds. John Ackerman and David Coogan. Columbia: University of South Carolina Press, 2010. 175–93. Print.

Deegan, Marilyn, and Willard McCarthy. *Collaborative Research in the Digital Humanities*. Farnham: Ashgate, 2012. Print.

DeVoss, Dànielle Nicole, and James E. Porter. "Why Napster Matters to Writing: File-sharing as a New Ethic of Digital Delivery." *Computers and Composition* 23.1 (2006): 178–210. Print.

DeVoss, Danielle Nicole, Ellen Cushman, and Jeffrey T. Grabill. "The When of New-Media Writing." *College Composition and Communication* 57.1 (2005): 14–44. Print.

Diehl, Amy, Jeff Grabill, Bill Hart-Davidson, and Vishal Iyer. "Grassroots: Supporting the Knowledge Work of Everyday Life." *Technical Communication Quarterly* 17 (2008): 413–34. Print.

"The Digital Dead Sea Scrolls." *Digital Dead Sea Scrolls at the Israel Museum, Jerusalem*. N.p. 2012. Web. 27 June 2012.

Doberneck, Diane N., Chris R. Glass, and John Schweitzer. "From Rhetoric to Reality: A Typology of Publically Engaged Scholarship." *Journal of Higher Education Outreach & Engagement* 14.4 (2010): 5–35. Web. 08 Dec. 2013.

Dobkina, Liza. "UNESCO Grants Funding, Heritage Status to Bethlehem." *Reuters*. Thomson Reuters, 29 June 2012. Web. 10 July 2012.

Dobrin, Sidney I. *Postcomposition*. Carbondale: Southern Illinois UP, 2011. Print.

Doumani, Beshara. "Scenes from Daily Life: The View from Nablus." *Journal of Palestine Studies* 34.1 (2004): 37–50. Web. 1 Nov. 2014.

Dragga, Sam. "The Ethics of Delivery." In *Rhetorical Memory and Delivery: Classical Concepts for Contemporary Composition and Communication*. Ed. John Frederick Reynolds. Hillsdale: Lawrence Erlbaum Associates, 1993. 79–95. Print.

Dubisar, Abby M., and Jason Palmeri. "Palin/Pathos/Peter Griffin: Political Video Remix and Composition Pedagogy." *Computers and Composition* 27.2 (2010): 77–93. Print.

Egerton, Lady Francis. *Journal of a Tour in the Holy Land in May and June, 1840*. London: Harrison and Co., 1840. Print.

Elliott, Charles B., M.A. F.R.S. *Travels in the Three Great Empires of Austria, Russia and Turkey*. Vol. 2. London: Richard Bentley, 1838. Print.

Enoch, Jessica, and David Gold. "Seizing the Methodological Moment: The Digital Humanities and Historiography in Rhetoric and Composition." *College English* 76.2 (2013): 105–14. Print.

Estrin, Daniel. "A West Bank Bid for Heritage Claims Holy Land." *National Public Radio*. NPR, 08 July 2012. Web. 10 July 2012.

Eubanks, Virginia. *Digital Dead End: Fighting for Social Justice in the Information Age*. Cambridge: MIT Press, 2011. Print.

Everson, Michael, and Mark Shoulson. "Proposal to Add the Samaritan Alphabet to the BMP of the UCS." *UC Berkeley Script Encoding Initiative (Universal Scripts Project)*. Universal Multiple-Octet Coded Character Set, 25 Jan. 2008. Web. 25 Nov. 2013.

Eyman, Douglas. *Digital, Rhetoric: Ecologies and Economies of Circulation*. Unpublished dissertation. East Lansing: Michigan State UP, 2007. Print.

Fara, Raqheb. Personal interview on Mount Gerizim. 23 May 2012.

Field, Henry M., D.D. *Among the Holy Fields*. New York: Charles Scribner's Sons, 1884. Print.

Fine, Steven. *The Israelite Samaritan Version of the Torah: First English Translation Compared with the Masoretic Version*. Trans. Benyamim Tsedaka. Eds. Benyamim Tsedaka and Sharon Sullivan. Grand Rapids, MI: Eerdmans, 2013. xiii–xiv. Print.

Finn, James. "The Samaritans." *The Sunday Magazine for Family Reading*. London: Daldy, Isbister & Co., 1875. 225–32. Print.

Florentin, Moshe. *Late Samaritan Hebrew: A Linguistic Analysis of its Different Types*. Leiden: Brill, 2005. Print.

Flower, Linda. *Community Literacy and the Rhetoric of Public Engagement*. Carbondale: Southern Illinois UP, 2008. Print.

Franklin, Stephen. "In an Angry Land, Samaritans Find Peace." *Chicago Tribune*, April 5, 1990, p. 8.

Fredal, James. "The Language of Delivery and the Presentation of Character: Rhetorical Action in Demosthenes' Against Meidias." *Rhetoric Review* 20.3/4 (2001): 251–67. Print.

Gaster, Moses "The Story of My Library." *The British Library Journal*. Vol. 21, no. 1 (1995): 16–22. Print.

Getto, Guiseppe, Ellen Cushman, and Shreelina Ghosh. "Community Mediation: Writing in Communities and Enabling Connections through New Media." *Computers and Composition* 28.2 (2011): 160–74. Print.

Golb, Norman. "The Oriental Institute of the University of Chicago." *The Current Controversy Over The Dead Sea Scrolls, With Special Reference To The Exhibition At The Field Museum Of Chicago*. The Oriental Institute at University of Chicago, n.d. Web. 07 Aug. 2014.

"Good Samaritans in Jerusalem Join in Prayers for Persecuted Jews of Europe." *Palestine Post*, January 31, 1944. 3.

Graban, Tarez Samra, Alexis Ramsey-Tobienne, and Whitney Myers. "In, Through, and About the Archive: What Digitization (Dis)Allows." *Rhetoric and the Digital Humanities*. Eds. Jim Ridolfo and William Hart-Davidson. Chicago: University of Chicago Press, 2015. 233–44. Print.

Grabill, Jeffrey T. *Community Literacy Programs and the Politics of Change*. Albany: State University of New York, 2001. Print.

Grabill, Jeffrey T. *Writing Community Change: Designing Technologies for Citizen Action*. Cresskill: Hampton, 2007. Print.

Grabill, Jeffrey T. "Infrastructure, Outreach and the Engaged Writing Program." *Going Public: What Writing Programs Learn from Engagement*. Eds. Shirley K. Rose and Irwin Weiser. Logan: Utah State University Digital Commons @ USU, 2010. 15–28. Web. 08 Dec. 2013.

Haas, Angela M. "Wampum as Hypertext: An American Indian Intellectual Tradition of Multimedia Theory and Practice." *Studies in American Indian Literatures* 19.4 (2007): 77–100. Print.

Hanley, Jeremy, MP. "Thank You for Your Letter of 3 August about the Samaritans."

Letter to The Lord Avebury. 22 Aug. 1995. In Benyamim Tsedaka and Efrat Tse-daka. "MEMO: The Samaritans Between the Israeli, Palestinian, and Jordanian Raindrops." Holon, Israel: A.B.-Institute of Samaritan Studies Press, 1998. N.p. Print.

Harviainen, Tapani, and Haseeb Shehadeh. "How Did Abraham Firkovich Acquire the Great Collection of Samaritan Manuscripts in Nablus in 1864?" *Studia Orientalia* 73 (1995): 167–92. Print.

Hayles, N. Katherine. *How We Became Posthuman: Virtual Bodies in Cybernetics, Literature, and Informatics.* Chicago: University of Chicago Press, 1999. Print.

Helsley, Sheri L. "A Special Afterword to Graduate Students in Rhetoric." *Rhetorical Memory and Delivery: Classical Concepts for Contemporary Composition and Communication.* Ed. John Fredrick Reynolds. Hillsdale: Lawrence Erlbaum Associates, 1993. 157–59. Print.

Holtzblatt, Karen, and Hugh R. Beyer. "Apprenticing with the Customer." *Communications of the ACM* 38.5 (1995): 45–52. Print.

Holtzblatt, Karen, and Sandra Jones. "Contextual Inquiry: A Participatory Technique for System Design." *Participatory Design: Principles and Practices.* Eds. Douglas Schuler and Aki Namioka. New York: Routledge, 1993. 177–210. Print.

Hoobler, Ellen. "To Take Their Heritage in Their Hands: Indigenous Self-Representation" *American Indian Quarterly* 30.3/4 (2006): 441–60. Print.

Howe, Craig. "Keep Your Thoughts Above the Trees: Ideas on Developing and Presenting." *Clearing a Path.* Ed. Nancy Shoemaker. New York: Routledge, 2002. 161–80. Print.

Jenkins, Henry, Sam Ford, and Joshua Green. *Spreadable Media: Creating Value and Meaning in a Networked Culture.* New York: New York University Press, 2013. Print.

Jowett, Rev. William, M.A. *Christian Researches in Syria and the Holy Land in 1823 and 1924 in Furtherance of the Objects of the Church Missionary Society.* Boston: Crocker and Brewster, 1826. Print.

Kartveit, Magnar. *The Origin of the Samaritans.* Leiden: Brill, 2009. Print.

Kaufman, Stephen. "Samaritan Political Identity." Thesis. Tel Aviv University, 1998. Web. 08 Dec. 2013.

Kershner, Isabel. "Unesco Adds Nativity Site in Bethlehem to World List." *New York Times.* 29 June 2012. Web. 10 July 2012.

Kirschenbaum, Matthew. "What Is Digital Humanities and What's It Doing in English Departments?" *Debates in the Digital Humanities.* Ed. Matthew K. Gold. Minneapolis: Minnesota UP, 2012. 3–11. Print.

Knoppers, Gary N. *Jews and Samaritans: The Origins and History of Their Early Relations.* Oxford: Oxford UP, 2013. Print.

Leaver, Simon. "Thank You for Your Letter of 24 December to the Prime Minister." Letter to Professor Cyrus Gordon. 12 Jan. 1998. In Benyamim Tsedaka and Efrat Tse-daka. "MEMO: The Samaritans Between the Israeli, Palestinian, and Jordanian Raindrops." Holon, Israel: A.B.-Institute of Samaritan Studies Press, 1998. N.p. Print.

Levinson, Chaim. "Samaritans Seek Opening of Holy Site Found in IDF Dig." *Haaretz.* 11 June 2010. Web. 10 July 2012.

Lindquist, Julie. *A Place to Stand: Politics and Persuasion in a Working-class Bar.* Oxford: Oxford UP, 2002. Print.

Lyons, Scott Richard. "Rhetorical Sovereignty: What Do American Indians Want From Writing?" *CCC* 51.3 (2000): 447–68. Print.

"MA Digital Humanities." King's College London, 2012. Web. 12 July 2012.

Magen, Yitzhak. "Mt. Gerizim." Judea and Samaria Civil Administration: Israel Nature and Parks Authority (2000): 1–11. Brochure.

McCorkle, Ben. "Harbingers of the Printed Page: Nineteenth-Century Theories of Delivery as Remediation." *Rhetoric Society Quarterly* 35.4 (2005): 25–49. Print.

McCorkle, Ben. *Rhetorical Delivery as Technological Discourse: A Cross-Historical Study.* Carbondale: Southern Illinois UP, 2012. Print.

"Mercy for Samaritans." *Palestine Post*, Dec. 10, 1947. 3.

Merriman, Helena. "The Modern Trials of the Ancient Samaritans." BBC News, Nablus. 3 Jan. 2011. Web. 10 Jan. 2012.

Mignolo, Walter D. "Epistemic Disobedience, Independent Thought and Decolonial Freedom." *Theory, Culture & Society* 26.7–8 (2009): 1–23. Print.

"The Ministry of Tourism Condemns the Declaration of Mt. Gerizim as an Israeli Nature Reserve." Ma'an News Agency. 4 July 2012. N.p. Web. 5 July 2012.

"Minutes of the Meeting of the Michigan State University Board of Trustees, November 14, 2013." Michigan State University. N.d. Web. 08 Dec. 2013.

Mitev, Nathalie. "Are Social Constructivist Approaches Critical?" *Handbook of Critical Information Systems Research: Theory and Application.* Eds. Debra Howcroft and Eileen Moore Trauth. Northampton: Edward Elgar, 2005. Print.

Montgomery, James. *The Samaritans, the Earliest Jewish Sect: Their History, Theology and Literature.* Philadelphia: John C. Winston Co., 1907. Print.

Môr, Menaḥēm. *Samaritans: Past and Present: Current Studies.* Berlin: De Gruyter, 2010. Print.

Morgenthau, Henry. "All in a Life-Time: Chapters from an Autobiography." *The World's Work* XLII (1921–1922): 57–71. Web. 08 Dec. 2013.

Mountford, Roxanne. *The Gendered Pulpit: Preaching in American Protestant Spaces.* Carbondale: Southern Illinois UP, 2005. Print.

"Mukurtu CMS." *Mukurtu CMS.* N.p. 2013. Web. 09 Dec. 2013. http://www.mukurtu. org/.

National Review. "Postal Communication, Past and Present." *The Living Age* (1887): 284–92. Print.

Nelms, Gerald, and Maureen Goggin. "The Revival of Classical Rhetoric for Modern Composition Studies: A Survey." *Rhetoric Society Quarterly* 23 (1993): 11–26. Print.

Newman, David. "From Bilateralism to Unilateralism: The Changing Territorial Discourses of Israel-Palestine Conflict Resolution." *The Israel-Palestine Conflict: Parallel Discourses.* Ed. Elizabeth G. Matthews. Abingdon, Oxon: Routledge, 2011. 51–66. Print.

Ng, Kwong B., and Jason Kucsma. *Digitization in the Real World: Lessons Learned from Small and Medium-Sized Digitization Projects.* New York: Metropolitan New York Library Council, 2010. Print.

Oliphant, Laurence. *Haifa or Life in Modern Palestine.* New York: Harper & Brothers, 1887. Print.

"One-Sixth of 160 Surviving Samaritan Jews Enter Israel for Permanent Resettlement." Jewish Telegraphic Agency. N.p., 15 Sept. 1949. Web. 13 Feb. 2015.

Pentek, Stephen P. "William E. Barton Collection of Samaritan Materials, School of Theology Library, Boston University." *Boston University School of Theology Library RSS.* Boston University. July 2000. Web. 29 Sept. 2013.

Porter, James E. "Recovering Delivery for Digital Rhetoric." *Computers and Composition* 26.4 (2009): 207–24. Print.

Potts, Liza. "Archive Experiences: A Vision for User-Centered Design in the Digital Humanities." In *Rhetoric and the Digital Humanities*. Eds. Jim Ridolfo and William Hart-Davidson. Chicago: University of Chicago Press, 2015. 255–63. Print.

Powell, Malea. "Rhetorics of Survivance: How American Indians Use Writing." *CCC* 53.3 (2002): 396–434. Print.

Powell, Malea. "Dreaming Charles Eastman: Cultural Memory, Autobiography, and Geography in Indigenous Rhetorical Histories." *Beyond the Archives: Research as a Lived Process*. Eds. Gesa Kirsch and Liz Rohan. Carbondale: Southern Illinois UP, 2008. 116–27. Print.

Pratt, Mary Louise. *Imperial Eyes: Travel Writing and Transculturation*. 2nd Ed. London and New York: Routledge, 2008. Print.

Prendergast, Catherine. *Buying into English: Language and Investment in the New Capitalist World*. Pittsburgh: University of Pittsburgh Press, 2008. Print.

Presner, Todd S, David Shepard, and Yoh Kawano. *Hypercities: Thick Mapping in the Digital Humanities*. Cambridge, MA: Harvard UP, 2014. Print.

Prime, William Cowper. *Tent Life in the Holy Land*. New York: Harper & Brothers, 1857. Print.

Prior, Paul, et al. "Re-Situating and Re-Mediating the Canons: A Cultural-Historical Remapping of Rhetorical Activity." *Kairos: A Journal of Rhetoric, Technology, and Pedagogy* 11.3 (May 2007). Web.

Pummer, Reinhard. *The Samaritans*. Leiden: E.J. Brill, 1987. Print.

Pummer, Reinhard. *Samaritan Marriage Contracts and Deeds of Divorce*. Vol. 1. Wiesbaden: Harrassowitz, 1993. Print.

R., T., and M. S. "Palestinians Welcome Including Bethlehem on World Heritage List." *Palestine News and Information Agency*. 30 June 2012. Web. 5 July 2012.

Randall, David Austin. *The Handwriting of God in Egypt, Sinai and the Holy Land: The Records of a Journey from the Great Valley of the West to the Sacred Places of the East*. Philadelphia: John E. Potter & Co., 1868. Print.

Ratcliffe, Krista. *Rhetorical Listening: Identification, Gender, Whiteness*. Carbondale: Southern Illinois UP, 2005. Print.

"Reflector." *Palestine Post*, Aug. 5, 1938. 6.

Rehberger, Dean. *Digging into Image Data to Answer Authorship Related Questions*. National Endowment for the Humanities Office of Digital Humanities, 2010. Web. 09 Dec. 2013.

Reynolds, John Fredrick. *Rhetorical Memory and Delivery: Classical Concepts for Contemporary Composition and Communication*. Ed. John Fredrick Reynolds. Hillsdale, NJ: Lawrence Erlbaum, 1993. Print.

Ridolfo, Jim. "Hello and a Question from a Researcher at Michigan State University." Message to Benyamim Tsedaka. 3 Jan. 2008. E-mail.

Ridolfo, Jim. "Rhetorical Delivery as Strategy: Researching the Fifth Canon through Practitioner Stories." *Rhetoric Review* 31.2 (2012): 117–29. Print.

Ridolfo, Jim, and Dànielle Nicole DeVoss. "Composing for Recomposition: Rhetorical Velocity and Delivery." *Kairos: A Journal of Rhetoric, Technology, and Pedagogy* 13.2 (2009). Web. 08 Dec. 2013.

Ridolfo, Jim, and William Hart-Davidson. "Introduction." In *Rhetoric and the Digital*

Humanities. Eds. Jim Ridolfo and William Hart-Davidson. Chicago: University of Chicago Press, 2015. 1–12. Print.

Ridolfo, Jim, Kendall Leon, Stacey Pigg, Amy Diehl, Martine Courant Rife, Douglas Walls, and Jeffery T. Grabill. "Collaboration and Graduate Student Professionalization in a Digital Humanities Research Center." *Collaborative Approaches to the Digital in English Studies.* Ed. Laura McGrath. CCDP/Utah State University, 2011. Web. 08 Dec. 2013.

Ridolfo, Jim, and Martine Courant Rife. "Rhetorical Velocity and Copyright: A Case Study on the Strategies of Rhetorical Delivery." *Copy(write): Intellectual Property in the Writing Classroom.* Eds. Martine Rife, Shaun Slattery, and Dànielle Nicole DeVoss. Anderson, SC: WAC Clearinghouse and Parlor Press, 2011. 223–44. Print.

Ridolfo, Jim, William Hart-Davidson, and Michael McLeod. "Balancing Stakeholder Needs: Archive 2.0 as Community-centred Design." *Ariadne* 63 (2010). Web. 08 Dec. 2013.

Ridolfo, Jim, William Hart-Davidson, and Michael McLeod. "Rhetoric and the Digital Humanities: Imagining the Michigan State University Israelite Samaritan Archive as a Thriving Social Network." *Journal of Community Informatics* 7.3 (2011). Web. 08 Dec. 2013.

Risam, Roopika, and Adeline Koh. "Mission Statement." *Postcolonial Digital Humanities.* #dhpoco, n.d. Web. 07 Aug. 2014.

Rockwell, Geoffrey, and Andrew Mactavish. "Multimedia." *A Companion to Digital Humanities.* Eds. Susan Schreibman, Ray Siemens, and John Unsworth. Oxford: Blackwell, 2004. 108–20. Print.

Ross, Dan. *Acts of Faith: A Journey to the Fringes of Jewish Identity.* New York: St. Martin's Press, 1982. Print.

Rothschild, Jean-Pierre. "Samaritan Manuscripts: A Guide to Collections and Catalogues." *The Samaritans.* Ed. Alan D. Crown. Tübingen: Mohr Siebeck, 1989. 771–95. Print.

Rude, Carolyn. "Toward an Expanded Concept of Rhetorical Delivery: The Uses of Reports in Public Policy Debates." *Technical Communication Quarterly* 13.3 (2004): 271–88. Print.

Sacy, Silvestre de. "Correspondence des Samaritaines de Nablouse." *Notices and Extraits des manuscrits de la Bibliotheque du Roi.* Paris: Imprimerie royale, 1831. xii. Print.

Sacy, Silvestre de. "On the Samaritans." *The Jewish Expositor, and Friend of Israel* 1 (1816): 87–95. Print.

Samaritan Documents: Relating to Their History, Religion, and Life. Ed. and trans. John Bowman. Pittsburgh: Pickwick, 1977. Print.

"The Samaritan Medal Foundation." *The Samaritan Medal Foundation.* N.p. 2013. Web. 25 Nov. 2013.

"Samaritan Museum." *Facebook.* N.p. 9 July 2012. Web. 10 July 2012.

"Samaritans." *JewishEncyclopedia.com.* The Kopelman Foundation, n.d. Web. 29 Sept. 2013.

"Samaritan to Visit." *Palestine Post,* Sept. 15, 1949. 3.

Sarrawi, Sameer Yousef. Personal interview on Mount Gerizim. 25 July 2012.

Sassoni, Osher. Personal interview in Tel Aviv, Israel. 13 August 2014.

Sayare, Scott, and Steven Erlanger. "Palestinians Win a Vote on Bid to Join Unesco." *New York Times.* 5 Oct. 2011. Web. 10 July 2012.

Schniedewind, William M. *A Social History of Hebrew: Its Origins through the Rabbinic Period.* New Haven: Yale UP, 2013. Print.

Schur, Nathan. *History of the Samaritans.* Frankfurt Am Main: Peter Lang, 1992. Print.

Schwartz, Hillel. *The Culture of the Copy: Striking Likenesses, Unreasonable Facsimiles.* New York: Zone Books, 1996. Print.

Scott, Richard Lyons. "Rhetorical Sovereignty: What Do American Indians Want from Writing?" *College Composition and Communication* 51.3 (2000): 447–68. Print.

Sedaka, Israel. "Izhak Ben Zvi, David Ben Gurion and the Samaritans." In *Samaritans: Past and Present.* Ed. Menachem Mor and Friedrich V. Reiterer. Berlin: Walter de Gruyter, 2010. 239–45. Print.

Selfe, Cynthia. "Computers in the English Departments: The Rhetoric of Technopower." *ADE Bulletin* 90 (1988): 63–67. Print.

Sheridan, David, Jim Ridolfo, and Tony Michel. "Beyond Snap, Crackle, and Pop: Toward a Theory and Pedagogy of Multimodal Public Rhetoric." *JAC* 25 (2005): 803–44. Print.

Sheridan, David, Jim Ridolfo, and Tony Michel. *The Available Means of Persuasion: Mapping a Theory and Pedagogy of Multimodal Public Rhetoric.* Anderson, SC: Parlor Press, 2012. Print.

Skinner-Linnenberg, Virginia. *Dramatizing Writing: Reincorporating Delivery in the Classroom.* Mahwah, NJ: Lawrence Erlbaum Associates, 1997. Print.

"Studying Beowulf." *Electronic Beowulf,* 3rd ed. Ed. Kevin S. Kiernan. University of Kentucky, 2011. Web. 13 Feb. 2015.

Suchman, Lucy. "Practice-based Design of Information Systems: Notes from the Hyperdeveloped World." *Information Society* 18.2 (2002): 139–44. Print.

Huatong Sun and William F. Hart-Davidson. "Binding the Material and the Discursive with a Relational Approach of Affordances." In Proceedings of the SIGCHI Conference on Human Factors in Computing Systems (CHI '14). New York: ACM, 2014. DOI=10.1145/2556288.2557185, http://doi.acm.org/10.1145/2556288.2557185.

Svensson, Patrick. "Envisioning the Digital Humanities." *DHQ: Digital Humanities Quarterly* 6.1 (2012): Web. 08 Dec. 2013.

Theimer, Kate. "Archives in Context and as Context." *Journal of Digital Humanities* 1.2 (2012). Web. 08 Dec. 2013.

Thomson, Rev. J.E.H. "The Samaritan Pentateuch, Its Date and Origin." *The Biblical Review* 6.1 (1921): 72–93. Print.

Trimbur, John. "Composition and the Circulation of Writing." *College Composition and Communication* 52.2 (2000): 188–219. Print.

Tristram, Henry B., MA. F.L.S. *The Land of Israel; A Journal of Travels in Palestine: Undertaken with Special Reference to Its Physical Character.* London: Society for Promoting Christian Knowledge, 1865. Print.

Tsedaka, Benyamim. "The Four Principles of the Israelite Samaritan Faith." *A.B. Samaritan News.* Vol. 1103–1104. February 15, 2012. 58.

Tsedaka, Benyamim. "The Jewish and Samaritan Legends about the Lost Tribes." *A.B. Samaritan News.* Vol. 1109–1110. 2012, 95.

Tsedaka, Benyamim. "Medal: Samaritan Medal for Achievement in Peace, Humanitarian, or Samaritan Studies." http://www.israelite-samaritans.com/medal/. A.B. Samaritan Institute, 2008. Web. 11 Feb. 2015.

Tsedaka, Benyamim. "Re: Hello and a Question from a Researcher at Michigan State University." Message to Jim Ridolfo. 4 Jan. 2008. E-mail.

Tsedaka, Benyamim. Personal interview in Holon, Israel. 16 Feb. 2012.

Tsedaka, Benyamim. Personal interview in Holon, Israel. 28 Feb. 2012.

Tsedaka, Benyamim. Personal interview on Mount Gerizim. 4 April 2012.

Tsedaka, Benyamim. Personal interview on Mount Gerizim. 19 April 2012.

Tsedaka, Benyamim. Personal interview in Holon, Israel. 8 June 2012.

Tsedaka, Benyamim. Personal interview on Mount Gerizim. 25 July 2012.

Tsedaka, Benyamim. "Why Are Samaritan Antiquities That Belong to the Samaritans in the Good Samaritan Inn Museum?" *Facebook*. N.p. 23 April 2013. Web. 23 April 2013.

Tsedaka, Benyamim. "Response to Jim Ridolfo's post 'Creating a Samaritan Keyboard layout for OS X based on a combination of the Hebrew and Arabic keyboard layouts.'" Facebook. 2 May 2013.

Tsedaka, Benyamim. "Panel on the Samaritan Version of the Torah." *Facebook*. N.p. 25 Nov. 2013. Web. 25 Nov. 2013.

Tsedaka, Benyamim, trans. *The Israelite Samaritan Version of the Torah: First English Translation Compared with the Masoretic Version*. Ed. Benyamim Tsedaka and Sharon Sullivan. Grand Rapids, MI: Eerdmans, 2013. Print.

Tsedaka, Benyamim, and Efrat Tsedaka. *MEMO: The Samaritans Between the Israeli, Palestinian, and Jordanian Raindrops*. Holon, Israel: A.B.-Institute of Samaritan Studies Press, 1998. Print.

Twain, Mark. *Mark Twain's Pleasure Trip on the Continent: The Complete Work Previously Issued Under the Title of "The Innocents Abroad" and the "New Pilgrim's Progress."* London: John Camden Hotten, 1871. Print.

"University College London Centre for Digital Humanities." *University College London Centre for Digital Humanities*. University College London, 2012. Web. 12 July 2012.

US Department of State. Fulbright Program. West Bank Travel and Residency Rules for American Fulbright Grantees, 2011–12. N.p. Web. April 2011.

Weaver, Warren, and Claude Elwood Shannon. *The Mathematical Theory of Communication*. Urbana-Champaign: University of Illinois Press, 1963. Print.

Weissenberg, S., Dr. Trans. J. H. *The Advocate: America's Jewish Journal* 46 (1913): 274–79. Web. 08 Dec. 2013.

Welch, Kathleen E. *Electric Rhetoric: Classical Rhetoric, Oralism, and a New Literacy*. Cambridge, MA: MIT Press, 1999. Print.

Welch, Nancy. *Living Room: Teaching Public Writing in a Privatized World*. Portsmouth, NH: Boynton/Cook, 2008. Print.

Welch, Nancy. "Living Room: Teaching Public Writing in a Post-publicity Era." *College Composition and Communication* 56.3 (2005): 470–92. Print.

Whiting, John D. "The Last Israelitish Blood Sacrifice: How the Vanishing Samaritans Celebrate the Passover on Sacred Mount Gerizim." *National Geographic* (1920): 1–46. Print.

Wilson, James. *The Lands of the Bible: Visited and Described*. Vol II. Edinburgh: William Whyte and Co., 1847. Print.

Wolff, Joseph. "Intelligence." *The Christian Herald and Seaman's Magazine* 9 (1822): 238–41. Web. 08 Dec. 2013.

Yancey, Kathleen Blake. *Delivering College Composition: The Fifth Canon*. Portsmouth, NH: Boynton/Cook, 2006. Print.

"Yazidis I. General." *Encyclopedia Iranica*. Encyclopedia Iranica. 20 July 2014. Web. 08 Sept. 2014. http://www.iranicaonline.org/articles/yazidis-i-general-1.

Index

Note: Page numbers in italics refer to figures.

Printed and bound by CPI Group (UK) Ltd, Croydon, CR0 4YY

13/04/2025

14656532-0005